THE FAIR SEX IN TRIBAL CULTURES

THE FAIR SEX IN TRIBAL CULTURES

Problems and Development

SAMITA MANNA

GYAN PUBLISHING HOUSE

NEW DELHI - 110002

The Fair Sex in Tribal Cultures
(*Education, General*)

ISBN: 81-212-0643-X

Published in 2000 in India by
Gyan Publishing House
5, Ansari Road
New Delhi-110 002

Laser Typeseting: Durga Computers
Printed at: Chawla Offest Printers

CONTENTS

PREFACE

Liberal and progressive intellectuals, throughout the world, have been organising movements, for equal human rights of the women. Different developmental programmes, related especially to health, education and occupation have also been initiated to raise the status of this subjugated section. Many developmental programmes have failed to change the life of women. Irrespective of social and community affiliations the number of beneficiaries varies, particularly the impoverished group is still lagging behind. So all macro level programmes are not sufficient to attain the goal or to remove the real problems faced by the women. Therefore, a micro level study, related to developmental aspects is necessary to find out the obstacles that remain in the way of their development.

Real development of society cannot be achieved if we ignore the backward communities and the importance of their fullest participation in various developmental programmes. In tribal societies also, women are much more backward than men. To eradicate the problems of the backward community, women should be brought into the limelight. It is expected that they must assume the prime responsibility to socialize and educate their children by which the new generation would be awakened to the changing social systems and play important roles to adjust themselves with the new socio-economic situations.

Illiteracy is one of the important reason which may act as an hindrance to the development of tribal women. If women are illiterate, society cannot prosper, specially girls should be enabled to understand the positive role of education. It is because of their indifference and lack of enthusiasm a large number of dropouts and a negative stance is found as regards to attending schools. As a result many unhealthy practices such as child marriage, high infant mortality rate. etc are prevalent in society.

For the overall development of the country the educated people, administrators and social scientists, have to be much more alert about the actualities and conditioning of the tribal women of our society. The present study entitled *The Fair Sex is Tribal Cultures* may have some modest claims for being regarded as distinctive micro-level study. It reflects as a mirror, the true picture of the society under consideration.

The project has been financed by the Ministry of Welfare (Tribal Development Division), Government of India. I express my deep sense of gratitude to all the officials of that department, specially Sri P.R. Mahanty, IAS, and Dr P.K. Mahanty. I am also thankful to my Project Assistants, Sri Asuthosh Mallick and Smt. Sumita Bhattacharyya who have sincerely collected the data for this project. I am also grateful to my Research Scholar Sri Soumyajit Patra and Sri Swapan Kumar Koley, who helped me a lot to process the data and to finish the report. I shall be failing in my duty if I do not express my indebtedness to Prof P.K. Deb and Prof A.K. Mallick of the University of Kalyani for their kind advice and suggestions. My sincere thanks are also due to the Panchayat Officials of all the districts, local leaders and, villagers who have extended their cooperation to collect the information for the project. I shall be extremely happy if the problems which have been focussed in this monograph can be overcome by the administrators and political leaders of our country.

Samita Manna

1

Introduction

India's first Prime Minister Jawaharlal Nehru once "stated", "In order to awaken the people it is the woman who has to be awakened." Socio-economic position of women is low in many countries with special reference to the tribal communities. After fifty years of Independence inspite of many welfare projects set by the Government, it is high time to examine the situation carefully and to suggest the remedial measures, if needed. Naturally to raise the status of women, the women at home should be given prior emphasis. A major section of the women including Scheduled Castes, Scheduled Tribes and some other castes people of varied natures— live in rural areas as well as in jungle-covered rugged terrains. Actually in rural areas, sometimes it is very difficult for an unknown passer-by to feel and to differentiate between a poor Scheduled Caste woman and a Scheduled Tribe woman. As it appears, most of the time they are under the same cruel buffet of poverty. It is a fact that the tribal people who are more nature-based, live sometimes in an isolated way or in the areas of less contact. Though apparently there is very little difference in identifying the tribal women from the rural folk, in reality the tribal culture has its separate identity pigmented with many traits.

While considering the issue in general we find that the tribals have to face many difficulties. Due to the low level of their education, the modern process of development touched their culture only partially and as such they are recoiled to the age-old traditions and have very little urge to overcome this problem.

Of course this study is an attempt to reflect the ethnography of a few tribal people who have echoed their lifestyles with rhythmic vibrations. It is true that any individual has to react with three situations: man with nature or geography, man with man in bewildering situations, man with supernaturals. Thus, all these interactions moulded the character as well as the image-profile of the people and in course of time, these have become culturally isolated manifesting their distinctiveness-indicating differences.

In tribal life, women have to play a vital role, they have to take the main role in economic activities, household work, child rearing activities and to look after many more aspects which help the community to combat dangers and tide over the problem of extinction.

II

After Independence constitutional facilities were extended to overcome the difficulties of the so-called weaker sections by providing for them facilities in the form of grants and employments. During that time the tribals had also been awakened by the administrators, policy makers, and high officials of bureaucratic organizations, along with social workers and social scientists. All of them have argued that the total development of the nation cannot be possible without the development of these downtrodden people who are scattered in various parts of this country. Actually, they were considered to be the original inhabitants of this country and known as early settlers or autochthones.

Das and others (1990) wrote:

> The evideces of pre-historic period reveal the existence of man in India from Paleolithic period (old stone age). The culture of early man through an evolutionary process reached a climax during Chalcolithic period in the formation of Mohenjodaro and Harappa Civilization about 3500 BC.

But due to upheavals of many new migrant groups from different historical periods, these original settlers might have been uprooted and with many difficulties had to take shelter in different inaccessible areas where nobody would disturb them. In this circumstantial exigency these people developed a culture of their own, where modern civilized traits had little impact on their lifestyles. Except this, during the time of colonial administrations, the Britishers had exerted little influence on them. They actually did not want to bring them up among the mainstream population.

> The British administrations in our country did not seriously think about the development of these down-trodden and hapless communities, rather they preferred to keep them aloof and in isolation. This in due course of time created an emotional gap between the tribals and the so called *bhadralok* or the affluent people[1].

By this time many more developmental works had been done through government patronage, by the Ministry of Welfare or through voluntary organizations or the Missionaries, just to overcome their immediate problems. But in many cases no scientific, systemic attempt had been made to ameliorate the plight of these people.

Naturally, it is expected to get a clear picture of the situation and an attempt has been made to distinguish the groups as well as the impact of ecology, environment and surrounding social groups of varied nature. The amazing conglomeration of traditions, beliefs, philosophies and materialistic activities for the survival, of course, vitalizes this lifestyle just to combat the difficulties which may appear in their struggle for existence. The nature of reaction of the people at different ecology either in the scorching rays of the sun, torrential rainfall areas or in the waning moon, their essential activities continued when we get the nature of differences of the six tribal groups.

But it has been found that the amount of real change in the lifestyle of the tribal people has been very insignificant. Still now they are the most unprivileged section of the society and have been suffering from illiteracy, poverty, health problems, housing problems and a number of allied problems at every moment of life. The situation is more frustrating in case of the tribal women. Their progress is not much satisfactory. One of the important reasons of this relative backwardness of the tribal women is that their participation in educational institutions is very poor. According to Basu Roy (1992):

The strength of a nation is thought to be hampered with

the backward section of its population (Scheduled Castes, Scheduled Tribes etc.). Similarly, the counterpart of the developing males will hinder in faster progress if remains backward. Hence, education as a tool is supposed to change the outlook, to accept new ideas, to grow with broader worldview and to brush off old prejudices, superstitions and misconceptions.

A number of decades have passed after Independence leaving little impact on the actual position of the women of our country. It has been reiterated that only a little section of them are getting the fruits of various developmental schemes and welfare projects. The Government is trying and encouraging to ensure their progress through different welfare measures by starting girl hostels, training programmes and extending many facilities but the results obtained so far are not upto satisfaction. Thus, Ministry of Welfare, Government of India restructured their setting, encouraging researchers to pinpoint the problems, i.e., where shoe pinches. In this respect Professor Sachidananda (1985) pointed out:

> The impact of development on different sections of tribal women in our country has not been even. For a small number of tribal women who have taken advantage of education, new vistas of employment have opened up and they have realized self-fulfilment.

III

Women throughout the world play the most important role in the part of the socialization process where social self of the individuals are developed. The initial parts of the socialization process like feeding habits (including breast feeding), weaning and toilet training are most imporant for the children where the role of women is immense. The children are considered to be the future citizens of a nation and the total personality system of the children mainly develop through the nature of interaction between mother and child. Women's education, awareness, social positions, healthy body and minds are undoubtedly considered as different inputs for the total development of the nation.

Though the status of women is not equatable with that of the men yet the status enjoyed by the women varies from society to society and group to group.

> It is a matter of great disgrace that tribal women are still in darkness. Their progress is not at all satisfactory. Only a small section of women is getting education. The increased number of literates in each decade depicts the picture of enhanced male participation in education. If we try to get the impression from different parts of West Bengal, that will show the same scene—females are in the backlog. They are unable to keep pace in equal steps with the males[2].

It is generally observed in tribal societies that though the tribal women are less educated they are more free to liberate themselves from their social bindings. Social norms are not so rigid as to bring about their confinement to the non-lovable ways of life. In many tribal societies they enjoy the right to divorce; to select their own partners and even after the death of a husband they can choose a new one. Poverty is there but it does not destroy their human qualities.

Singh, Vyas and Mann (1985) observed:

> ....The tribal women in general and in comparison with caste women enjoy more freedom in various walks of life. Traditional and customary norms are comparatively liberal to women.

In each and every society women are regarded as indispensable partners of men but their position or importance varies from society to society. Women in the global context are not equatable with men. The variations are observed in consideration of the nature of society—developed, or least developing countries.

> In general women in India suffer on numerous fronts. By and large their concentration is in low skills and they are low-paid. Since they are, in general, not involved in decision-making, they are not found holding many positions in political and economic institutions. For various handicaps based on religious elements, including their impurity and subsequent pollution, the women are again debarred from holding positions in the religious hierarchy and sphere. On many accounts they are discriminated against in day-to-day life. Illiteracy is rampant among women and so social and cultural taboos....purdah (veiling) system, with all its attending impositions and restraints, hinders the progress of women in various walks of life[3].

Women receive less than one-tenth of the world income, but do two-thirds of the world's work. ... When house work and child care are taken into account women on average have a 60 to 70 hour week[4].

Irrespective of country women are considered to be a weaker section of the society. Physically they are not fit like men, they have to take special care and to spend much more time for their family, specially for their children. Women have three distinctive roles in society — Reproductive, Productive and Community management[5].

Child rearing is the most effective role for women in all aspects of economic development[6].

The woman plays the role of an affectionate mother, loyal wife, beloved daughter and loving sister but the status held by the woman differs basically from her male partner in the society in which they live. The sex roles of male and female attached with various customs and activities differ from one society to another. Men are characteristically assigned to the work according to their physical strength and ability which take them far off from their homes.

The fair sex or women are therefore, shaped and processed in accord with the cultural patterns. The role and status of women, their ethics and world views are the outcome of the age long traditions of the cultural groups in which they are born and brought up. Thus to understand and measure the extent of the problem of women folk in relation to any society, the concerned cultural patterns are needed to be focussed accurately.

IV

Many important studies have been conducted by Malinowski (1949), Lowie (1920), Majumdar and Madan (1969), and others by concentrating on the issue of the status of tribal women. No consensus has developed regarding their opinions. To evaluate the status of women one has to judge and explain it in terms of the particular cultures and economic activities on which they depend. Generally in tribal society the status of women is dependent on the nature of the social organisation. It is observed that if the socio-economic condition of women is high in a particular culture her status will be high automatically. For example, in case of the Toda, South Indian Tribe, the status of women is not high because they do not take upon themselves the direct economic burden as men do. The women are not allowed to do all economic activities like the men, whereas among hunting-gathering tribes, like, the Andamanese, Birhor, Lodha, women enjoy parallel status with the men because they also take part in their daily economic activities[7]. Gond women enjoy better status and greater freedom, specially in the choice of a husband, premarital sex licence, seeking of divorce and so forth. But women form a depressed lot in other areas.

The husband's authority is largely curtailed among the matrilineal clans. A woman's initiative is foremost in family affairs. Again the women command high respect and freedom in case of the tribals of Lahaul, Spiti, Ladakh, Kinnaur and Arunachal Pradesh. In social matters the tribal women enjoy considerable freedom of movement compared to their non-tribal counterparts.

The Dhebar Commission Report (1961) mentions that the tribal women are not a drudge or a beast of burden but exercise a firm hand in family matters. The tribal women are treated more humanly and humanely than the non-tribal women. The male partners are not allowed to take dowry. Naturally dowry deaths, brideburning etc. are totally absent in most of the tribal societies. Boys and girls are treated equally. Women in some society also inherit parent's property.

Elwin (1975) remarked:

> The tribal is no, generally subject to early child-bearing. She is married when she is matured and if her marriage is a failure she has the right of divorce. The lamentable restrictions of widowhood do not await her. ... She is allowed even enjoyed to remarry.

As primitivism persists along with modernity, since Independence, a countrywide attempt has been made in every corner, in every accessible or inaccessible part, to locate the downtrodden groups and to underscore their problems. So the tribal women who were once the gift of nature are no more so much dependent on it. Due to deforestation and the impact of industrialization and urbanization the plain living tribal communities have been adversely affected. With the changing ecological setting, the tribal women also have to accept the new social status and role in which often they are confused and feel gloomy. But the slow process of acculturation and absorption with the greater Hindu Society often lead them to be the victims of it.

The socio-economic condition of tribal women is not good. Most of them are illiterate and have drinking habits. Lack of awareness in their ways of life often proves detrimental to the governmental projects. Various efforts are now being made to develop the tribal communities and thus there is a growing need for knowing and assessing the life of the tribal women and its allied problems for their overall welfare and betterment of the whole society in a spirit of harmony.

> In general, development means removal of poverty, improvement of productivity and consequently raising the quality of life in a given society. This means better education, health and nutritional status for population backed by purchasing power and access to well developed social services[8].

The term 'development' is very often bracketed with the term 'social progress'. Tribal people are identified as "Scheduled" as per the Constitution, considering their nature of illiteracy, poor socio-economic position and the low level of representations in different types of job. So these groups are lagging behind from the others. Development of these groups is only possible through various welfare measures. Of all developmental items, education plays the key role. It can change the way of life of the people. From time to time the concept of development comes through various dimensions in the minds of the people. After the mid-seventies the concept of development includes the per capita income with the assurance of an improved quality of life.

Development of women with special reference to the tribals is an integral part of social or human development. Development comes through alternations in the major social institutions—like changing the family's income, opening formal and informal educational institutions, introducing new co-operatives and banking services for giving loans as well as improving the rural economy. Medical and health services are also essential for better medical help specially for the children and the mother. Except these, general awareness should be increased to improve their quality of life. As a whole, development indicates the new social adjustment of the people with the changing improved environment where majority of them express their happiness.

V

The main thrust of this project is to locate the problems of the fair sex of six tribal groups settled in the same ecological zone. These groups are not pursuing the same type of economy, though economy is the most important determinant to understand the status of any population. Although in this present worked the economy of the tribal people does not play a significant role to determine their problems like poverty, illiteracy, exploitation, lack of opportunities, idleness, which are important factors to hinder their attainment of goals and to make interactions with other groups in their day-to-day life processes.

Among these six tribal groups, two tribal groups, the Birhor and Lodha, belong to gathering-hunting group, the Mahalis are the basket makers, the Santal, form the agricultural tribe, the Mundas constitute the migrant agricultural community, while the Bhumij tribe is the Hinduised tribe— all these tribal groups have been selected for this work. They all live in the same setting of ecology, i.e., lateritic undulating zones clothed with dwarf trees in patches, having less communication facilities of the Bengal -Bihar-Orissa region.

The problems of the tribal people are numerous and it is very difficult to categorize these problems quite distinctively because in most of the cases their problems are interrelated and interwoven with each other. These six tribal groups are basically the people of Austro Asiatic language group and are concentrated in the border districts of Midnapur and Purulia (W.B.), Singbhum and Hazaribagh (Bihar) and Mayurbhanj (Orissa). There are, of course, other ethnic groups who have a strong impact on their lifestyle. The recent development programmes initiated by the Government have also similar impact on them. But these development programmes are not implemented equally in all areas, even after the implementation of these programmes very little changes can be found and in some places no change can be noticed in their day to day life. These impoverished groups still suffer from the problem of isolation due to their poor education or lack of education, and low social position in the social hierarchy. However, the major problems generally faced by them are:

(i) *Underdeveloped economy.* Most of the tribal women under study are agricultural labourers or casual labourers in the off season. Naturally there are hungry mouths to be fed during the lean period. For cultivating they have to depend on rain. Inadequate money for purchasing better seeds and fertilizers and inadequate knowledge to maintain a happy life are important factors for their low level of living.

(ii) *Hygiene, communication and lack of awareness.* Socio-economically they are generally considered a backward community. Poor economic condition does not permit them to maintain a decent life. The villages hardly get sufficient drinking water and good medical facilities. In most of the cases good medical practitioners are not available and hospitals are not seen in town areas. Governmental efforts are also considered very poor to make them aware of the application of modern medicine and to arrange for them proper medicine also.

(iii) *Education.* Proper education can only bring a new light and a refined life to the backward community. Formal ways of education are very poor which distinguish them from the general level. Lack of education, rather a detached attitude to formal education separates them from the mainstream population, so they are lagging behind. Now there are provisions (special seats) for employment, they have a minimum standard of education which can provide them with some jobs, which undoubtedly improve their economy and the pattern of social interaction.

(iv) *Conflict between tradition and modernity.* It creates many problems in their day to day life. Considering all these basic general problems, the researcher has designed the following objectives:

(*a*) find out the problems of the fair sex of six tribal groups separately.

(*b*) locate the point of difference and similarities in the problems of the fair sex of six tribal groups and to find out the real causes for understanding these.

(*c*) understand the nature of the problem of women of each tribe belonging to two different states of same ecology, as ecology offers common geo-physical background which in its turn provides economic facilities.

Reference

1. *Bhowmick*, 1985.
2. *Basu Roy*, 1992.
3. *Ibid.*, 1985.
4. *Rowobothom*, 1992.
5. *Piza Lopez*, 1991.
6. *Moser*, 1991.
7. *Singh and others*, 1985.
8. *Paul Chowwdhury*, 1991.

2

Research Design

The present report covers six tribal groups of different economies and cultures living in a common ecological setting on the western fronts of West Bengal comprising the districts of Midnapur and Purulia, of Orissa including the district Mayurbhanj and of Bihar having the two districts of Singbhum and Hazaribagh. The researcher has an idea that common ecological background and different social settings might be considered to understand the group meaningfully.

Data have been collected through participant observation and direct interview method to know their socio-economic background as well as various problems of their life. Data collection started in September, 1995 and ended in February, 1996.

Through this project the researchers has tried to explore different problems of the fair sex in six tribal cultures. Females throughout the world irrespective of society—developing or non-developing, tribal or non-tribal, black or white are facing much more problems than the males. So to highlight their problems in a vivid way the researcher has framed a structured schedule with four important parts. Each part contains specific questions on particular problems like occupation, education, livelihood and finally attitude towards and awareness of better life and finally offered her suggestions for their development.

From amongst the population of the Lodha, Mahali,

Santal, Munda and Bhumij, 100 for each group have been chosen from the bordering district of Midnapur in West Bengal; but the Birhors are selected from the district of Purulia where only 37 cases are studied, due to some political disturbances 13 cases are left out where the requisite size of the population was 50. But 100 families of Birhor are selected from the district of Hazaribagh, Bihar, one of the concentrated zones of the Birhor.

Fifty families of the Lodha and Santal have been selected from the district of Mayurbhanj, Orissa. Fifty families each from the Mahali, Munda and Bhumij have been selected from the district Singbhum, Bihar. For this study, the tribal population of the districts have been selected to make a comparative analysis and to understand the problem in a better way.

Table 2.1 depicts the distribution of population state and district wise and Table 2.2 shows the distribution of population village and police-station wise.

For data collection, the villages under Police Stations were surveyed. In this phase to get accurate information the local Panchayat offices and Anchal Panchayat offices were contacted. The lists of the tribal population have been collected for each and every village of the same region. An attempt was made for complete enumeration of the villages. But actually it was not possible due to following reasons:

First, during the time of data collection many informants were not available because of seasonal agricultural work.

Secondly, some villages are far away from the road-side and communication facilities are not good.

Thirdly, a few respondents hardly utter any word.

Table 2.3 describes the age distribution of the respondents.

TABLE 2.1
DISTRIBUTION OF SAMPLE STATE WISE

Tribe	State	No. of Family	Total
BIRHOR	West Bengal	37	137
	Bihar	100	
LODHA	West Bengal	100	150
	Orissa	50	
MAHALI	West Bengal	100	150
	Bihar	50	
SANTAL	West Bengal	100	150
	Orissa	50	
MUNDA	West Bengal	100	150
	Bihar	50	
BHUMIJ	West Bengal	100	150
	Bihar	50	
Total			887

TABLE 2.2
DISTRIBUTION OF SAMPLE VILLAGE AND POLICE STATION WISE

State	Police Station	Village	No. of Family	Total
		BIRHOR		
West Bengal	Bagmundi	Bhupatipalli	29	
	Jhalda	Mangaltaur	8	37
Bihar	Chari	Banchitao	34	
	Hazaribagh	Daru	9	
	Mandu	Gobindapur	5	
		Baladoharatola	6	
	Churchu	Jhumri-Mahua colony	6	
		Jarga	5	
	Ichak	Khijura	11	
		Tilra	21	
	Vishnugarh	Tantijharia	3	100

(*Contd.*)

State	*Police Station*	*Village*	*No. of family*	*Total*
		LODHA		
		Padampur	2	
		Parulia	5	
	Narayangarh	Daharpur	8	
		Kajla	9	
West Bengal	Belda	Bardai	26	
		Maliara	5	
	Dantan	Shakharidanga	9	
		Panchrol	15	
	Keshiari	Kukai	21	100
Orissa	Morada	Chittamatiya	50	50
		MAHALI		
	Narayangarh	Kotaigarh	23	
		Maynapara	1	
West Bengal		Chotamatkatpur	3	
	Belda	Sarisasaraidihi	7	
		Ektal	27	
		Shaorapich	1	
	Dantan	Maghalmari	4	100
		Jayrampur	34	
		Old Potomda	8	
Bihar	Potomda	Bidra	15	
		New Potomda	27	
		SANTAL		
	Narayangarh	Chakmakrampur	1	
		Belda	3	
		Chotomatkatpur	3	
		Dakshinkhatnagar	6	
		Sabujpalli	6	
	Belda	Babalpur	7	
West Bengal		Deuli	9	
		Haldia	9	
		Susinda	9	
		Maynapara	14	
	Dantan	Maghalmari	9	
		Baganshahi	12	
	Keshiari	Kalabani	3	
		Bahna	6	
	Nayagram	Kharika	3	100
Orissa	Morada	Chorabandha	9	
		Sannyasi	41	50

(*Contd.*)

State	*Police Station*	*Village*	*No. of family*	*Total*
		MUNDA		
		Kotaigarh	1	
		Deulchak	10	
		Gobindapur	10	
West Bengal	Narayangarh	Hirapari	11	
		Daharpur	13	
		Pichabani	15	
		Abhirampur	16	
	Keshiari	Gaganeswar	24	100
Bihar	Potomda	Paglabera	50	50
		BHUMIJ		
	Narayangarh	Abhirampur	1	
		Deuli	10	
	Belda	Gan-Belda	17	
West Bengal		Vinodpur	29	
	Dantan	Monoharpur	6	
	Keshiari	Kanchanpur	5	
	Kharagpur	Shikharpari	32	
Bihar	Potomda	Gadigram	50	50

The population is distributed in six groups starting from '10-20' years to '60 years and above'. Majority of the respondents in all the three states, West Bengal, Orissa and Bihar are within the two age groups of '20 to 30' and '30 to 40'. Out of 887 respondents 525 (59.19 per cent) respondents are in the age group '20 to 40'.

TABLE 2.3

AGE GROUP

Tribe	State	Age (in Years)						
		10-20	20-30	30-40	40-50	50-60	60 +	Total
BIRHOR	W.B.	4	9	9	6	6	3	37
		(10.81)	(24.32)	(24.32)	(16.22)	(16.22)	(08.11)	(100.00)
	Bihar	12	32	34	10	7	5	100
		(12.00)	(32.00)	(34.00)	(10.00)	(07.00)	(05.00)	(100.00)
LODHA	W.B.	5	30	31	14	15	5	100
		(05.00)	(30.00)	(31.00)	(14.00)	(15.00)	(05.00)	(100.00)
	Orissa	5	22	7	5	8	3	50
		(10.00)	(44.00)	(14.00)	(10.00)	(16.00)	(06.00)	(100.00)
MAHALI	W.B.	7	33	27	17	8	8	100
		(07.00)	(33.00)	(27.00)	(17.00)	(08.00)	(08.00)	(100.00)
	Bihar	2	13	10	10	10	5	50
		(04.00)	(26.00)	(20.00)	(20.00)	(20.00)	(10.00)	(100.00)
SANTAL	W.B.	4	29	32	17	11	7	100
		(04.00)	(29.00)	(32.00)	(17.00)	(11.00)	(07.00)	(100.00)

(Contd.)

Tribe	State	Age in years						
		10-20	20-30	30-40	40-50	50-60	60 +	Total
	Orissa	1	9	16	11	8	5	50
		(02.00)	(18.00)	(32.00)	(22.00)	(16.00)	(10.00)	(100.00)
MUNDA	W.B.	7	37	28	14	10	4	100
		(07.00)	(37.00)	(28.00)	(14.00)	(10.00)	(04.00)	(100.00)
	Bihar	-	12	11	11	6	10	50
			(24.00)	(22.00)	(22.00)	(12.00)	(20.00)	(100.00)
BHUMIJ	W.B.	5	42	29	11	8	5	50
		(05.00)	(42.00)	(29.00)	(11.00)	(08.00)	(05.00)	(100.00)
	Bihar	1	12	11	15	9	2	50
		(02.00)	(24.00)	(22.00)	(30.00)	(18.00)	(04.00)	(100 00)
	Total	53	280	245	141	106	62	887
		(05.98)	(31.57)	(27.62)	(15.90)	(11.95)	(06.99)	(100.00)

N.B. *Figures in the parentheses indicate percentages.*

TABLE 2.4
MARITAL STATUS

Tribe	State	Married	Unmarried	Widow	Divorcee	Total
BIRHOR	W.B.	35	-	2	-	37
		(94.59)		(5.21)		(100.00)
	Bihar	97	2	1	-	100
		(97.00)	(2.00)	(1.00)		(100.00)
LODHA	W.B.	92	-	6	2	100
		(92.00)		(6.00)	(2.00)	(100.00)
	Orissa	45	-	4	1	50
		(90.00)	(8.00)	(2.00)	(100.00)	
MAHALI	W.B.	91	2	7	-	100
		(91.00)	(2.00)	(7.00)		(100.00)
	Bihar	46	-	4	-	50
		(92.00)		(8.00)		(100.00)

(Contd.)

Tribe	State	Married	Unmarried	Widow	Divorcee	Total
SANTAL	W.B.	77	5	13	5	100
		(77.00)	(5.00)	(13.00)	(5.00)	(100.00)
	Orissa	46	-	4	-	50
		(92.00)		(8.00)		(100.00)
MUNDA	W.B.	81	6	11	2	100
		(81.00)	(6.00)	(11.00)	(2.00)	(100.00)
	Bihar	46	-	4	-	50
		(92.00)		(8.00)		(100.00)
BHUMIJ	W.B.	87	1	11	1	100
		(87.00)	(1.00)	(11.00)	(1.00)	(100.00)
	Bihar	48	2	-	-	50
		(96.00)	(4.00)			(100.00)
	Total	791	18	67	11	887
		(89.18)	(2.03)	(7.55)	(1.24)	(100.00)

N.B. *Figures in the parentheses indicate percentages.*

TABLE 2.5
EDUCATION

Tribe	State	No. of illiterate	Can sign	Can read	Can read &	Primary Write	Middle	IX-X	S.F.	H.S.	Graduate	Total
BIRHOR	W.B.	37	-	-	-	-	-	-	-	-	-	37
		(100.00)										(100.00)
	Bihar	100	-	-	-	-	-	-	-	-	-	100
		(100.00)										(100.00)
LODHA	W.B.	81	15	-	-	1	3	-	-	-	-	100
		(81.00)	(15.00)			(1.00)	(3.00)					(100.00)
	Orissa	49	1	-	-	-	-	-	-	-	-	50
		(98.00)	(2.00)									(100.00)
MAHALI	W.B.	82	8	4	-	5	1	-	-	-	-	100
		(82.00)	(8.00)	(4.00)		(5.00)	(1.00)					(100.00)
	Bihar	45	-	-	-	4	-	1	-	-	-	50
		(90.00)				(8.00)		(2.00)				(100.00)

(Contd.)

Tribe	*State*	*No. of*	*Can sign illiterate*	*Can read*	*Can read &*	*Primary Write*	*Middle*	*IX-X*	*S.F.*	*H.S.*	*Graduate*	*Total*
SANTAL	W.B.	73	10	4	-	5	2	3	-	2	1	100
		(73.00)	(10.00)	(4.00)		(5.00)	(2.00)	(3.00)		(2.00)	(1.00)	(100.00)
	Orissa	49	-	-	-	1	-	-	-	-	-	50
		(98.00)				(2.00)						(100.00)
MUNDA	W.B.	47	34	-	-	11	7	1	-	-	-	100
		(47.00)	(34.00)	-		(11.00)	(7.00)	(1.00)		-	-	(100.00)
	Bihar	39	-	-	-	10	1	-	-	-	-	50
		(78.00)				(20.00)	(2.00)					(100.00)
BHUMIJ	W.B.	66	19	-	-	8	7	-	-	-	-	100
		(66.00)	(19.00)			(8.00)	(7.00)					(100.00)
	Bihar	45	-	-	-	2	2	1	-	-	-	50
		(90.00)				(4.00)	(4.00)	(2.00)				(100.00)

N.B. *Figures in the parentheses indicate per centages.*

Table 2.4 depicts the marital status of the respondents. It shows that in all the selected tribal communities of three states, majority of the respondents are married. Out of total respondents 7.55 per cent respondents are widow whereas only 2.03 per cent are unmarried. Divorcee women are very few (1.24 per cent).

Table 2.5 describes the educational status of the respondents. It is observed from the Table that in case of the Birhor community all the respondents of both West Bengal and Orissa are illiterate. In case of the Lodha only 19.00 per cent are literate in West Bengal and 2.00 per cent literate in Orissa. The rate of illiteracy of the Mahali in West Bengal (82.00 per cent) is lower than the illiteracy rate (90.00 per cent) of Bihar. In the Santal community of Orissa 98.00 per cent women are illiterate. But in West Bengal 27.00 per cent Santal women are literate, among them 3.00 per cent have higher education. In case of the Munda community only 47.0 per cent are illiterate in West Bengal, whereas it is 78.00 per cent in Bihar. In the Bhumij community the rate of illiteracy among the women of West Bengal (66.00 per cent) is lower than that of women (90.00 per cent) of Bihar.

So from the foregoing analysis it is observed that the rate of literacy of women is highest in the Munda community of West Bengal and lowest (i.e., nil) in the Birhor community of West Bengal and Bihar.

Table 2.6 represents the sex ratio of the sample. It can be observed from the Table that the highest sex ratio i.e. females per 1000 males (1133) is in the Santal community of West Bengal, and the lowest (758) in the Mahali community of Bihar. The sex ratio is 1000 in the Lodha community of Orissa and the Birhor Community of Bihar. The average size of the family of each tribe varies from 4 to 5 members. So the family size is not found to be very large among them.

TABLE 2.6
POPULATION STRUCTURE

Tribe	*State*	*No. of Family*	*Male*	*Female*	*Total*	*Sex Ratio*	*Average size of the family*
BIRHOR	W.B.	37	82	76	158	927	4
	Bihar	100	196	196	392	1000	4
LODHA	W.B.	100	251	236	487	940	5
	Orissa	50	106	106	212	1000	4
MAHALI	W.B.	100	241	225	466	934	5
	Bihar	50	124	94	218	758	4
SANTAL	W.B.	100	241	273	514	1133	5
	Orissa	50	143	132	275	923	6
MUNDA	W.B.	100	257	250	507	973	5
	Bihar	50	128	133	261	1039	5
BHUMIJ	W.B.	100	231	240	471	1038	5
	Bihar	50	150	116	266	773	5

A poor scenario has been observed regarding the land distribution pattern among these tribal communities. A good number of landless (agricultural) families have been observed among the Birhor (40.54 per cent), Santal (39.00 per cent), Bhumij (35.00 per cent) of West Bengal. Except landless families, majority of the families have not more than 1 acre of agricultural land, only 7.00 per cent Bhumij families have agricultural land measuring more than 4 acres (Table 2.7).

The land holding pattern of the Lodha and Santal of Orissa shows a miserable picture where 66.00 per cent Lodha and 36.00 per cent Santal have no land at all. Besides these landless families most others among rest have agricultural land upto 2 acres. But in case of Bihar an improved land holding pattern among the tribes like the Birhor, Mahali, munda and Bhumij has been observed. The maximum number (34.00 per cent) of the Mahali community are landless but on the other hand, the Bhumij and Munda communities have good amount of agricultural land (40.00 per cent and 36.00 per cent have more than 4 acres respectively). The rest of the population have land between 1 acre to 2 acres.

Regarding the distribution of non-agricultural land (homestead) in West Bengal the landless families are very few except for the Santal (20.00 per cent). But in Orissa there is not a single Lodha or Santal family who has no homestead land but in Bihar, except 2.00 per cent Birhor, all the families have homestead land. In majority of the cases except a few communities they have more than 3 kathas of homestead land.

Table 2.8 depicts the types of family where the respondents live in the three states—West Bengal, Orissa and Bihar. There are two major types of family, joint and nuclear, over which the families are distributed. It is evident from the Table that nuclear families dominate in all tribal communities irrespective of the state to which they belong. Among all these tribal communities the Birhor and Munda communities of Bihar exhibit domination of nuclear families (93.00 per cent and 92.00 per cent respectively), whereas in the Lodha community of West Bengal, nuclear families are seen only in 58.00 per cent cases, 42.0 per cent families live in joint family structures.

TABLE 2.7
LAND HOLDING

State	Tribe	No. of Family	Agricultural (in acres)					Non agricultural (in katha)			
			Landless	Marginal (0–1)	Small (1.1–2)	Medium (2.1–4)	Large (4.1+)	Landless	1-3	3-6	6+
	Birhor	37	15	2	20	-	-	1	22	12	2
			(40.54)	(05.41)	(54.05)	-	-	(2.70)	(59.46)	(32.43)	(5.41)
	Lodha	100	19	37	8	5	1	6	33	38	23
			(19.00)	(37.00)	(08.00)	(05.00)	(01.00)	(06.00)	(33.00)	(38.00)	(23.00)
West	Mahali	100	26	51	20	3	-	1	39	46	14
Bengal			(26.00)	(51.00)	(20.00)	(03.00)	-	(01.00)	(39.00)	(46.00)	(14.00)
	Santal	100	39	41	9	11	-	20	31	24	25
			(30.00)	(41.00)	(09.00)	(11.00)	-	(20.00)	(31.00)	(24.00)	(25.00)
	Munda	100	9	41	23	20	7	2	25	37	36
			(09.00)	(41.00)	(23.00)	(20.00)	(07.00)	(02.00)	(25.00)	(37.00)	(36.00)

(Contd.)

	Bhumij	100	35	46	15	2	2	8	43	28	21
			(35.00)	(46.00)	(15.00)	(02.00)	(02.00)	(08.00)	(43.00)	(28.00)	(21.00)
Orissa	Lodha	50	33	3	14	-	-	-	39	11	-
			(66.00)	(06.00)	(28.00)	-	-	-	(78.00)	(22.00)	-
	Santal	50	18	26	3	2	1	-	17	33	-
			(36.00)	(52.00)	(06.00)	(04.00)	(02.00)	-	(34.00)	(66.00)	-
	Birhor	100	17	21	62	-	-	2	59	39	-
			(17.00)	(21.00)	(62.00)	-	-	(02.00)	(59.00)	(39.00)	-
	Mahali	50	17	23	7	3	-	-	19	28	3
			(34.00)	(46.00)	(14.00)	(06.00)	-	-	(38.00)	(56.00)	(06.00)
Bihar											
	Munda	50	-	3	7	22	18	-	12	25	13
			-	(06.00)	(14.00)	(44.00)	(36.00)	-	(24.00)	(50.00)	(26.00)
	Bhumij	50	1	4	12	13	20	-	9	25	16
			(02.00)	(08.00)	(24.00)	(26.00)	(40.00)	-	(18.00)	(50.00)	(32.00)

N.B. *Figures in the parentheses indicate percentages.*

TABLE 2.8
FAMILY TYPE

State	*Tribe*	*No. of family*	*Type*	
			Joint	*Nuclear*
West Bengal	Birhor	37 (100.00)	4 (10.81)	33 (89.19)
	Lodha	100 (100.00)	42 (42.00)	58 (58.00)
	Mahali	100 (100.00)	29 (29.00)	71 (71.00)
	Santal	100 (100.00)	33 (33.00)	67 (67.00)
	Munda	100 (100.00)	32 (32.00)	68 (68.00)
	Bhumij	100 (100.00)	19 (19.00)	81 (81.00)
Orissa	Lodha	50 (100.00)	8 (16.00)	42 (84.00)
	Santal	50 (100.00)	12 (24.00)	38 (76.00)
Bihar	Birhor	100 (100.00)	7 (7.00)	93 (93.00)
	Mahali	50 (100.00)	8 (16.00)	42 (84.00)
	Munda	50 (100.00)	4 (8.00)	46 (92.00)
	Bhumij	50 (100.00)	11 (22.00)	39 (78.00)

N.B. *Figures in the Parentheses indicate percentages.*

TABLE 2.9

FAMILY SIZE

State	Tribe	No. of family	Size			
			Small 1-3	Medium 4-6	Large 7-9	Very large 10-up
West Bengal	Birhor	37 (100.00)	12 (32.43)	23 (62.16)	2 (05.41)	-
	Lodha	100 (100.00)	19 (19.00)	60 (60.00)	20 (20.00)	1 (01.00)
	Mahali	100 (100.00)	21 (21.00)	67 (67.00)	11 (11.00)	1 (01.00)
	Santal	100 (100.00)	22 (22.00)	53 (53.00)	21 (21.00)	4 (04.00)
	Munda	100 (100.00)	16 (16.00)	70 (70.00)	10 (10.00)	4 (04.00)
	Bhumij	100 (100.00)	25 (25.00)	59 (59.00)	16 (16.00)	-
Orissa	Lodha	50 (100.00)	18 (36.00)	30 (60.00)	2 (04.00)	-
	Santal	50 (100.00)	10 (20.00)	26 (52.00)	12 (24.00)	2 (04.00)
Bihar	Birhor	100 (100.00)	44 (44.00)	49 (49.00)	6 (06.00)	1 (01.00)
	Mahali	50 (100.00)	19 (38.00)	24 (48.00)	7 (14.00)	-
	Munda	50 (100.00)	7 (14.00)	35 (70.00)	7 (14.00)	1 (02.00)
	Bhumij	50 (100.00)	9 (18.00)	29 (58.00)	12 (24.00)	-

N.B. *Figures in the parentheses indicate percentages.*

Data regarding the distribution of tribal families by their family size are furnished in Table 2.9. Here families have been classified into four groups. These are small-sized family (1-03) members, medium-sized family (4-6) members, large-sized family (7-9) members and very large-sized family (10 and above) members.

Considering the nature of family structure it has been observed that the maximum number of families in all tribal coummunities belonging to all three states show the same picture where mojority of the families are medium-sized (4-6 members). Very few families belong to very large sized (10 and above) group. As compared to all other tribal communities in all three states, the number of small-sized family is maximum in the Birhor community of Bihar (44.00 per cent) followed by the Mahali in Bihar (38.00 per cent), the Lodha in Orissa (36.00 per cent) and the Birhor in West Bengal (32.43 per cent).

3
Ethnographic Account

Tribal communities in general are considered as the simple children of nature. Many of them are characterised by qualities like gentleness, tolerance and hospitality and take no interest in material possessions and power. Despite many problems and difficulties, they seem always cheerful without any grudge against anybody. They envy none, and covet nothing. In actuality, the women—the fair sex—have some special values gradually accumulated in varied situations. Of course, in urban areas they are in a process of change, their activities are regulated by altered situations and in this way they are found to adjust themselves with the changed social contexts. So in course of time some new traits are incorporated in their cultural matrix.

It has been reiterated that six tribal groups represent almost six models through differentials and variations: the gathering-hunting Birhors and Lodhas, the basket-making Mahalis, the agriculturist Santals and Mundas and the Hinduised tribe—the Bhumij, who are gradually losing interest in their languages and exhibiting different lifestyles. Thus we can expect variations in their modes of living though they are found to be placed against a more or less similar geographical background.

BIRHOR

The Birhors, one of the most primitive tribes of Chhotanagpur, are nomadic hunters, food gatherers and rope makers. They belong to Mundari family and have their own dialect. The Birhors are generally found in the Bihar districts of Hazaribagh, Manbhum, Singbhum and Palamau, in the Orissa districts of Sundargarh, Sambalpur, Keonjhar, Dhenkanal and Mayurbhanj and in a few districts of West Bengal and Madhya Pradesh.

The word Birhor is made of two Mundari words - *bir* and *hor*. *Bir* means jungle (forest) and *hor* means man. So it means man of jungle. Birhors are also famous for rope making from indigenous fibres of trees and creepers known as Chop. Sometimes they use the surname as Chopdar which is derived from Chop. Linguistically they belong to Austo-Asiatic Mundari Group. The Birhor's dialect is more closely connected with Mundari than that of Santhali.

The Birhors always like to settle not far away from the villages of peasants because they sell their ropes and forest products to the villagers. Particularly in Bihar they prepare very durable ropes from the fibres of a jungle creeper which show great demands among the peasants.[1] In Orissa the Birhors are locally known as Mankidi, Mankria or Mankar Khia Kol which denote their habit of eating and sharing monkeys. In Oriya dialect *Mankar* means monkey and *Khia* means the habit of eating.[2]

Generally there are two main sections of the Birhors:

(i) Uthlu Birhor or Nomadic Birhors;

(ii) Jagghi Birhor or Settled Birhors.

But recently another section of the Birhor community has developed. It is known as Basalu or Semi-nomadic Birhor.

Uthlu Birhors are nomadic and roam about from one forest to another in search of food, shelter and comfort. Generally the people of this group like to move from one place to other place. Sometimes they move only with their own family but in other cases all family members belonging to one lineage and sometimes members of different lineages. They move in a cyclical way around and within the forests because they know when and where the natural things will be available, but now-a-days this type of migration often fails to fulfil its complete needs. Forests are gradually becoming thinner and the easy accessibility of this tribal people are sometimes restricted. For this reason, this tribal group is gradually alienated from their work. Except in the rainy season, the Uthlu Birhors move about from jungle to jungle in small groups with their families, their scanty belongings, and their gods or spirits represented by stones and wooden pegs and carried in baskets by one or two young bachelors who walk at the head of the party. Other boys carry fowls meant for occasional sacrifices to the gods; the men follow with their nets and tools and weapons; the women carry on their heads palm leaf mats, and wooden mortars and pestles. Dried *Mahua* (*Madhuka latifolia*) flowers and grains contained baskets are carried out by both men and women. The girls carry earthen pots for cooking and carrying water. They keep no cattle nor even cow or any other beast of burden to carry their belongings at the time of shifting from one camp to another. They ordinarily stop and hunt at one jungle for about a week or two and then move on to another jungle and form similar camp. In this way at last they come back to their original starting point. Generally it takes two years or little less or more.

The Jagghi Birhors, on the other hand, are those families who have settled down for a comparatively long period generally on some hilltop or the outskirts of some jungle. Birhors, both Uthlu and Jagghi, sometimes grow a scanty crop of maize or beans by burning a patch of jungle, and sowing seeds there. Generally, a Jagghi Birhor after his marriage with an Uthlu wife, sooner or later, joins the group of his Uthlu father-in-law and leads a nomadic life. The Uthlus have retained more of their primitive customs and usages than Jagghis.

II

The settlements of Jagghi groups as well as the temporary encampments of Uthlu groups are both known as *tanda.* A *tanda* usually consists of about half a dozen or more huts. They live in family groups—father, sons, daughters, grandsons and family members of such near relatives. In this way half a dozen to a dozen families live at a time in some temporary settlement. They put up their huts on the gentle slope of a commanding height at the fringe of a jungle on the outskirts of a village cultivation, near which the jungle begins. Their settlement is always very near to the place from where they can get water easily, either from a brook or a natural stream or a village well. They do not encamp within the deep forest. The hut is the basic economic unit both for the consumption and production. Sometimes in Birhor's settlement a kumbha (hut) may not have enough space for cooking. Usually two or more kumbhas are combined together and they form a common place used as a kitchen. The houses in the Jagghi tanda are a little more pretentious. Although the roofs of their huts are generally made of branches covered with leaves, they have better walls. Their huts usually possess slightly raised floors. Each family has generally one hut partitioned with two compartments, one serving as lumber room in which they keep one or more iron axes, hunting nets, rope making tools, and a few earthen pots containing dried mahua fruit grains. And the other compartment is generally used as sleeping room and for the purpose of cooking. A corner of the larger room is generally used as a pen for fowls or for goats or cattle. Some clans, such as the Ludumba, erect close to their dwellings a miniature hut. In this hut sometimes may be seen a small bamboo box called *bonga-peti* or spirit box. Some clans also have their spirit seats adjoining the settlement, where lumps of clay, pieces of stone, or wooden pegs represent the tutelary deities of the clan. By the side of the Jagghi settlement a sacred grove is called the Jayar. This is the seat of the sendra-bongas or spirit presiding over the hut. Before hunting all hunter's tools are kept to this place and a fowl is sacrificed to this place. At one end of the settlement, *a giti-ora* or sleeping hut is exclusively used by the young bachelors of the Birhor. The young maidens sleep with some old widows in a similar hut usually at some distance from the boys' *giti-ora*.

III

Birhors are basically hunters and food gatherers. Their economy is still traditional and mainly based on forest. Forest plays a vital role in their life. Birhors collect a number of wild roots, fruits, flowers, leafy vegetables and mushroom from the forest. Rope and rope-made articles are also produced by them from the jungle resources and it is one of the important primary occupations of the Birhors. They have great specialization in making ropes from different types of bark of creepers and trees. Different types of rope fibres, like Mahulan, Sisit, Udal, Tarparasi, Beri etc., are collected by both the male and female partners. Among these Mahulan fibre is the best, which they call chop. Trapping nets are mainly made of chop fibre. For these products the non-Birhor agricultural communities are fully dependent on the

Birhors.

Besides rope making, hunting or trapping is also important source of livelihood. They hunt by nets and during rainy season it is very difficult to hunt by nets. Hare's meat is in great demand among the non-Birhors. The subsidiary games are pig, deer, squirrel, porcupine, parrot etc. They also collect horns, bones, skins and other parts of rare wild dead animals from jungles and sell them in the neighbouring society for magico-religious purposes. Hunting party usually consists of eight to fifteen persons in which male, female and children take part. Sometimes they fail to hunt. In this situation they have to live without food or in starvation for a few days. Besides their occupational hunting, ceremonial hunting (*Disum sendra*) also takes place in their life.

It is a special type of hunting which is held once in a year on Baisakh Purnima (fullmoon—April—May). All members of different Tandas come and share the hunted animals. The Naya and other elder members also take leadership in it. The Naya prays to the Sing Bonga to invoke his blessings for the success of the team. The fowls are sacrificed to the Biru Bhut and chawrashi haprom for the welfare of the team. The heads of the animals are roasted and eaten by the men excluding the pregnant wives' hushands. The Naya also shares good amount of flesh due to his leadership. The rest of the meat is divided in equal shares among the members of the Tanda.

The majority of the Birhors live from hand to mouth. They do not get sufficient food the whole year. In June, July and August a few of the Jagghi Birhors who have cultivable lands work on field. Women also work as day labourers and most of the Uthlus in this season select temporary spot and sell the wooden cups and bowls. In September and onwards the men begin to collect chop and prepare net and the women make plates, bedmats with wild date-palm. They are in great demand by other tribal and non-tribal communities. Almost in every *Tanda* one or two Birhors have great knowledge about the indigenous medicine which are made by different types of plants, shrubs, flowers, leaves, stems, roots, and flesh of different types of animals. They are considered to be the most efficient herbal doctors. All kinds of problems like headache, stomach pain, fever, dysentery, problem of pregnancy, fertility control are cured through their herbal medicines. It is one of the important sources of their income.

IV

Among the Birhor, clan generally known as *Killi,* is the most important kin group. It is an exogamous group, though the rule of exogamy is not maintained in all the cases. The origin of almost all the clans are found on some hills or mountains which are now regarded as the sacred abode of their ancestral spirits or Bonga. So it is totemic in nature.

The opinion of anthropologists regarding the number of clans varies. Different studies on Birhor show different figures of the existing number of clans in different regions. According to *Roy* (1925) there are thirty-seven clans among Birhor in Bihar, while Adhikari (1984) in his study observes thirteen clans which are existing in Orissa.

Generally marriage within the same clan is prohibited, but nowadays their rule of exogamy is not followed. Even the clans are divided into number of sub-clans after the death of the father belonging to that clan. If their sons follow the separate rituals and sacrifices to their ancestors, the separate clans automatically come into existence. As for example, *Hembram* clan is ritually separated from the *Chauli Hembram* and *Penre Hembram* for introducing different mode of worship to their ancestral spirits. In this way, two separate clans have been formed from the original *Lakurchuta* clan.

Birhor families are patriarchal and patrilineal. Their household unit is often referred as *Orha.* After marriage the newly married couple form another *Orha* or separate *Orha.* Husband, wife and children perform various roles in their economic and family life. Affectionate relationship is found between parents and children. Eldest son often takes the responsibility of his family after immediate death of his father. The widows are given proper respect and widow remarriage is also prevalent in their community. Female children are not neglected. They help their mother in doing chores. The brother-sister relationship is very strong.

Observing the death ritual of the Birhor it can be said that the Birhors like the Mundas, Bhumij and other tribes follow many death rituals and usage from the Hindu. They also use the term "Haribol" which means uttering the name of the Hari or God for final salvation.

V

Life cycle of each group starts with preconception and ends with post death rituals. They believe that one can get a child after the goodwill of the Bonga. If any woman inspite of her good health does not conceive they think that some of the spirits are not pleased, so they try to appease these spirits by offering worships and sacrifices. The *Naya* through his supernatural powers tries to please the spirits for her.

The pregnant woman gains a high social status in their society. In this period the woman has to maintain the taboos some of which are for her health. Through this prohibition she would get rid of doing some laborious task. She would not go in all places. She would not eat all edible things. She would not be allowed to go to forest because evil spirits are there. Through these taboos she would be protected and delivery would be safe.

The birth of a child takes place in her own *Kumbha* with the assistance of a mid-wife (*kusrain*) who is an aged lady. After the birth of the child they all beat *thalis* making great noise for protecting the child from being deaf. The mid-wife cuts the naval cord (*buka*) with the help of an arrow-head and buries it deep in the ground outside the *Kumbha* near the door. In many cases during delivery a new opening in the *Kumbha* is opened from back-side. On the following day at about noon the mother is given food with drinks and the husband of the woman takes bath in some spring and takes a jug of water and slowly pours the water standing with his face towards the sun and prays to *Sing Bonga* for sufficient breast milk. From the second day after delivery she is given a meal of hot rice and a soup of rahar pulse every evening. The Birhors believe that the future luck of the new born baby is determined according to the nature of hunt on that very day. The *Chhathi* or *Thathi* or the First day of purification is celebrated on the seventh day from the date of the birth of the child. This day is for the final purification of the other members of the *tanda* and the preliminary purification of the new-born child and its mother.[3] It is also observed by Sahu (1995) in his "Birhor Tribe" that *Chhathi* is the final purification.

The name ceremony of the new born child is one of the important ceremonies of the Birhor and generally this is celebrated on *Chhathi*. The name of the baby is finalised in the presence of the men of the *tanda*. They take a bowl of water and after shaking it up they drop *til* seeds and paddy grains into the water. Then they utter the name of their paternal grand father and their relatives one by one. At the very moment when *til* seeds and paddy grains touch each other then whose name is uttered, the child is immediately given that name. If the relative whose name is selected is present there he anoints the child with oil and performs certain rituals. He presents the child as gifts one or two copper coins and necklet of black beads. This man is called *Saki* (Sponsor) of the child. *Saki* may be the member of their clan or not. He is offered a dinner and rice beer. The child always follow his *saki*. If he is a *Mati* then the child will be a *Mati* in his future life. The child also has a second name. Generally his name is selected according to the name of the day, month, year etc. Nowadays, they use and prefer their second name than the *Saki* name.

On the *Thathi* day, men of the child's clan living in the *tanda* have their nails pared, and their beards and heads are shaved. Women of the clan also pare off their nails. The nails of the mother and the baby are also pared. Finally the baby's head is shaved and is taken for bath by the side of a river. There they worship Bonga on the river side for protecting him from evil spirits. Then the *Naya* with his face to the east offers a red fowl to the name of *Chowrasi Pahar Parbat* (the eighty-four hills and mountains) and one black fowl to *Mahali Chati* (who is said to be the mistress of the spirit of Lugu Pahar). At each of the two spots of sacrifice the rice beer is kept. It is believed that unless these sacrifices are offered, the birth taboo will continue and the men of the *tanda* will have bad luck. However, all the *tanda* members are invited on that day for dinner. They take cooked food and rice beer. They enjoy by singing and dancing and it continues till midnight. In some *tandas* twenty-first day after birth is considered for final purification ceremony. In that case the head of the family also sacrifices a red fowl with rice-beer to the spirits of his ancestors.

Marriage as a social institution helps the grown-up boys and girls belonging to different families to build up a new *Orha*. Generally adult marriage is practised in their society. Marriage by negotiation is mostly popular than marriage by exchange (*golat*) and intrusion (*dhuku*). Except these, levirate and sororate marriages are not uncommon. Monogamous family is the general form, but polygamous family is not totally absent in their society.

Society provides no restriction to negotiate marriage among the kin groups. Only three generations individuals either on father's side or on mother's side are prohibited. Bride price is the system which prevails in their society. Generally after selection of the bride and bridegroom from both the parties before marriage, the bridegroom's parents talk to the bride's parents to fix up the bride price which varies from Rs. 8 to Rs. 24 only. Except this cash payment ornaments made of brass, clothes, chickens and rice beer are also given as bride price. After fixing the bride price the marriage date is settled. Generally it is observed that they prefer the time after harvesting from January to April to arrange marriage when they fully depend on hunting, rope-making and food gathering.

In the morning before starting the procession in the bride-grooms' family, ceremonial water is brought from the spring and each of the two spinsters carries the earthen pitcher. One of them carries a sword and another carries a bow and an arrow. The mouth of the pitcher is tied with the yellow thread dyed with turmeric and brought to the bridegroom's hut. The mother of the bridegroom comes out with potsherd containing some live charcoal and sprinkles a handful of mustard-seeds on the fire. After burning the mustard-seeds the potsherd with its contents is left upside down on the courtyard and the objects, sword and bow and arrow appear to scare away evil spirits. They perform various marriage rituals where sister and sister's husband play important role. Before starting the journey the bridegroom puts on his bridal dress of a *dhoti* dyed yellow with turmeric. If possible *chadar* or wrapper for the body or *pagri* are sometimes used. Then the bridegroom accompanies with female folk including his mother and one of the females also carries a *lota* full of different articles like vermilion, thread, leaf plates etc. Then his sister's husband takes the bridegroom to a mango tree. He puts vermilion marks and ties a thread on it, and chews some leaves. Then he starts his journey.

Reaching there a few women of the bridegroom's party go to the bride's house and anoint her with oil and turmeric.

She then takes bath and puts on bridal clothes presented by the bridegroom's party. A few women of the bride's party also do the same thing to the bridegroom. Then the marriage rituals are performed mostly by the female members.

In case of widow's or widower's marriage, the marriage ceremony is simplified. Other forms of marriage like levirate and sororate marriages are also prevalent among them. Sister exchange marriage is very popular among them. There is also a form of marriage in which a girl decides to marry a young man and intrudes into the father's house with her own bundle of clothes. In another form a young man waits in a market place for his sweetheart and applies vermilion mixed with oil to the forehead of the girl.

The marriage ceremony takes place in the bride's house. The bride and bridegroom take seats set in the courtyard in front of *Naya* facing towards east. *Naya* spells *mantras* (incantations) and asks the bridegroom to apply vermillion on the forehead of the bride with the thumb and first finger of the right hand. Next morning chicken and rice-beer which are received from the bridegroom's house are distributed among the participants. They enjoy the day with great amusement.

The *mari* (cooked rice) and chicken are served to the newly wed couple. After marriage the bridegroom brings the bride to his father's house. When they reach their *tanda* the *Naya* worships the spirits and deities of *marai* for the well being of the newly married couple. If they construct the separate *Kumbha* before marriage they enter to their new *Kumbha* and worship their ancestral and family spirits. Except this some detailed marriage ritual is performed in some *tanda* by the female members of both the parties.

Perhaps the most important incidence in the life cycle of the Birhor is the cessation of life, which is believed to be caused by some evil spirits. Death, naturally involves some supernatural beliefs and demands some rituals to be performed. It is the temporary separation of the soul from the body. In fact the Birhor believe that every individual has two souls. These souls are of opposite sexes, i.e., one is male and the other is female. They, when the individual dies, come out together from the body and enter into a new one. However, not only the evil spirits but also when different Bongas are not worshipped properly they become angry and this may cause the death of any of their family members. The Birhor also believe that the spirits of their ancestors move around their huts till the end of the death rituals.[4]

Cremation is the general practice among the Birhor, but the dead bodies of the children and pregnant women are buried. Also in some exceptional situations the custom of burying the dead body is allowed. The Birhor believe that death conveys pollution and therefore when the dead body is taken out they clean the place where it was laid by water and the cooked food, drinking water etc. are thrown out.

The members of the same tribe carry out the dead body to the cremation ground by uttering "*Bolo Hari Hari Bol*". In this procession the women are not allowed. However, in the cremation ground the corpse is laid on the pyre pointing the head to the south after taking rounds three times Mounds the pyre. The eldest son sets fire for the first time. After the burning is over a tooth, a finger bone, thigh bone and some of the other bones are taken into a earthen pot. This pot is kept on a tree in the courtyard of the deceased house until the shaving ceremony. This ceremony takes place on the seventh day of the death. Restrictions regarding eating are imposed on the members of the family until the shaving ceremony. During this period they are not allowed to take alcohol.

In case of burial, the dead body is kept in the grave pointing the head to the south. The eldest son of the deceased first touches fire in the body and moves three times round the grave. Some articles like axe, tabocco, brass plate etc. are put into the grave.

However, in the evening of the shaving ceremony a feast is arranged. During this time the religious head of the community takes some rice and throws it in the name of the deceased. He is followed by other members also. Thus the pollution period is over.

The Birhor think that pollution comes through death. When the corpse is taken out of the hut, all water, cooked food, ashes in the hearth, burning charcoal are thrown away. Even the spirit hut is considered infected with death pollution. After the death of a person all the ingredients in the spirit box are seemed to be polluted and thrown away and new ingredients are replaced in it. When the pall bearers return home after burial or cremation, all old fires in the *tanda* are extinguished and thrown away, and every Birhor in the settlement takes a bath and the new fire either friction of two stones of wood or the new fire from separate *tanda* is brought for the same. Until the *Hoyon* or shaving ceremony which takes place on seventh day from death no Birhor of the settlement will shave. Amongst the Uthlus no one will go for hunt upto *Hoyon.* But the Jagghi Birhors are allowed to go for hunting but they do not take any flesh of the game. Singing and dancing are not allowed in the *tanda.*

The corpses of children and women dying in time of childbirth are buried. During the rainy season and in poor economic condition they do not follow cremation. On death, the corpse is washed and anointed with oil mixed with pounded turmeric. Married deceased is put vermilion marks on the forehead. The corpse is then stretched out and bound on an improvised wooden bier to the cremation ground. When a corpse is to be cremated, a funeral pyre is arranged by the men. The corpse is carried three times round this pyre and then the dead body is laid flat on it with its head pointing south. The son or grand-son touches the fire into the mouth of the corpse and straightway leaves the ground without looking backwards and goes to some stream or spring where he bathes and then returns home. When the corpse is wholly burnt, the women of the *tanda* bring jars of water from some stream and pour the water over the members with a winnowing. Then the women with their left hands pick up first a tooth, next a finger-bone, then a thigh-bone and finally the remaining bones. These they carefully wash in water and put into a new earthen jug. This jug with the bones is carried at home and hung up on some tree near the deceased's hut to remain there until the *Hoyon* ceremony. They all take bath in some nearby stream.

Food offering for the deceased is one of the death rituals. On the evening of the day they offer food to the spirit of the dead at the outskirts of the settlement. On the seventh or ninth day death the bones of the cremated corpse are buried in a small hole under some tree and covered up with stone or slab.

VI

The religious life of the Birhor is coloured with different gods, goddesses and spirits. They think that the whole universe is created and controlled by *Sing Bonga* or the Sun God and his wife *Chandu Bonga* or the moon. *Sing Bonga* is regarded as their supreme deity which is extremely powerful. He is thought to be benevolent. It is worshipped once a year usually in the months of *Paus-Magh* (Jan-Feb). *Chandu Bonga* is also worshipped in the same month but in case of her worship a black hen is sacrificed. At the time of worshipping *Sing Bonga* a white cock and a he-goat are sacrificed. Besides, there are other deities. *Dhatri Mai* or *Devi Mai* is one of them and she also plays a significant role in their life. She is known as the earth goddess. She is worshipped usually in the month of *Agrahayan* (Nov-Dec). A black hen or a black she-goat is sacrificed during her worship.

The Birhor have supernatural beliefs on different types of beast-gods. *Bagh-bir* (tiger-god) is the presiding deity over the tigers. Cocks of mixed colour are sacrificed to Him. *Hunder-Bir* (Wolf-god), *Bir-Banhey* (Orang-Outang god), *Bandar-Bir* (Monkey-god and Hanuman-Bir (Baboon-god) are also propitiated. They are all the presiding deities of wolf, orang-outang, monkey and baboon respectively, and they are sacrificed with cocks and fowls of different colours in various occasions. *Mahadeo, Kali Mai* and *Burhi Mai* are also the deities of the Birhor who are superior to man. The concept of these deities has been generally borrowed from the Hinduised neighbours who were in the agricultural stage. These are the gods and the rest in the supernatural worlds are different spirits. The Birhor like many other tribes call themselves as the Hindu and there are number of Hindu supernatural powers. There are four main groups of common deities: *Kando Bonga* is very common and can be seen in each *tanda*. He is absolutely benevolent; *Ora Bonga* is a lineage god. He gives prosperity and happiness and special puja or sacrifice is done when any one sees dreams of his; *Hapram Bonga* is a ancestral god. *Hapram* means respect for an elderly male, ancestor of a lineage. He is not individually worshipped but a communal worship is arranged for the general welfare of the community as well as the family; *Tanda Bonga* includes a number of gods, goddesses and spirits. During the time of any ritual or any worship their names are uttered.

Except these there are different types of spirits which

have immense effect in their day to day life. Each and every spirit is explained by them and these spirits are also controlled by the magical performance of the *Mati.* Many bad incidences in the societies are happened due to these evil spirits. Some sort of sacrifices and magical performances are required to avoid the evil effects of these spirits. Area to area the nature and type of evil spirits differ. But their life is fully controlled by these spirits and their effect is either good or bad.

The main sacred head among the Birhor is called *Naya.* The *Naya* is not only a religious head of a particular *tanda* but he is incharge of all other activities of the Birhor of that *tanda.* For this reason he is called the *Malik* of the *tanda.*

Generally the post of a *Naya* is hereditary but this rule is not followed always. If a *Naya* is issueless then other nearest relative will occupy that post as *Naya.* In every *tanda* there is a sacred place which is called *Marai.* In most of the cases the worship and sacrifices are offered to that place. By birth a *Mati* or a magician occupies his religious post. Some men from childhood are found more sensitive to supernatural influences than others. And such sensitive persons slowly and gradually become and act as *Mati* by possessing the magical power.

The Birhor celebrate a number of festivals throughout the year of which a few important are to be mentioned like *Sarhul, Karam, Dasai, Jitia, Sankrant, Fagua* (Holi) etc. These festivals are very important in their day to day life. These festivals break the monotony and enliven them with new spirit. *Sarhul* and *Karam* festivals are the observation of fertility rites. These are celebrated for good crops. The common belief behind the *Sarhul* festival is the marriage between the earth and the sun. During *Karam* in the month of Bhadra, a *karam* branch is brought and ceremonially planted in the open space of the house. *Dasai* festival takes place in the month of *Aswin.* Goats are sacrificed. For the welfare of the family this festival takes place. *Jitia* festival generally takes place twelve days after the *Karam* festival. *Jitia pipar* tree, and a branch of *sekre* or *sidha* tree and a twig of the *mahua* tree are tied together and planted. *Jitia Kahini* (story in the form of poetry) is recited by someone who knows it. The *Arua* rice, milk, molasses, clarified butter, rice flour cakes and flattened rice are offered to the *Jitia* plants and its associates. Generally the *Naya* is appointed to perform the worship and sacrifices are offered for the general welfare of the family and entire community.

THE LODHA

The Lodhas of West Bengal are one of the ex-criminal tribes of India. The Criminal Tribes Act was passed by the British Government of India as early as 1871. An individual of any community who was considered to be a habitual criminal or who committed systematic crimes came under the purview of the Criminal Tribes Act for constant surveillance. Eventually in 1952, this law was repealed. The Lodhas were badly involved with a good number of major and organised crimes like dacoity, robbery, burglary, theft etc., in the district of Midnapur around 1900. Many of them were sent up for trial and some of them were put under surveillance. The Lodhas were declared as a criminal tribe in 1916 under Governmental Notification No. 7022-23 dated 20th May 1916, Calcutta.[5]

In earlier days the Lodhas were engaged in hunting and food gathering economy. They fully depended on forest and forest products. But that situation did not continue forever. Many restrictions were gradually imposed for utilisation of the forest products. The primitive people, who were once brought up around the forest which provided the raw materials of their lifestyles and the joys and sorrows of their lives and were automatically tuned with the forest environment, were gradually alienated from the forest by losing their free entry into it. Before that, they thought that forest was quite inseparable from them. Gradually they started working as agricultural workers and engaged themselves in cultivation.

But basically they are lazy and avoid hard work. They are poor and their socio-economic conditions are very bad. The local people also exploit them. They have no future plan. So when they can get any help from the government they are incapable of utilizing it and become the victims of local people. In this way their agricultural implements are used by the local people, their lands are purchased and cultivated by the money-lenders and they become the landless labour of their own land which once belonged to them. The stigma of "criminal tribe" also helps the local people to make isolated from the mainstream of population. Different types of anti-social activities are committed by them partly due to their criminal identity.

II

Savara is a generic term which is often used by many tribes of this region. This Savara group, known as primitive and forest dweller, used to live in forest and were widely known as hunters. We got ample references to this group from our early epic periods. Sometimes members of this Lodha community also identify themselves as "Savara".

The Lodhas live in villages. In most of the cases they live with other castes and communities. Generally the huts of the Lodhas are clustered in two rows in a haphazard fashion. These are all thatched huts made up of mud-wall and straw-roof. The Lodhas in jungle settlements are quite different. The huts have a rectangular ground plan, the four walls are constructed by branches of the tress or bamboo placed vertically or sometimes mud-walls are also constructed in a jungle area. Majority of these jungle huts have no window but small doors without plank shutters are found in every hut. The single room which constitutes the hut is used by them for every domestic purpose. A raised earthen platform called *isan* is constructed near the hearth where offerings are made to ancestral spirits. But in village areas the families are a little better off. They build mud-build thatched huts with more than one room, small windows are there. Sometimes they have courtyard and kitchen gardens which are attached to their huts. They have also one verandah covered by bamboo sticks, where they keep the domestic animals like goats and hens.

The Lodhas are strictly endogamous family. In a few cases inter-caste marriage takes place. Clan organisation is an important feature of the Lodha society. All individuals belong to one clan or another. Each clan has a totem name, strict taboos or restrictions are observed with regard to them. Marriage within the clan is prohibited. Clans are not hierarchically arranged. All have equal status. Only members of the *Kotal* clan receive some extra respect from others as the task of serving as *bailiff* in the village is regarded as the monopoly of this clan. The Lodha clan is a patrilineal unit. After marriage girls are initiated into the respective clans of their husbands. Generally the following clans are observed among the Lodhas.

Name	Totemic objects
1. *Bugta, Bhakta*	*Chirka alu,* a kind of Yam available in the jungle.
2. *Mallik*	*Makar,* a kind of Shark or sea-monster. The *Salfish* is treated as totem.
3. *Kotal*	'Moon' and Grasshopper.
4. *Laik, Layek*	*Salfish* (ophicaphalus marulius)
5. *Digar*	Propoise.
6. *Paramanik*	A kind of bird named *Manik.*
7. *Dandapat or Beg*	*'Bagh'* or tiger.
8. *Ari or Ahari*	*Chanda* fish. (Ambasisis ranga).
9. *Bhuiya or Bhunia*	*Salfish.*

(Bhowmick, 1963)

III

Poor socio-economic conditions compel them to live in nuclear families with one of their parents. Children are brought up under the direct care of their parents. No special preference is given to boy or girl. Though now a days many of them prefer male child. Senior girl children look after their brothers and sisters when their parents are in field. Side by side, when they are grown up they also take many responsibilities of their families including cooking. Old persons are also respected in their families. Grand-children are often cared by them. Old male persons are most responsible persons of their families as well as the society where they live in. Grandfather and grandmother and other older persons of a family are given due respect by the younger generation. The nature of grandparent and grand child relationship is full of affection. They sometimes tell jokes, folk tales, ghost stories etc. Elder brother is highly esteemed by the wife of the younger brother and the custom is that they should not talk to each other and she should not be exposed in front of him. Reversely a jocular relation exists between the elder brother's wife and the younger brother. A few people are found to marry the wives of the deceased elder brothers. Mother-in-law is respected like one's own mother. Husband's sister is looked upon like one's own sister.

Child marriage is not uncommon where the age of the bride varies from 10 to 12 years and that of the bridegroom from 15 to 25 years. But generally the marriage unions are settled at the matured age (15-20 years) of the girl after attaining puberty. Negotiations for such marriages are conducted by a person who acts as a go-between amongst the parties of the marriageable boys and girls of different families. At the final stage a bride price is settle. The bride price is received by the bride's mother before the wedding ceremony. But the custom of bride price is now only prevalent in the Lodha families those who live near jungle or interior places. But in other cases the system of bride price is automatically changed and in its place dowry system has been introduced. According to the status of bridegroom's family the demand of dowry either in cash or in kind or in both is to be claimed. The wedding ceremony consists of a series of rites and rituals. Levirate is permissible in the Lodha society but it is not obligatory.

Divorce is freely practised in the Lodha society. No formal intimation or ceremony is required for divorce. Adultery or indolence on the part of a wife are generally the two main factors which lead to divorce. In every case of divorce, the general complaint of the wife is the alleged ill-treatment by the bridegroom's family. Another cause of divorce is that a bride of tender age being immature in sex. When such a divorced wife is remarried, this marriage contract is called *Sanga.* This is less costly and the rites of usual marriage ceremony are performed in this case. The permission of village headman is required to make such arrangement of marriage. Widow remarriage is also called *Sanga.* Besides the usual wife and the wife of the *Sanga* marriage there is also a form of concubinage.

IV

Nowadays interference of political parties is greater, yet the older persons take crucial roles to solve different disputes which take place in their day to day life. Except the village panchayat they have their own political organisation (panchayat) where three important office bearers are seen. These are *Mukhia*—the headman of the village, *Dakua*—the village messenger or bailiff and the *Paramanik*—village cook for the ceremonies. Some important disputes of their community are settled by the Mukhia with the help of other male members of Lodha village panchayat. He also performs certain important functions and lead the community. All members of their community and the members of other neighbouring communities also show their respect to him. Generally the Dakua like *Mukhia*—convene the meeting at a common place. He is also very respected person in the Lodha community and some important functions in connection with marriage is performed by the *Dakua.* Dakua generally comes from the *Kotal* clan. The paramaniks are the professional cooks of the Lodha community and are engaged for ceremonial cooking.

V

Stoppage of menstruation is taken as the sign of pregnancy. Gradually the outer symptoms of pregnancy are noticed by others. During this period women are abstained from hard working. Some restrictions are also imposed to her. Some of these are as follows:

(i) Fish caught in a basket trap should not be eaten by them.
(ii) The pregnant woman will not be allowed to sew torn pieces of cloth with a needle.
(iii) Unholy places like a cremation ground should not be treaded by a pregnant woman.

Besides these restrictions, the gurdians of the pregnant women observe *Manasiks* or take vows to offer fruits, goats or fowls as sacrifices to the local deities for the safety of the baby and the mother and a trouble-free delivery.

At the time of delivery, generally a *Hadi* woman, one of the untouchable castes is asked to serve as a mid-wife. Delivery is generally held in a home. There is also not any separate apartment for delivery. In most of the cases delivery takes place successfully by the mid-wife. In serious cases, medicine men are sent for as expectant mothers are generally thought to be spirit-possessed. They sacrifice a fowl or a goat to the deity for her safety. But nowadays they generally prefer local doctors or hospital for any critical case.

After the child's birth the mid-wife cuts the umbilical cord by a sharp bamboo slip from the navel of the baby and then ties it by a thread. After a while the placenta comes out of the womb and is kept inside an earthen pot covered with an earthen plate and it is buried in the south-west corner of that room. The floor is cleaned by the mid-wife with a solution of earth, cowdung and water already prepared by the elderly females of that family. The barber and washerman are informed. The nails of the baby and her mother are pared off first then other family members follow the same rite. All of them take bath including the newborn baby and the mother. The barber is paid Rs. 25, 1 kg. rice and the washerman takes the used clothes and remuneration. Mother-in-law cleanse the kitchen with cowdung. For purification all used earthen cooking articles are thrown away in a fixed place. One *kajalpata,* i.e., a pot full of collyrium is kept on the bed of the child. This day is called *sajlat, a* i.e, the day of child birth. On this day the mother takes only a little hot water and the baby is fed with two or three drops of honey. From the second day to twenty-first day, the mother of the new born baby is given rice gruel without salt to eat and the baby is fed with breast milk. Twenty-one days from birth are considered as unclean period.

On the twenty-first day called *Ekushia* certain purificatory measures have to be observed again. The barber and the washerman come and they are given their remuneration. The mid-wife is also given a saree. A few well-wishers are invited and entertained on that day according to custom. After the period of pollution the mother is allowed to do every work and to eat every food item.

At the age of six months of the child first rice-feeding ceremony takes place. The village priest takes milk, sugar, sun-dried rice and new earthen pot to the shrine of goddess Sitala. He cooks these in a newly purchased earthen pot and makes a gruel which he offers to the deity and utters some sacred words and pray for the sound health and longevity of the baby. Then he hands over the *khir* to the head of the family. During that time baby's head is shaved and the baby is taken to the side of the pond to complete his bath. The body is smeared with a mixture made of turmeric paste and mustard oil. After taking bath a new cloth is worn to the baby and some members of their own clan and the members of the clan of his maternal uncles are also invited and the ritual is over.

The marriage rituals of the Lodhas are not so

complicated. There are four important phases to complete them. First, Negotiation through which marriage proposals are placed to both the parties by a go-between or some elderly person; Second, Selection of the bride and bridegroom, bride price, the date of marriage; Third, Wedding day preparations which include the following phases:

(i) *Gai-halud* or anointment of turmeric paste of both the bride and bridegroom in their respective houses, ceremonial bath and worship;
(ii) Construction of earthen platform or alter;
(iii) Starting of the wedding procession;
(iv) Dressing of the bridegroom;
(v) Procession to go to bride's home. Last part of the marriage ritual ends with the dinner of the couple;

Fourth, Return journey of the bridegroom with bride to the groom's house which also includes the following phases:

(i) Starting for the bridegroom's village and meeting the reception;
(ii) Blocking the way of entrance or *Batghera;*
(iii) Wearing of the iron bangle by the bridegroom or *Kharu-Parano;*
(iv) Undoing the wedding knot and the sacred thread on the wrist of the groom.

After completing the rituals the couple maintain their marital life and on the eighth day after the wedding ceremony the bride and bridegroom return to the bride's house. Sometimes for an under-aged girl another ceremonial arrangement of marriage has to be arranged. This is known as Remarriage or *Punarbibaha.*

Disposal of the dead is associated with performance of elaborate rituals by the Lodhas. There are two traditional ways of disposing of the dead body. Deceased adults are cremated but children are buried. After death the dead person is laid upon a mat with only a piece of old cloth spread over the body. All nearest kingroups and the villagers are informed. Only a sickle is placed on the bed of the dead to protect the body from being possessed by spirits. Some of the members of the bereaved family apply the oil and turmeric paste to the dead body. In the meantime a bier made of bamboo is prepared to carry the dead body to the cremation ground. Before taking the dead body to the cremation ground it is garlanded and a few *tulasi* leaves (*Oscium bacilicum*) with rice are put into the mouth of the dead body. The cremation ground is used by other people also. The funeral pyre is prepared with logs of wood. The dead body is placed on the pyre with its face downward and head towards the north. The eldest son takes the fire and walks seven times round the pyre. After that he puts fire to the dead man's face. During this time they cry and utter the word *Haribol.* After the eldest son, the other brothers also do the same rites and apply the fire to the face of the dead body. After that before returning from the cremation ground the bier is tied with a tree by a rope for the assumption that the spirit of the dead will not return from the cremation ground to the locality. All members of the deceased cross that rope and reach by the side of a pond or river. They take bath and utter *Haribol* three times and return home.

One place is cleansed with cowdung in the northern side of the courtyard and one *Bena* plant (*Operculina turpethum*) is brought and placed on that place. Some rice curry and water are offered and kept in that place each day for the spirit of the dead. It is continued upto the tenth day. On the fourth day the boys of the deceased visit the cremation ground with one earthen pitcher, a new piece of cloth, one *tulasi* plant, four bamboo sticks and the sickle used previously. The eldest son prepares a human image on the pyre after removing the halfburnt wooden pieces. *Tulasi* plant is planted on the head of this image. Four bamboo sticks are inserted on the four corners of the figure and the new piece of cloth is tied to the tops of the sticks forming a canopy and the earthen pitcher is used for carrying water from the tank and before preparing the image the water is pouered thrice on the pyre. Before their return journey they make a hole in the new earthen pitcher. On that day a new earthen pot is used for cooking. The vegetarian diet is taken until the period of mourning is over. On the tenth day the ceremonial feast is held and the barber and the washerman come and perform several rites and *Pret Hanri* or spirit pot is removed in that morning. The *Bena* plant is also removed and thrown into the water. On the eleventh day the *Sradh* ceremony takes place. That day a clarified butter and dried mango twigs are collected and burnt by a *Vaishnava* on that spot where the person breathes his last. The Vaishnava is duly paid for his service. Thus the *Sradh* ceremoney is over. That day a feast is given to the people of his community. The custom is prevalent in the police station of Sabang, Narayangarh and Kharagpur.

VI

Like other tribal people the Lodhas also believe the role of supernatural for their mysterious power possessed by certain objects and persons. There are two types of powers—maleficent. or beneficent. The interaction with the supernaturals is not an uncommon thing in their daily life. The good spirit and evil spirit always take part in their community affairs. For this reason different types of gods and goddesses are worshipped in their day to day life. On the other hand the spirit-doctor called *Ojha* or *Gunin* also plays an important role in their society. They know the technique to control the spirits or ghosts. Unnatural events or ill lucks stand for the evil spirit or ghosts. For the welfare of the community the *Deheri* conducts prayers, sacrifices and offerings to different gods and goddesses.

The Lodhas recognise the existence of *Bhagawan* or a *Supreme God* over all of them. This concept they develop from the Hindu neighbours. *Basumata* or Mother earth is considered to be a very important deity. She is propitiated with simple prayers along with *Dharma Devata* at the marriage ceremony before ceremonial bath is performed after anointment with turmeric paste. She has no shrine or residence of her own. Thus in the Lodha society the worship of *Basu Mata* is a common rite. For worshipping no particular date is fixed. She is also invoked before the communal dance which is performed with music.

Like mother earth, *Dharam Devatas* or god of righteousness is worshipped and invoked in all the ceremonial occasions. He lives in heaven and observes all the activities of men and animals. For this deity there is no temple or any sacred place, nor any offerings or sacrifices. This deity is only worshipped during the ceremonial bath of the marriage. Some sand or mud is piled for high image. Betal leaf and betal nut are placed on it to show reverence. Vermilion marks are made on it.

Sitala is considered to be the chief deity of the Lodhas.

She is worshipped with awe and fear as she is controlling deity of epidemic diseases like cholera, small pox. Sitala becomes a benevolent goddess when proper worship, prayer and sacrifice are made for her. She is worshipped once, twice or thrice a year. One on the last day of *Chaitra* (March-April), then on a day in *Vaishak* (April-May) and lastly on a Saturday or Tuesday in *Magh* (January-February), in the lunar fortnight. The deity resides in the shrine which is locally called the *Than* or *Maro.* The shrines are treated as communal property. The shrines are rectangular with mudwalls and thatched with straw. There is only one door for each shrine facing the east. Almost in every village such shrines can be seen. Inside the hut there is an earthen platform, locally called *Bedi,* where pots filled with water are placed before any worship.

Baram or *Garam* is the chief deity of the woods. Baram is the tutelary deity of the Lodhas. Baram is supposed to reside, in a grove or a tree near the jungle. Big *Sal* tree (*Shorea robusta*) or *Mahua* tree (*Madhuka latifolia*) or mango tree is the dwelling place of Baram. Baram is worshipped on the last day of the month of *Chaitra* (March-April) during the *Jathael* festival and on the last day of the month of *Paush* (December-January). Generally earthen elephants, horses etc. are offered at the foot of this abode. Perhaps the earthen elephants are the symbol of the deity. He appears in human form but is taller than average man. His body is covered with long hair. He holds a long axe in his hand. He rides on a tiger or an elephant. If he becomes furious or feels disturbed tigers may visit the village or elephants may come in the locality.

Chandi is also considered a mighty deity by the Lodhas. Literally the term *Chandi* means 'the terrible one'. For a short distance she travels on foot but her favourite conveyance is a lion or a tiger. She appears in various shapes. If she gets annoyed she may do harm to the people otherwise she controls serious diseases. Her blessings are invoked through prayers and vows. Generally, fowls and goats are sacrificed to her. *Chandi* is worshipped thrice or four times a year. Generally at the time of *Makar Sankranti,* the last day of *Paush* (December-January). *Chaitra Sankranti,* the last day of *Chaitra* (March-April) and the annual *Sitala* is worshipped in the month of *Vaisakh* (April-May). *Chandi* has got separate priests for her worship. Generally, earthen horses are offered in her name.

Yugini is the most dreaded of all spirits. She is one of the maids of the goddess *Sitala.* When *Sitala* is displeased or enraged, epidemic diseases like cholera, small-pox etc., occur. She has no head, but her eyes are fixed on her breast. Each *Sitala* worship is followed by the worship of *Yugini.* Generally a black fowl is sacrificed in her name.

Except these, three are different types of ghosts and other evil spirits like *Kundras, Chirguni, Pretasini, Kalpuras, Baghoa, Gomua* etc., who are believed to be vicious spirits. They are the souls of men who died accidentally and unnatural death like suicides or sudden attacks of snakes or wild animals.

The faith in witches of *Dains* and their evil influence is widely prevalent in Lodha society. They are both male and female. Witches are hated and feared by the Lodha society. Some amulets or charms are worn to avert the evil influence of a witch.

A detailed analysis of their religious beliefs and practices reveals that a process of Aryanisation is prevalent among them, where some of their deities are gradually being incorporated in the pantheon of their upper class Hindu neighbours.

Throughout the year the Lodhas are engaged with different types of worship of gods and goddesses of which some are malevolent and others are benevolent. Generally for the welfare of the community and community's people all such belief patterns develop. Sometimes centering this worship different festivals are arranged for their recreation. Generally these festival cycles are not enjoyed only by the Lodhas but also by the other community members.

The Lodhas are not the isolated group. Most of the Lodha population live in multi-ethnic villages. In their day to day life many of the Hindu cultural traits are automatically merged with their culture. Even in census the Lodhas are described as one of the Hindu groups. But the detail ethnographic study easily points out their tribal affinity. As they are very closed to Hindu caste group, they follow many cultural traits of their lifestyles. Festival cycles of the Lodhas easily reflect their close interaction pattern with other caste and community people. Sometimes they are set apart from other community but in most of the cases a close affinity is observed among them.

Generally, in the month of *Phalgun* (February-March) new mango or *mahua* flowers are offered to the deities near a tank by the head of the family. This is the ceremony in which the first fruits of the year are offered to the deities, *Basumata* and *Dharma Devata*. But this ceremony is mainly performed by the Lodhas those who live in jungles or near jungle area.

Worship of *Baram* or *Garam* is prevalent in almost all the Lodha villages except a few. In the same way, a few agricultural festivals like the worship of *Bani, Sar, Lakshmi* and *Kali* (Hindu gods and goddesses) are prevalent in particular Lodha villages. As a result, all these festivals are not strictly followed by the Lodha but also all the villagers of different castes and communities.

Worship of *Bani* takes place on the first day of the harvest ceremony. On this particular day the unseen deity is first saluted by the astrologer with folded hands and holding the plants with his left hand cut them with the sickle and makes a bundle of it. This grain represents *Lakshmi* or the goddess of Wealth. He lifts this bundle on his head and returns home. On his way back speaking to anyone is a taboos for him. When the women of the household see him returning, they blow conch-shells to welcome the August arrival of paddy. He keeps it on the thatched roof of his house. After that all family members take puffed rice and sweets only. Thus the ceremony is over. *Lakshmi* is propitiated in every Hindu home on each Thursday starting from harvesting time onwards, during the months of *Agrahayan* (November-December) and *Paush* (December-January). Worship of *Sar* is also an agricultural festival mainly celebrated by the agrarian communities. The Lodha families those who are very close to that community also perform this festival. On the last day of the harvest, i.e., the last day of *Paush* (December-January) the worship of *Sar* is celebrated. The bundle of ripe plant is carried and taken in the home as is done in the worship of *Bani*. Then they worship the bundle of ripe plants with agricultural implements in their courtyard and the process is continued till they hear the howling of jackals. The members of the family take puffed rice and fruits. Worship of Goddesses like *Sitala, Chandi, Manasa* and *Kali* (Hindu goddesses) are also performed by the Lodhas as a part of the great Hindu tradition. Partly they follow the Brahmanical pattern and the Lodha usages (tribal).

Goddess *Sitala* is also worshipped in the Lodha villages by a Brahman priest where no cooked rice and curry are offered to deity. But Yugini is not worshipped separately at the outskirts of the village with the sacrifice of black fowl by any caste other than the Lodhas. In the same way the goddesses *Chandi* and *Manasa* are worshipped by the Lodhas with the help of a special *dehri* (priest). *Bandana* is a cattle-caressing festival celebrated with the worship of cattle. This is a festival of the Mahatos and the Koras. The Lodhas those who live in Mahato-Kora concentrated areas perform this ritual. *Tusu* is also a regional festival and performed by the Lodhas. It is a social festival where only female members take part in it through singing and dancing. In this festival generally they worship the wedding festival of dolls. After the ceremony pan cakes are distributed among the community members for their enjoyment and recreation.

THE MAHALI

The word 'Mahali' was originated from the two words: 'Mah' means bamboo and 'Ali' means specialized. Etymologically the word 'Mahali' indicates those people who are specialized in bamboo work. They are also known as traditional bamboo workers. They have many tribal attributes of their own. Present researches also show that the Mahalis have greater tribal affinity to that of the Santals and they are also originated from the big Santal or Hor race.[6] Considers them as one of the branches of the Santal separated in comparatively recent times from the parent tribe. The Bedia group of people also assert them as 'Mahali'. Again, Risley opines that Mahali's rank might be equated with that of the Bouris. Both the Santal and the Mahali share common surnames, this also indicates their same origin, that is Austro-Asiatic linguistic group. The Mahalis are one of the Scheduled Tribes (as per Scheduled Caste and Scheduled Tribe Act, 1956) of West Bengal.

In early days the Mahalis were engaged as *Kheroal* specially in times of battle with the outsiders. All these groups, i.e., the Santals and the Mahalis have to work together during battle. It is said that the Mahalis provided the soldiers with prolectors, bows and arrow shafts made of bamboo. This particular group of people, ultimately in initiation of the caste system, are specialised in bamboo work.

Risley (1891) in his *Tribes and Castes of Bengal* mentions, the Mahalis as 'Dravidian castes of labourers, palanquin bearers, and worker in bamboo, found in Chhotnagpur and western part of Bengal'. He also describes them as,

> .... Branch of Santals, separated at a comparatively recent date from the parent tribe.... The exact causes of sepearation are, of course, lost in the obscurity which enshrouds the early history of all the tribal movements. But the fact is that the Mahalis make baskets and carry palanquins, the occupations which every Santal would deem degrading, suggest that the adoption of these pursuits may have given the first impulse to the formation of a new group ...

II

About fifty per cent of the Mahalis are distributed in different districts of West Bengal like Jalpaiguri, Midnapore, West Dinajpur, Burdwan etc. The rest are found in different parts of the states of Bihar and Orissa.

The Mahalis are the traditional bamboo workers. They are also cultivators. They participate in agriculture in different ways as owner-cultivator, share-cropper, contract-cultivator and also agricultural labourer. At present, they mainly prepare bamboo baskets which are used by the betel-leaf dealers in large quantities to pack the leaves for disposal. The men, women and children all are engaged in various types of economic activities throughout the year.

But in Mahali society the women are not allowed to plough and sow seeds. *According to Sengupta* (1969), " ... the Mahali economy portrays a small scale non-monetary or partially monetized economy." The Mahali women prepare baskets and at the same time they sell these baskets.

After harvesting and thrashing which end in January-February, the Mahalis are engaged full time with the production of basketry. Hunting is also a part of their economic life. The Mahalis are good hunters also. But large scale deforestation in recent times has compelled them to hunt occasionally instead of taking to regular hunting of small or big games.

(*Bhowmick* (1991) opines:

> They are hunters as well, and they prepare traps of bamboo splinters and large varieties of fishing traps, both for personal use and for sale among the neighbouring tribes and castes.

Young members go for hunt with bows and arrows made by them. Nowadays wild games are not available but they collect dove, wild goose, crane, squirrels, rabbits, rats etc., from the neighbouring areas and distribute them among the participants.

The Mahali society is patriarchal. But the position of women in the Mahali society is not regarded so much degraded. This is mainly due to their participation in the productive process. Both the males and females earn for the dependent members of the families. This relative economic self-sufficiency has enabled the womenfolk to secure prestigious status in the Mahali community.

Family is the smallest social institution of the society where the children of every community are reared and cared. The Mahali tribal community is not an exceptional one. Their society is patrilocal. After marriage the bride goes to the bridegroom's house. Previously bride price is given during the time of marriage. But at present, with the process of interaction and assimilation, the dowry system also has developed. The nature of dowry varies according to the economic status of the family.

Among the Mahalis the father is the owner of the property and he controls the whole family members. After his death the property is divided among the male lines. The girls of their society are highly emotional. At the time of difficulties they may take shelter to their father's family. Majority of the families are nuclear families and in many cases after marriage the son lives separately with his newly married wife. One of the major causes of leaving father's family is due to his poor socio-economic condition. In some cases after the death of their father, all the brothers live together and run a common household. Mahali families are not an exception from the local caste families. Conflicts are common scene. In many cases quarrel between mother-in-law and daughter-in-law is almost a common occurrence among the Mahalis.

III

The Mahali clans are patrilineal. They have elaborate clan organisation. Clans are totemistic in nature. It has been found that thirteen totemistic clans are present in the Mahali society. Marriage in the same clan is strictly prohibited. It is important to note that the clan names are closely related to Santal clans, but there is also little variation. Clan names are like, (i) Besra (Hawk), (ii) Hansda (Wild goose), (iii) Hembrom (arecanut), (iv) Kisku (king fisher), (v) Mandi (a kind of blue bird), (vi) Baske (a kind of herbal vegetable), (vii) Murmu (a kind of fish), (viii) Soren (the constellation pleiades), (ix) Tudu (ground rat), (x) Chore (uzard), (xi) Samah (grass), (xii) Pirhi (round pumkin) and (xiii) Khangar (Jackdaw).

Of course, Risley (1981) referred thirty-four clans among the Mahalis. The clans have no discrimination and all of them are equal in status. A few clans are again divided into sub-groups, like Mandi (totem: a kind of blue bird, locally known as *Nilchakra*). This clan has two sub-clans—Sada Mundi and Mur Mundi. The members of Sada Mundi sub-division wear white clothes without dyeing with turmeric during the time of marriage and Mur Mundi use clothes dyed with turmeric. In the same way, Murmu has six sub-groups. Again, Baske clan has three sub-divisions as the case of Besra. Hembrom and Handsa also have three sub-divisions. Tudu and Socren have two sub-divisions as the case of Kisku. Chose, Samah, Pirhi and Khangar clans have no sub-division.

The clans of the Mahalis conform to their traditional norm, i.e., they are fully exogamous. Marriage within the clan is considered as a punishable offence, i.e., breach of customary laws. The clan members consider themselves as brothers and sisters. As a result, marriage with the same clan is strictly prohibited. Even emotional love within the same clan never happens. Emotional love or any sort of sexual offence within the same clan is strictly prohibited because there might be super-natural punishment.

It is also found that some clans have little privilege in their village life. Most of the village headmen are from the Mandi clan. Headman is known *Manjhi.* Next to the Headman is called *Gorait* who is generally selected from the Besra clan. Again village priest or *Naike* and the ceremonial cook, i.e., *Paranik* belongs to a particular family of the Mandi and Baske clan respectively. Besides the *Pargana* is elected from Murmu clan and his main function is the ceremonial immersion of the bones of the dead. Clan names are generally followed by the members of the descent. The fundamental obligation is that the Mahalis should bear the clan names as their surnames except a few who have embraced Christianity. It is reported that in olden days they had to use different types of dresses but now-a-days these customs are not prevalent.

It is also reported that specific types of clan have to observe specific rites and obligations at the time of worship specially during communal sacrifice. The Sada Mandi sub-division does not use vermilion during the time of worship and recites sacred formulae in a very low tone. On the other hand, the Mandi clan uses vermilion and recites sacred formulae in a loud tone and sacrifices white coloured fowl. The members of the Murmu clan first sacrifice a red fowl and in the same way the members of the Baske clan sacrifice a mixed colour (*baranunia*) fowl to the worship of their *Orak Bonga*. Members of the Besra clan sacrifice a red cock for propitiation of some deities. While offering he sits in folded knees. Members of the Tudu clan at the time of offerings before the deities often sit with folded knees touching the ground, while that of the Kisku clan after offering the articles to their deities sit with folded knees touching their breast on the ground. Thus, it is clear that almost all the clans have to follow a traditional system of offerings and sacrifices even today. These are not yet changed though some of the members have received higher education.

Risley (1981) found five sub-groups among the Mahalis, they are as follows :

(i) Bansphor Mahali or basket makers and bamboo workers;

(ii) Pator Mahali or cultivators as well as basket makers;

(iii) Sulunki Mahali or cultivators and labourers;

(iv) Tanti Mahali or palanquin-bearers;

(v) Mahali-Munda, their occupation not mentioned.

On local enquiry it is found that in Midnapur areas the common Mahalis are Bansh-Mahali (Bamboo worker) which might have been indicated by Risley as 'Bansphor Mahalis'.

IV

The Mahali community has its own village council where different types of disputes among individuals and families are settled for justice. All adult members of that village are the members of this village council. Before the Panchayati Raj system, this village council played a very important role for maintaining village solidarity, peace and harmony. But after implementation of the present form of three-tier system of Panchayat by the State Government all such local traditional village Panchayats of different tribal communities are going to be very weak. Still they persist with their traditional leadership pattern. The headmen and elder persons of their community possess various roles and try to solve minor disputes which are exclusively of their own. But nowadays major decisions are mostly taken by the local self-government, where different castes and community members participate in that decision making process.

The Mahalis have three important office-bearers in the village council who are: (i) *Manjhi Haram,* (ii) *Gorait* and (iii) *Paranik. Manjhi Haram* is the headman of the village. *Gorait* is the village messenger or Bailiff. Generally he belongs to Besra clan and is associated with some rites and rituals during the time of marriage and death ceremonies. *Paranik* is the deputy headman of the Mahali village. Generally he belongs to Baske clan. All these members of Mahali community perform important function when the meeting is presided by the *Manjhi Haram.*

The post of the *Manjhi Haram* is hereditary and the headman is selected from the Mandi clan. After the death of the *Manjhi,* if he is without a son, his nearest kin group is generally selected for that post after making discussions with his two portfolios, i.e., *Gorait* and *Paranik.* His position is important and everyone in his community respects him, but sometimes he has to be dismissed from his post due to his unpleasant work. Generally *Gorait* acts as an assistant of the headman who fixes up the date of the meeting. He also summons all the adult members of their community to gather in a fixed place for attaining that meeting. The *Manjhi Haram* presides over the meeting as the chief of these office-bearers. The post of the *Gorait* and *Paranik* is also hereditary.

The three distinguished office-bearers of the Mahali community not only settle the disputes of the villagers, but also perform many important ceremonial functions of their day-to-day life. During the time of marriage, many essential obligatory functions are done by the *Manjhi Haram* and *Gorait.* As for example, the final settlement of the marriage ceremony is decided by the *Manjhi Haram* where he acts as one of the chief witnesses. Besides this, he also performs many other important functions of that ceremony. Like him the *Gorait* also does important functions such as inviting all the villagers to be present at the marriage ceremony, sprinkling water by mango twigs as blessings to the bride and bridegroom etc. The *Paranik* also acts as a cook for the wedding feast. All these greatmen are well respected by the villagers who offer ceremonial gifts, food and sometimes rupees in cash as their remuneration. In this way their positions are honoured.

V

Pregnant woman is highly welcome in Mahali family. The woman of their community are well aware of the pregnancy period that generally lasts 10 months. The relatives and the parents of the pregnant woman always make offerings to the deities and ancestral spirits (*Bongas*) for smooth delivery.

Some unholy places like cremation ground should not be visited by pregnant woman; this is because they believe some ghosts or spirits reside in those places and they may catch hold of the pregnant woman which may create danger to the baby in the womb. Distant travels are prohibited, and if necessary, generally a male member accompanies her. Fishes caught in a basket trap or in hook are strictly prohibited. Idea behind this is that there might be difficulty in delivery causing lingering pain. They are not advised to sew torn pieces of cloth with a needle which may cause blindness to the newborn baby. Preparation of cakes are prohibited with a belief that the baby may be of cleftlip. Jackfruit, wood-apple or pineapple eating is strictly prohibited.

At the time of delivery, generally a *Hadi* (Sweeper) woman of untouchable caste is sometimes asked to act as a midwife. In case of delayed birth or difficult birth, a *Gunin* or *Ojha* is asked for safe delivery. But now a days to avoid any type of complication the pregnant woman is taken to hospital.

During the time of delivery some senior women in the village always come to help the pregnant woman except the midwife. Unmarried girls are not allowed to go there. The popular Mahali conviction is that if unmarried girls see the childbirth, they will be either barren or give birth to the still born children. Before delivery the parents of the said woman take vows to offer fruits and fowls and sacrifices to the deities *Dharam* and *Garam* for the safety of the baby and the mother and for a trouble free delivery. Sometimes the spirit finder or the *Gunin* is called and he worships the *Orak Bonga* (family deity) and often sacrifices a fowl for safe delivery.

The *Hadi* woman acts as a midwife and cuts the umbilical cord with a blade and the placenta is taken and buried under a heap of cowdung in one corner of the courtyard. After that the child is taken for washing with hot water. Generally the baby is given the breast milk from the third day, the first two days milk is not given to the baby due to its thickness which may be a cause for diarrhoea. The first day the mother only takes some hot water. On the second day the mother takes some *Kurthi* pulses (*Dolichos Biflorus*) boiled in water without salt with a few pieces of garlic for flowing of sufficient breast milk. On the third day she has to follow some restrictions. On the tenth day a purificatory rite is performed by the husband. Village priest, i.e., degraded Brahman priest, is called on. The village deity is propitiated with rice beer. The midwife comes on the tenth day. She purifies again the mother and the baby. The mother is allowed to prepare food on that very day.

On the tenth day after birth a purificatory ceremony is performed—a room is sprinkled with fresh water—the mother is allowed to cook or to do little physical labour. On 21st day after the birth of a child a ceremonial feast is arranged to some members of the community. Barber has to pare off the nails of the mother and the child. At the time, name giving ceremony is held. A barber attends the ceremony.

In respect of marriage, there are certain prohibitions. Marriage in the same clan groups and immediate kin groups even with children of the ritual kins is strictly prohibited. Bride price is common in their society and the amount of it varies according to the economic condition of the groom's father and it is settled during the time of negotiation and paid in cash. On that particular day three pieces of clothes are brought and these are distributed among the bride's mother, foster mother or *dai* and the bride respectively.

Child marriage is almost obscure, and generally marriage takes place among the members when they are quite adult. Marriageable age varies among the members of the boys and girls. The girl's age is more or less fixed within 20 years. Husband's age at marriage is higher than that of the wife's.

The bride price is called *Bapla gonong;* which literally means marrieage money. *Bapla* is the most popular marriage which is fixed by negotiation. After accepting the marriage proposal first the groom's father with his party selects a date to go for fixing the bride price. That day a feast is also arranged by killing a goat or a fowl by the bride's party to entertain the groom's party and to make the marriage date valid. Similarly another date is fixed by the groom's father to entertain the bride's party and on that very day half of the bride-price is handed over to the bride' father through the village headman, i.e., the *Manjhi.* The go-between (Raihar) performs many functions in marriage ceremony starting from settlement to the end of it. Sometimes the kin members of both father and mother side and sometimes husband of the elder sister plays the role of go-between.

Three days before the of marriage, the ceremonial rituals start when the go-between carries turmeric powder and mustard oil from the groom's house to the bride's house and also brings these materials from bride's house to the groom's house. This ritual is performed with the help of village headman from both sides. In their community, *Nugti Bura* (groom's elder sister's husband) and *Nugti Buri* (bride's elder brother's wife) are the two important kin members, who perform different functions till the end of marriage. Another important ritual, i.e., the rice-feeding ceremony of the unmarried (*Aora Bhat*) is performed on the day of marriage where the *Nugti Bura* and *Nugti Buri* are invited by the neighbours and relatives and they accompany with the groom and bride in their respective villages. After eating *Aora Bhat,* ceremonial bathing of the bridegroom takes place. Then the bridegroom starts his journey by cart to the bride's house taking *Daora* (basket containing wedding materials) with him. The marriage party of the groom's side consists a few village members, relatives and friends. They arrive at the *Manjhi's* house and there the groom is cordially welcomed by the bride's mother and relatives. After this ritual the bride is taken by her mother, *Nugti Buri* and other relatives for ceremonial bath and after bathing she puts on a new saree and decorates herself. Before going to the wedding place for actual marriage, the bride gets married with a *Mahua* tree (*Madhuka Latifolia*) which is a marriage custom in the Mahali community. A similar marriage custom is followed in the groom's house where he gets married with a mango tree (*Mangifera Indica*). On completion of this rite, the real marriage takes place where a couple of rituals is also followed and finally the vermilion is put on the forehead and parting of the hair of the bride by the bridegroom. After this the marriage feast begins where invitees are served with meat of goat and fowl with country-made rice-beer (*Hanria*). Next day the couple starts their journey and reaches to the groom's house. The groom's mother heartily receives them in the *Manjhi's* house. From there they go to the bridegrooms house and sit there on a palm-leaf mat with *Nugti Bura* and *Nugti Buri* who take their seats on both sides of the couple. There also a feast is arranged. After taking bath all of them attend the feast and the next day they return from bridegroom's house to the bride's house. Spending two and half days there, the bridegroom, the bride and the *Nugti Bura* return to groom's house. Before returning on that very day bride's father gives a bow and arrow to the groom for killing a cock or hen by which a feast is also arranged and that day is also considered an auspicious day. *Nugti Bura* and *Nugti Buri* are well received by both the parties and are given new clothes for their services from both the houses.

Like the other Hindus the Mahalis cremate the dead bodies except in the case of death of a child, pregnant woman and a person affected by a contagious disease. Every village has its own cremation ground. After the death the family members of the deceased inform all the relatives, friends and kin groups. Before their of the deceased arrival they prepare the bier and collect wood and important necessary materials for cremation. The dead body is protected from the evil spirit by keeping a sickle and an axe near the corpse. The Mahalis are very much cautious and keep a watch at the domestic cat as they think that if the cat crosses the dead body then the it will turn into a ghost and harm the family members.

If the death takes place at night they wait for the morning. They carry the dead body by uttering the word *Hari Bol* three times in the room and throughout the path several times and finally reach the cremation ground. The pyre is built up with woods arranged in the ditch and the deadbody is placed on it and the face remains upward. The eldest son puts the fire on the mouth of the deceased three times and then other sons follow him. Fire is then set on the woods. Before returning from the cremation ground they take bath in a pond and later come to the house of the deceased person. The *Manjhi* also accompanies them and on his returning he keeps three branches of a *Kul* tree. (*Zizyphus Jujuba*) on the way, thereby the evil spirit of the dead cannot enter the village and does not do any harm to the members of the community. Before entering the house all the persons have to touch the burning coal which is kept in an earthenpot. The women relatives then also go to take bath and perform the death rituals accordingly. On that day all the earthen pitchers and the cooking utensils are thrown away and from the second day to tenth day they take vegetarian meal (rice, vegetables without oil) and maintain severe restrictions for remembering the soul of the dead. On the tenth day *sradh* ceremony takes place. All the relatives and neighbours are invited. After their arrival the deceased Person's sons shave head and pare off the nails with the help of a barber. The washerman also comes and performs his ritual to purify the house. After that they take all members for bath in a pond and anoint their body with turmeric and oil. Then they refresh themselves with some rice-beer (*Hanria*). In their community *paragana* is known as *Aguhandar* who conducts *Sradh* ceremony. According to the Mahali conviction the soul of the deceased enters in the new earthen pot which is taken by the *Pargana* to the village street where the thorns are kept by the *Manjhi*. The *Pargana* possesses some magical powers which make the deceased soul enter into the earthen pot. At that time the food is also offered to the spirit of the deceased. At night they bring the soul to the deceased house. At last the *Parganas* serves meat, fish and oil to the relatives of the deceased and breaks the pollution period. Then they all join in a feast arranged there. In this way the Mahalis perform *Saradh* ceremony.

VI

The concept of *Bonga* is very important in Mahali community. There are different types of *Bongas* like the *Sing Bonga, Orak Bonga, Age Bonga* and *Sima Bonga.* They are worshipped for specific reasons. All *Bongas* possess some supernatural power and do many good and evil acts for the people of their community. People generally think that if the *Bongas* are pleased, their blessings will fall on them and they will live happily and peacefully. But if they get angry, many evil incidents will occur and people will be affected by many diseases. For this reason the *Gunin* or *Ojha* performs many magico-religious activities to cure diseases and propitiate the *Bongas* by sacrificing a fowl or a goat, chanting *mantras* and sprinkling of holy water. Mahalis generally think that cholera, small-pox and other epidemic diseases break out due to the wrath of goddess *Sitala, Chandi* and *Yugini* or *Sima Bonga* and for their appeasement they arrange communal worship by collecting subscriptions from every member of their community.

The Mahalis profess Hinduism. All their life cycle rituals are performed as the Hindus. The Mahalis also depend on the caste groups as sacred specialists—the Brahmin, Washerman and Barber for conducting their rites and rituals in their day to day life. Throughout the year they are engaged in different festive occasions, like the other agrarian castes of their society. As they fully depend on agriculture naturally different festive occasions start from the sowing of the seeds and end until they bring the ripen food to their houses. All public places and temples are shared by other caste people so there is no such distinction.

The Mahalis are not in isolation. They always associate themselves with other caste and communities sharing their common beliefs, values, rites and rituals. Many common patterns of worship of Hindu gods and goddesses, some of the important birth rites, death rites and marriage rituals are followed by the Mahali community. The patron-client relationship between the agrarian community and Mahali community is still prevalent and reflected in their interaction pattern of their day to day life and also in times of different festive occasions held throughout the year. Naturally except their own deities the Mahalis accept many Hindu gods and goddesses and arrange their worship according to almanac. The Mahalis worship the deities *Dharam, Garam, Marang Buru, Joher Era* and also some Hindu gods and goddesses such as goddess *Laxmi, Manasa* and *Sitala* for the well-being of the members of the community. Some of the goddesses are worshipped regularly, while others occasionally. They also participate in many Hindu festivals like *Durga Puja, Kali Puja, Dol Jatra, Ratha Jatra, Maghi Parab, Bandana, Karam* and *Tusu*. A section of their community is Vaishnavites and they arrange puja of Sri Gourango Maha Prabhu on the day of *Dol Jatra* and they practise many rites and rituals of the Vaishnavas.

THE SANTAL

The Santals are one of the dominant tribes in India, mainly concentrated in the states of Assam, West Bengal, Bihar and Orissa. In West Bengal, the Santals constitute more than half of the total tribal population.[7] Except these states, a good number of Santals are also found in Tripura and in the neighbouring country, Bangladesh.

Originally the Santals were nomadic in nature and they roamed about from place to place in search of food and shelter. With the passage of time they gradually settled and established their permanent habitat in different parts of our country. According to Roy and others (1982), within historic times they settled in the Chhotanagpur plateau and in the adjoining districts of Midnapore and Singbhum and moved towards north at the close of the 18th century and made their home in Santal Parganas. Bhowmick (1992) points out that the name 'Santal' has come from 'Samanta Pal' meaning border force. According to him, the well-to-do families employed them as Samantapal. But Chowdhuri (1985) opines that the ancestors of the present day Santals lived for a long period in Samantabhum of Silda Pargana (Midnapur district of West Bengal) and in course of time they become popular as Santals. Before that they were known as Kharwars.

The dialect in which the Santals interact with their community members belongs to the Austro-Asiatic group. However, the Santals are in general bilingual. They speak in their own dialect known as 'Olchiki' and also use the local language to interact with the local non-tribal population. The Santals are a homogenous community. Strong sense of belongingness and group identity isolate them from the other tribal and non-tribal groups. They are very faithful, loyal, honest and hard working. For this reason in different rural, urban and industrial areas, a good number of Santals are seen to be engaged in different organised and unorganised sectors. Gradually, in those areas they have established their own settlements without destroying their traditional solidarity, which is so strong that they sometimes identify the others as *Diku*. Generally they consider the moneylenders, contractors and political infiltrators and such other exploiters as *Dikus*. They are also very much afraid of the *Dikus* (strangers) writes.

Bhowmick (1991) writes:

> Their truthfulness, simplicity and forthright conduct gave the tyrannical and scheming landlords and other employers to exploit them. When this exploitation surpassed all endurable limits they revolted...

II

The Santals are not restricted, in theory, to one fixed profession (Bodding, 1940). But at present most of the Santals are engaged in agriculture, though the method they apply and the tools they use are more or less backdated. So they often fail to get the maximum benefit from the soil. Actually rice is their staple food but they cultivate other cereals also. There are three types of agricultural land—*Barge, Goda* and *Khet. Barge* is cultivated mainly for the production of maize though other crops are also cultivated on *Barge.* Various types of millets are produced on *Goda. Khet* is the rice field. Besides their principal occupation, Santals are also engaged in hunting, fishing, collection of forest produce, honey etc. which to some extent help to increase their income and maintain the standards of their livelihood. But gradually their regular hunting of small or big games has been transformed into an occasional one. Their main trading craft was extraction of oil and manufacture of lime. But at present, due to massive deforestation and establishment of tea industry. West Bengal and Assam many Santals are employed as labourers in industries, mines, collieries, tea gardes and other places. Recently a good number of Santals have been recruited in various governmental and non-governmental departments and also they work as migrant agricultural labourer known as *Namal.*

A Santal dwelling consists of one or more huts usually made of bamboos or 'Sal' logs and are generally plastered with a thick coat of mud, and the roof is made of by the straw of rice plants. The construction of these huts depends upon the financial position of the owner of the household. Generally Santal houses are well decorated, having some floral designs in front side of the outer wall introduced by the female members. Their houses are without windows but in some cases little spaces are kept open to make the windows by fixing bamboo sticks there. In front of three or four houses there is a courtyard. Each and every house has also one provision for shed to keep cattle, pigs and fowls. But now a days a few Santal affluent families live in brick-built houses with all modern amenities. A good number of Santals have also converted their religion and turned into Christian. In most of the cases they are employed in different organizations where they live in quarters with all urban facilities.

III

According to the popular belief, the first human couple Pilcha Haram and Pilcha Buri divided the Santals into twelve ancestral clans one of which has been lost. These clans are totemic in nature and exogamous in character. The name of the clans are: Hasdak, Murmu, Kishku, Hembrom. Saren, Mandi, Tudu, Baske, Besra, Pauria, Chore and Bedea. The first eleven clans exist today excepting the last clan. Violation of rules regarding marriage is the greatest offence. Those who disobey these rules are expelled from the Santal society which is the highest social punishment. Previously the orthodox punishment known as '*Bit laha*' was prescribed but this occurs rarely at present.

The Santal society is patriarchal and the dominance of the males is found in every affair of life. But the females in the Santal society always play the active role in various household works and in the solution of various day-to-day familial problems. Thus they secure a prestigious position. They also join hands in economic activities and bear much of the financial responsibility of the family.

Generally in the Santal family the aged members are

honoured and respected by others. All decisions of the family are taken by the senior male members and often they take part in their traditional village panchayat which plays a dominant role for maintaining their cultural heritage and preservation of customary laws which even now restore their communal solidarity. Now a days due to migration in various places their extended families are disintegrating and small nuclear families are emerging for fulfilling their immediate needs. But in their traditional villages lineal joint families are visible and collateral joint families are rarely found. Children are also affectionately treated by the elders and in absence of their parents they are properly looked after by them.

The Santals have their own rules regarding the inheritance of property. Generally the son inherits the father's property after his death. But the daughters have no right in their father's property. When a Santal has no son but only a daughter, then she inherits the property. A daughter is generally maintained by her father or brother until her marriage. They also bear all marriage expenses. If a man dies without a son or a daughter, the widow is provided with one calf, one *Bandi* (10 to 12 *maunds*) of paddy, *bati* or one cloth and returns to her parent's house. In the Santal society the widow is sometimes kept by her husband's younger brother and does not return to her father's house after the death of her husband. A widow with minor sons keeps all the property in her possession but the senior members of her in-laws' house keep a watchful eye on her. If the widow gets remarried before her sons' marriage, the grandfather and uncles take possession of all the property; the mother has no right to get anything but sometimes a calf is given to her. However, the widow has the right over the property which she brings from her father's house during marriage. The customary laws of Santals regarding the inheritence of property have not yet been codified.

IV

The present village or the smallest political unit of the Santals is a vestigial form of the traditional political system. In every village there is a village council which consists of five officers each with distinct functions. The headman is known as *Jagmanjhi,* who is assisted by a *Paramanik,* an assistant *Paramanik,* or *Jog Paramanik,* a *Naiki,* the village priest and *Gorati,* the messenger. Nowaday the minor disputes are generally decided by the village Panch, though it has lost its past influence. The '*Manjhi Than*' is the usual place for communal talks and council meetings. Previously, above the village council there was the *Pargana* Council which had its jurisdiction over a number of villages. The headman of the Pargana Council was known as *Parganait.* But at present there are some hereditary *Parganaits* and a *Dihaj* for each large district who is responsible for calling the annual hunts and who presides over the Lo Bir or Santal 'High Court'. This ceremonial hunting is generally held in the month of April. However, *Lo Bir* is the highest Council recognised by the Santals. All sorts of disputes are placed before the council for getting judgements and these are followed with strict observance of laws.

The modern Panchayat system, introduced in the villages after Independence, has put a parallel administration and as a consequence the relevance of this traditional institution is deminishing day by day. In fact, with the introduction of Panchayati Raj an era of conflict, tradition - vs - modernity has been emerged. After the official recognition of the Statutory Panchayat, the old system is fading away. In the village level Panchayat the tribals are gradually losing their traditional power, prestige and privileges which are often overshadowed by certain external forces. The traditional political power of the tribals is getting infused into the local Panchayat bodies, and this creates an inevitable conflict between the tribal people and local political leaders.

V

A strong community feeling is observed in all important and crucial stages in the life cycle of the Santals. These are marked by the performance of certain rites in which the cycle of the Santals are—*Janam Chatiar* (ceremonial cleaning after birth), *Chacho Chatiar* (ceremony performed for giving full social rights) *Bapla* (marriage ceremony), and funeral ceremony. Through the '*Janam Chatiar*' a Santal child is socially recognized as one of the family members but he is not conferred any social right. The social rights are given through *Chacho Chatiar* when the child is four to twelve years old. This ceremony enables an individual to take part in all social, religious and ritual activities of the Santal society. In this way he occupies a rightful place in their society. This rite is performed before marriage and it is only for males.

The new born baby is highly welcome in a Santal family. Generally, a midwife with the help of elderly women relatives attends on the parturient woman. In case of difficulty, *Ojhas* are summoned to perform rites so as to expel ghosts supposed to be creating difficulties.

When the child is born, the umbilical cord is severed by the midwife with an arrow blade. The baby is then given bath in lukewarm water and the naval string is buried near the main door of the room. Birth pollution period varies from place to place. Generally, it continues either for seven days or twenty-one days. During this pariod the mother is allowed to eat warm rice with salt, leaves of Murai arak (an edible leaf, the radish) and garlic. Not only the members of the house, where the child was born are considered polluted, but also the members of the whole village are regarded as polluted. No festivity or sacrifice is held in the village and nobody dines in the house of childbirth till purification.

Usually the Santals observe the name ceremony (*Narta*) between the third and fifth day after the childbirth. But in some places this ceremony takes place at any day before the child is one year old.

On the day of the ceremony all friends and relatives of the family are invited. They come with small presentations of cloth, *bandia*, necklaces of beads (*mala*), *dora* (string worn round the waist, and rice beer, for the newborn child. Midwife who delivers the baby is also invited. She sits with the baby and the baby is anointed with turmeric paste, *mahua* oil. After that the midwife takes the baby to the side of the river or tank for ceremonial bathing.

An old man of the village offers the rice beer to the chief presiding deity, Maran Buru, and ancestor spirits of the family, uttering some incantations so that the baby may be made free from all types of diseases.

The male child generally receives his name after his grandfather, and the female child after her grandmother on the paternal side. The midwife is offered a fee in rupees or in kind, the rice beer and food for dinner and after then she returns. Between the third and the fourth year, children of both sexes have their ears bores by their grandmother or elderly female relative by means of a brass needle. It is quite a domestic ceremony.

The second critical period in the life of the Santal is sought to be guarded by a purificatory ritual called *Chachochatiar*. This ceremony may be observed at anytime before marriage and after that the male child is given the full rights and responsibilities of adult manhood. Without this ceremony, the marriage is not permitted and if he dies (without going through the ritual) the dead body is not cremated and bones are not thrown into the river.

The very day of the ceremony rice beer is prepared. The Headman and Paranik drink rice beer first and then they send it for the villagers. The *Naik* performs the rituals. The ceremony concludes with these utterings "We were black like crows, now we are white as white paddy ... you five men are our witness". In the twelfth year of age another magico religious rites are performed — Cicatrization for boys and tattooing for girls. In this way they are protected from all evil spirits throughout their life.

Bapla is the term generally used for marriage by the Santals. It means mutual strengthening of two families. Monogamy is the general profile of the society. Polygamy is practised to a limited extent. It is culturally favoured but relatively infrequent. They follow patrilocal residence, i.e., after marriage bride generally comes to live with husband's kinsmen.

The Santals generally follow adult marriage, the age of the bridegroom generally ranges between 18 to 22 years. Nowadays the incidence of premarital sexual intercourse is not prevalent as it was in the past. However, if an unmarried girl becomes pregnant, the man who is responsible for it, is compelled to marry her or provide her with a husband who would give the child a clan name. Regarding the arrangement of marriage three types are visible in Santal society: (a) the marriage which is arranged by 'Raibar' (marriage maker), is more prevalent, (b) the marriage which is arranged by the couple themselves. The incidence of this type of arrangement is generally increa-sing in number, (c) the of marriage which is performed between a widower or a divorce man and a widow or a divorced woman. Both the girl and the boy are consulted for their mutual consent before the marriage. Equal value is placed on the opinion of both the parties.

During the time of marriage it is strictly forbidden for a

Santal to marry within his own clan including the clan to which his mother belongs. Again there are some clans which never intermarry with one another due to some quarrel in ancient time between them. Premarital sex relation is tacitly recognized. Husband and wife have a well balanced role in sexual matter though husband plays the role of aggressive partner. Active participation in sex matter by both the husband and wife is culturally favoured.

Payment of *Conong* (bride price) is in vogue in Santal society. The Santals who are economically poor and are not able to pay bride price to the bride's family, can be allowed to live with their fathers-in-law and serve them for few years without any wages. Later on they set up their house with the assistance of the brides fathers and start living with wives. *Bapla* form of marriage is generally practiced by the economically well-off and high status Santals. In *Ghardi-jawa* form of marriage, the bridegroom lives with the bride in the bride's parent's house. Among the Santals, when a man has only one child, specially the daughter, he gives his daughter in marriage to a man who wishes to settle with his wife in his father-in-law's house and looks after the parents-in-law in their old age and at the time of crisis. This type of marriage is confined to only economically poor Santals. In marriage ceremony *Sindur Dan* (offering the vermilion) and serving marriage feast are the essential features.

The marriage ceremony of the Santals takes three days when the bride becomes the member of the bridegroom's family. On the first day the bridegroom with his party consisting of friends and relatives starts his journey for the bride's village. The party take rest in a grove just outside the village. After a time they participate in the essential rite of the marriage ceremony, i.e., *Sindradan* which takes place on the village street outside the house of the bride, so that each and everybody can have a glimpse of it. After then they are invited to return to the house of the bride and offered a goat to provide them with food. The father of the bride offers libations of rice-beer to the deity *Marna Buru* and to the ancestors after which all are served rice-beer.

On the second day the bridegroom's party return to their village. The newly married couple visits each house of the village where they are offered molasses and water to drink.

When they reach the village headman' house they pay tribute to the last departed headman. Next day a goat is killed, and a feast is arranged in honour of the bride's brothers.

On the death of a person the village headman is informed. Some elderly persons come at the house of the deceased person. The dead body is smeared with oil and turmeric and the corpse is taken out of the house in a khatia or bier (a stringed bedstead) and placed in the courtyard. Then the dead body is taken to the cremation ground. A fowl is sacrificed before the funeral and some *Mahua* twigs are placed on its chest, navel, waist. Teeth are brushed and lime and tobacco are kept to its mouth. The eldest son of the deceased first applies fire on the pyre. After that the face of the dead body is turned, so that the flame touches the mouth of the corpse. Everyone then throws a piece of firewood on the pyre.

After the cremation, water is poured on the pyre by the eldest son and then by the other members. A piece of the frontal portion of the skull and two bits from the collar bone are washed and placed in a new earthen pot. It is buried under the earth near a *sal* tree. After completion of these rituals the funeral party returns home after bathing in a pond. Entering in the house of the deceased they perform several rituals. After that the pollution period starts. It continues for nine days. During this period they restrict themselves from doing certain works and to eat certain food. Each day they also offer food to the ancestral spirits which also include their deceased. On the expiry of the period, the headman arrives at the house with some elderly village men. A Santal barber comes and joins the members of the family. They take bath after rubbing their bodies with oil and oil cakes. Then they propitiate and make prayer to the chief deity *Maran Buru,* the deceased and the dead ancestors with some purificatory articles like tooth sticks, oil, cakes, *narkan basa* (a kind of earth to wash the hair) for releasing the spirit. At that night fowl is sacrificed and offered for the *Maran Buru* and the deceased. Some rice and vegetables are kept in a leaf plate and it is hung from a rafter of the deceased's house for its eating.

Another important death ritual among the Santal is *Jan Baha,* the immersion of the bones' in the river Damodar, but now a days this ritual is performed in any nearby river also. During the day of *Jan baha* the previously buried bones are collected by the eldest son from beneath the *sal* tree and kept in a pot. He then goes down into the water and while diving he turns his face towards east and immerses the bones into the river. After the *Jan baha,* on the bank he prepares a lump of food with mud, toothpicks, parched rice and sweet-meats and is kept on three *sal* leaves for the deceased and the ancestral spirits (Pildha Haram and Pildha Budhi). The Santals.believe that through these offerings the spirit of the deceased will come into contact with the ancestral spirits and from this day the spirit will be honoured by the Santal at the time of any festive occasion like their ancestral spirits.

VI

The supernatural world of the Santal is classified under three categories — Thakur or High God, *Bongas* or spirits and non-human monstrous beings or impersonal powers.

In Santal society the Thakur as a Supreme Deity, creator and preserver of the universe is well respected. He is a benevolent deity and the Santals recognise Him with greatest regard and remember him in every important festive occasion by offering sacrifices for his appeasement. The Santals identify Thakur with different names such as *Cando, Sin Cando, Cando Bonga,* or *Sin Bonga.*

Next to Thakur, the rcle of *Bongas* (spirits) is very important for their malevolent power to do harm and to spread diseases among the people. They often reside in hill, forest, river, pond, tree, etc. *Bongas* are worshipped through the sacrifice of animals blood or rice beer. Among them the six chief of the *Bongas* are the *Maran Buru, Moreko-Turuiko, Jaher Era, Gosae Era, Pargana Bonga* and *Manjhi Bonga.*

Maran Buru is the leader of the Bongas and usually resides at the hill. The literal meaning of it is the *Bonga* of the Great Mountain (*Maran*—great, *Buru*—hill). He is propitiated in all festivals and crisis of life. He is associated with both benevolent and malevolent spirits and worshipped with the sacrifice of either a white fowl or a white goat and offering of rice beer. Through his instruction the first Santal couple Pilcha Haram and Pilcha Budhi learned how to brew rice beer and how to indulge in sex.

Literally the term *Moreko Turuiko* comes from two words—*Moren* means five and *Turu* means six. It is believed that five brothers got married to six sisters. Now *Moreko Turuiko* is considered as a single entity known as village deity worshipped for the village welfare, and they often control rain, crops and epidemics.

Jaher Era or 'the lady of the grove' is the presiding spirit of the sacred grove of *Jaherthan.* She is referred as the sister of the mother of the (Moreko - Turuiko) Five brothers and she is mainly worshipped during the time of cattle epidemic and also propitiated for the general welfare of the village. *Gosae Era* is considered as the younger sister of *Moreko Turuiko* and worshipped against sores by sacrificing a white fowl. *Pargana Bonga,* the spirit is of great significance as he is believed to have some power over the witches. He has been propitiated whenever there is an outbreak of some serious illness in the village. He protects the society from all sorts of miseries and misfortunes.

According to O' Malley *Manjhi Bonga* is considered as the spirit of the Manjhiship in general. Except *Jaherthan,* this spirit lives inside the village in the place known as *Manjhithan,* specially constructed for him by the side of the house of *Manjhi* or the headman of the Santal village. Being the spirit of the original headman of the village and a benevolent one, this spirit acts as the adviser to the present headman in all matters concerning the welfare of the village. The heads of the sacrificed pigeons are eaten only by the headman. Through this ritual communication the headman drives his authority from the predecessors.

The *Abge Bongas* are considered on the tutelary spirits of the Santal *Khuts* or sub-clans. Each and every sub-clan has the same *Bonga.* A Santal cannot remain without *Abge Bonga,* he must get the *Bonga* from his father. The *Abge Bongas* are the most personal spirits of the Santals and are given high respect. The Santals usually abstain from disclosing the name of these *Bongas.*

Orak Bongas are considered as the household spirits. They are benevolent in nature and very much personal spirits to the Santals. They are propitiated to make the family trouble free. Only the head of the household knows the name of the spirit. Before dying he will disclose the name of *Orak Bonga* to his eldest son. Every Santal house has a small place called *Bhitar* meant for the *Orak Bonga* and the ancestors. These spirits are also worshipped once a year with sacrifice and offerings.

Hapramko Bongas are the ancestral spirits known as *Burha Burhi.* They are worshipped with sacrifice of fowl and with the offering of the rice-beer by the household members only. The Santals believe that only after the natural death one becomes a *Hapramko Bonga.*

Sim Bongas are another class of benevolent *Bongas* about forty-four in number. All of them are worshipped at the time of Jom Sim festival.

Deko Bongas - Three Hindu deities are quite prominent and these are *Kali, Durga* and *Ganga Mai.* Besides, some other deities such as *Lakshmi, Mahadev* (Shiva), *Parvati, Rama, Krishna* etc. have also got place in the Santal pantheon.

Hill Spirits or *Pats* or *Buru Bongas* delight in human blood. These hill spirits reside in the surrounding hills and mountains and are responsible for ruining crops and for causing accident if they get displeased. There are number of such spirits, Like *Berha Pat, Budha Pahar, Pauri Pat, Chandra Pat* etc. *Besumata* is worshipped for bumper crop and fertility of the agricultural field.

Besides, there are some impersonal spirits and powers such as *Curins, Bhuts, Ekagaudias* etc. who are not required to be worshipped or sacrificed but through magic their activities are controlled.

The Santals are the agricultural tribe. Throughout the year they are engaged in different types of agricultural work for the production of crops. Different festivals associated with agricultural production make their life joyful, romantic and full of energy. Otherwise their life will be dull, monotonous and mechanical. For this reason, they always celebrate these festivals from the core of their heart. Most of these festivals are associated with the production of agriculture, except a few. The *Naike,* the priest or the sacred headman of the village presides over the ceremony. The most important of these festivals are *Sahrae, Magh Sim, Baha, Erok Sim, Hariar Sim, Iri-Gundi, Nawai* and *Janthar.* All these festivals are connected with some agricultural activities.

The sowing of paddy in the month of *Asar* (June-July) is performed by the Santals as their first agricultural festival known as *Erok Sim.* This festival takes place in the *Jaherthan* where the *Naike* sacrifices fowls in the name of chief deities. The members of all neighbouring communities celebrate this festival for sufficient rains and bumper crops.

In the month of July they observe the *Hariar Sim* when thanks are offered to the gods as the festival of transplantation of paddy seedlings. The celebration of this festival is similar to that of *Erok Sim*. On behalf of the whole village, fowls are sacrificed by the *Naike* to all the *Bongas* of the village including *Maran Buru* and others. After the festival, the villagers start transplantation of paddy seedlings.

Iri-Gundhi Nawai festival is held in the month of *Bhadra* (August-September) when the millert crops are offered to various deities and spirits. No Santal will taste millets unless these are first offered to the spirits.

Generally in the month of *Agrahayan* (November-December) all the paddy fields are filled with ripened crops (Paddy). *Janthar* festival takes place in this time. It is the festival of first fruit of the winter rice. Nobody can take the rice before this festival. Early in the morning of this festival day, some paddy is brought from the paddy field to *Jaherthan* with some other articles, which are offered to the *Paragana Bonga*. Then a ram or a fowl is offered to the deity. The new paddy is also offered to other spirits. After this festival they take the new paddy for their consumption.

Sohrae is the harvest festival and most important festival of the Santal. This *Sohrae festival* is also known as *Badna Parab*. It is celebrated in the month of *Pous* (December-January) after the winter paddy is harvested but it must be completed before the last day of the month of *Pous* (mid January) or before the full-moon night of the *Pous*. Actually it is the thanks giving ceremony. The *Naike* offers sacrifices of fowl to the village spirits and the ancestral spirits. In the first day of the festivity the Got puja is celebrated in which rituals are performed through offerings. *Daka Hilok* or food day ceremony is observed on the second day when the ceremony starts with a ritual called *Gadoe*. A puja is performed in the cowshed when a sacrifice is made for *Marang Buru*. In the third day a ceremony know as *Khantau Hilok* is performed by exciting a bull after cleaning it and tying it to a pole and beating drums near it. During the fourth day *Jale Hilok* ceremony is performed and on that day the youngsters collect food grains from every house, prepare meal, eat it with plenty of rice beer. On the fifth day *Hako Katkom Hilok* ceremony is observed by catching fish and crab and eating them for a prolonged life.

Sakrat festival is performed at the time of Hindu *Makar* or *Pous Parab* or the local *Tusu Parab*. This is an imitation of the Hindu *Pous Sankranti* festival. It takes place in the last day of the month of *Pous* (January) just after the *Sohrae* festival when *Chida* (flattened rice) and *Gur* are offered to the ancestors and also to *Maran Buru*.

The month of *Magh* (January-February) is the end of the Santal year. They celebrate it through the festivals known as *Magh Sim* by cutting of jungle and mowing of thatching grass.

Karam festival is celebrated by the Santals in the month of *Aswin* (September-October) in order to have increased 'wealth of progeny' and to get rid of the evil spirits. During this festival, two youths fetch two branches of *Karam* tree from the forest and plant them just outside the house. The head of the household offers rice beer and other articles to *Manjhi Haram* and *Maran Buru* and prays for the prosperity of the house. This worship is followed with singing, dancing and playing of instrumental music with rice beer.

Jom Sim is the festival through which the Santals pay their homage to the *Sun god* or *Sin Bonge*. The festival is usually celebrated in the full moon day of *Falgun* (February-March) or *Baisakh* (April-May). *Jom Sim* is usually celebrated by the clan members usually after five years. It is a worship restricted to a particular clan group. The first day's festival is known as *Um Narak* or purificatory ceremony when the members of the clan purify themselves and offer *puja* to the *Bongas*. The second day's festival is known as *Sardi* when the clan members sacrifice fowl to the *Bongas*.

Baha is the *Sal* blossom annual festival celebrated in the month of *Falgun* (February-March) when the *Sal* trees start blooming. The Santals will not collect *Sal, Mahua, Palas* or other flowers so long this festival is not over. The two festive days are followed be singing, dancing and drinking in the village. During this time they worship the deities for production of good crops and to protect themselves from harmful diseases.

Pata festival is like the *Chadak* festival of Hindus in which the Hindus worship *Mahadeo*. But the Santals, according to their tradition, observe this festival in the month of

Baisakh (April-May) when they pay their homage to *Pata Bongas,* i.e., *Mahadeo* and *Parvati.*

Chata (umbrella) festival takes place in the month of *Bhadra* (August-September) to honour *Chata Bongas.* During this festival a pole is erected and an umbrella is tied with the pole. The worship is held there and sacrifices are made. After the *puja* rice-beer is served to the assembled guests and singing and dancing are followed.

The *Jatra* festival is celebrated by the individual household in the month of *Magh* (January-February). It takes place near *Jaherthan* where the *Jatra Bongas* are propitiated.

Observing the festival cycles of the Santals it is very clear that there is a very little difference between the Santal festival and the Hindu festival. Generally, the agricultural festivals, *Badna* and *Sakrat* are all done by the Hindus and the Santals both. During the time of *Durga Puja* and *Kali Puja* huge gathering of Santal families can be seen to join those festive occasions. Even in the *Chadak* puja a good number of Santals join with the Hindus in Hook swinging festival. Though the identity of a particular community is gradually fading away and in its place the unity of the greater society is slowly revived for the betterment of the humanity.

THE MUNDAS

The Munda hold a unique position in the tribal map of India. They are regarded as one of the indigenous races of the Indian Peninsula residing here from time immemorial. Except perhaps Santals, Oraons, Nagas etc. the Mundas are numerically most dominant tribal group of eastern India. Their main concentration is in the Chotanagpur Plateau of Bihar. They are also spread over in the adjoining states of Bengal, Orissa and Assam wherein they migrated a few generations ago in search of livelihood.

The name 'Munda' seems to have been given to these people by their ancient Hindu neighbours. The Munda call themselves *Horoko* (men) and their tribe *Horo* (mankind.) The Munda tribe consists of an elder and younger branch, the Mahali Mundako and the Kompat Mundako. Both branches are endogamous and the former is regarded as socially inferior to the later. The reason for this lower status of the former is attributed to the eating of a piece of umbilical cord by the progenitor of this group. But the real reason is to be found in the fact that this has come less under the influence of Hinduism.

There is no accurate history about the original habitat and migrations of the Mundari speaking people of middle India because the anthropologists do not have unanimous views regarding their original habitat or their ancestry. Traditional history of the Mundas, refers to north-western India, namely Punjab, as their earliest home, where they used to have a pastoral life. There are mentions of the Dasya Tribes in *Rig Veda* who fought a fierce battle with the Aryans on the bank of the 'five-rivers' which corresponds to the Mundari traditional story. References of these tribes are also found in the Hindu Puranas.[8(i)]

According to Sachchidananda (1979), the Munda migrated from the southern part of north India to modern Bundelkhand and middle India, spread over Rajasthan and north-western India and finally entered Chotanagpur through modern Rohilkhand and Oudh. Their last place of dispersal was Rohtas in the Kaimur hills. The Munda and the Santal crossed the river Sone and advanced towards the south-east and reached that place which now separates the district of Hazaribagh from Ranchi and Palamau, and here they parted. The Santals crossed the Damodar river and settled in Hazaribagh, later to Manbhum and Santal Parganas. The Mundas settled down in the forest-covered regions of Ranchi plateau defeating the Asuras, the iron-smelters, who were believed to be an older civilised race. The Asuras retreated towards a part of the present Ranchi district, leaving the Munda undisputed owner of the entire area.

The Mundari speaking people are called as Kolarians. Among them the Mundas, Hos and Bhumijs are main stocks.[8(ii)] In the epic literature the Mundas were referred as Nishadas and Mundari tribes are often called Mundari speaking people. The Mundas are Austro-Asiatic people having close linguistic affinity with the Santals. Nowadays the Mundari speaking people are rare and in most of the cases they come in close contact with other people who speak in either Bengali or Hindi. As a result they adopted those languages with the tune of their own dialect.

The Munda maintain a good interaction pattern and linek with other Mundari speaking people like Ho, Santal, Kheria, Birhor etc. and with other non-Mundari speaking people like Oraon and with other different castes and community people of same and neighbouring villages. Their society is patriarchal and patrilineal. Senior-most male member often acts as the decision-maker of each and every family. After marriage a woman has to go to husband's father's house. Bride price is still in vogue in their community. Unmarried sones and daughters live with their parents and sometimes the married sons also stay within the same family. Due to some economic crisis nuclear families are found in most of the cases where after marriage the newly married couple often form a separate household.

II

Generally the Munda live in villages. But their settlement pattern varies from area to area. In Ranchi district of Bihar the houses of the Munda are built on high lands and three or four houses are huddled together around a courtyard. Their homesteads are compartmentalized for various purposes. The sleeping place is known as *Giti Ora*. *Mandi Ora* is used as kitchen which is again divided into *Sara* and *Ading*. *Sara* is used for cooking purpose and *Ading* is the part where the Munda worship their ancestors. *Metron Ora* is made to keep goats and *Unri Ora* is used as cattleshed. This habitation pattern with little variation is also found in different parts of West Bengal.

Most of the houses are mud-built, having thatched roof and mud wall. Some of the well-to-do families build their houses with tiled roofs or sometimes corrugated iron sheets are also used as part of roofing. In front of their houses there is a verandah covered by bamboo sticks. All the houses have very small windows. But *Ading* is the darker portion of *Mandi Ora* having no window. Their ancestral spirits are kept there and no outsider is permitted to enter that place. Each and every household possesses a kitchen garden at the backyard where vegetables are grown. There are also cactus and tulsi (Basil) plants in each household which are worshipped by the Munda family. They worship these sacred plants like Hindu families. Cactus often stands as a symbol for Goddess *Manasa* and tulsi is the symbol of Hari or Lord Krishna. The village lands are classified into two types, *Don* and *Tanr.* The former indicates lowlands and the latter highlands. The staple food is rice which is grown both in *Don* and *Tanr.*

Agriculture is the most important occupation of the Munda. A very few Munda families have sufficient lands. So, most of them have to engage themselves in different occupations. Sometimes they work as agricultural labourers.

> Individual labourers are employed in different families as *Dhangar* who work all the year round. They are paid annually either in cash or in kind and housed and fed by their employers.[8(iii)]

Hunting as an occupation is subsidiary to agriculture. The Munda usually go for hunting when they are not engaged in agricultural operation. Nowadays hunting is decreased due to deforestation, but it is not completely extinct. Occasional hunting still takes place. *Phagu Shikar* and *Bisu Sendra* are such two important hunts. The first one takes place on the occasion of *Holi* and the latter is held in summer. A traditional rite is performed before the Munda start their journey for hunt: they worship the goddess *Chandi* at the house of the *Pahan,* the village priest. The hunting expedition is accompanied by a drummer. The games which they hunt are distributed among the participants and who kills the game generally gets the major share. They enjoy the night with feast and drink.

Fishing is also a subsidiary economy and is still done by all men, women and children from nearby, paddy fields (in rainy season), ponds, rivers and rivulets. During slack season they practise fishing.

A large section of the Munda go out as seasonal migrants to nearby towns where they work as industrial labourers. Nowadays due to various governmental programmes taken for the welfare of the tribal people, the Munda are getting higher education and are changing their occupations. Now they are employed as service-holders and sometimes they establish their own business.

III

Munda tribe is divided under a number of exogamous clans which are known as *Kili.* They consider all the members of the clan as the descendants of a common ancestor. Each clan of the Munda is divided into a number of sub-clans. Now there are about one hundred and fifty clans. The names of some Munda clan have been changed according to the name of Hindu *gotra*. Generally the Munda clans are named following the name of some animal, plant, soil or certain event.

Munda people think that each clan had an original land established by their ancestors. In course of time they spread into different directions and settled in new villages. In there original village of the clans, all members had equal right to the village land and were known as *Khutkatidars*. The members had equal access also to the village burial ground. At present, all the members of the clan are more or less united. They prefer to have separate burial ground or *sasan* of different clans, if possible.

The main function of the clan is to regulate marriage relationships. Generally, the marriages are performed outside the clans. In many cases the clan confers the surname on a person.

The clan of original settlers of a Munda village is considered as dominant clan. This dominant clan is further divided into two important lineages. These are *Munda Khut* and *Pahan Khut*. The members of these two lineages enjoy greater prestige than the rest of the village community. The members of one lineage are prohibited to take part in other's sacrificial ceremonies and are not allowed to take the sacrificial rice, meat etc. But the members of both lineages, belong to the same clan, have the same totem and they are not allowed to intermarry.

Most of the Munda families are nuclear in pattern. The families are comprised with the parents and their unmarried daughters and sons. The father and mother are termed as *Apu* and *Eanga* respectively. *Kora* and *Kuri* are used for son and the daughter respectively. In some cases vertically extended family may be found also. Such a type of family comprises of married couple with their unmarried children along with the parents of the hushand. In the laterally extended type of family we find married brothers with their spouses and their unmarried children. In few cases we can find the vertico-lateral extended family type. In such families married brothers their spouses and unmarried children live with their parents.

The father of a Munda family is the head of the family and considered to have almost absolute controlling power over the family property, family income and expenditure, like Hindu joint family system. Before the death of the father, the sons cannot get separation from the family. On the death of the father, the whole property is divided among his all sons in which the eldest son gets slight more than the equal share. Munda women generally are not entitled to inherit the family property. But the father may present some cash or anything except land to a daughter in his lifetime. If the partition takes place during the father's lifetime the unmarried daughter usually gets some land as a source of her maintenance till her marriage which is repositioned amongst the brothers after her marriage.

Being a patrilineal society, the rights of Munda women in certain fields are lower than that of men. But Munda women are respected as wife, mother, daughter and play important roles in social, cultural and economic and ritual fields of the families. They work both in the field and at home. Though women do not inherit property, the daughter of a sonless Munda father inherits the entire property. The Munda women lead a comparatively free life than other women of neighbouring community.

IV

The Munda families have their own traditional panchayats which settle village disputes and dispense justice before the introduction of British courts. *Hatu* Panchayat and *Parha* Panchayat are the two important institutions of the Munda polity. *Hatu* Panchayat works at village level, while *Parha* panchayat is a regional council of a group of villages. *Tola* panchayat is the smallest Panchayat in Munda community. It looks after disputes in one *Tola* or ward of a village. *Tola* Panchayat functions more effectively than *Hatu* Pnchayat. *Tola* Panchayat is convened regularly on a particular day of the week especially during the agricultural season when all the adult members attend the meeting. Appeals from *Tola* Panchayat go to *Hatu* Panchayat and if a dispute is not settled in a *Hatu* Panchayat, people move to *Parha* Panchayat to settle the dispute. It is the *Parha* Panchayat which can outcaste a person or readmit him to the community. The *Parha* Panchayat acts as a social, judicial and political body.

Each and every village constitution consists of a council, headman and priest. Each and every village office has at least a headman who is called a *Naik* and a ritual specialist and a number of assistants. The headman is usually aided by the deputies, messengers (often called Gorait) and village watchman. There are two main ritual specialists among the Munda. First is the village priest, called *Sisa, Pahan, Dihuri,* etc. who perform the familial rituals or the collective rites for the welfare of the family and the community as a whole. The second type of ritual specialists are *Shamans,* called *Ojha, Guniar, Mati,* etc, who possess magical power by which they control supernatural spirits. Both priest and *Shamans* have their assistants who also perform various functions.

V

The life of Mundas are marked by different types of ceremonies and rituals which are largely influenced by Hinduism. Each and every event of their life is marked by distinct taboos.

Such kind of rituals begin at the onset of puberty of the Munda women. Women are considered polluted during their menstruation. So they are not allowed to enter into the kitchen and to cook food. They usually do not sleep with their husbands and do not take bath or wash their clothes. They are not allowed to do agricultural works.

Childbirth is considered as an important event in every Munda's life. They think childbirth is an event that signifies the success in marriage. They perform different kinds of rituals and ceremonies from the pregnancy till the birth of the child and even upto child's three years of age.

For the first pregnancy of a married daughter a ritual is performed which is called *sutam daram.* At the fifth month of pregnancy this ceremony is held jointly by both the families—the daughter's father's family and daughter's husband's family. If the daughter stays at her father's house hen, rice, etc., are sent from daughter's husband's family in that occasion. During that occasion *Haram Buri* of both the families are worshipped and nearest relatives of both the families are entertained with *Handia* and different types of foods.

The delivery takes place at home. For this task during the birth of a child a midwife (*dai*) is engaged, from Hari community. She cuts the umbilical cord and watches the newborn. The placenta is usually digged under the ground in front of the house so that it cannot be touched by crow, cat, dog, jackal etc. The mother and newborn child usually stay at one corner of the sleeping room. The birth of a child brings joy to the parents and close relatives, but it puts the entire family in a state of ritual pollution. Usually it ends on the eighth day after birth but in special cases the period may be reduced to five days. The purificatory ceremony is called *chhati* if it is performed on 6th day after birth and it is called *nai-narta* if it is performed on 9th day after birth. The village barber and Washerman visit the house at that time for their own jobs. Each and every member of the family takes purificatory bath. After that the close relatives feast with foods and *handia* (rice-beer). When this purificatory ceremony is held on the 21st day after childbirth it is then called *ekusia.* The *dai,* barber and washerman are paid with one rupee and 5 kg. of rice each for their own duty.

The *sakhi* or the name giving ceremony is performed on the following day. In this simple ritual of name giving the female members become the exclusive participants. A small blade of *durba* grass and two paddies are dropped one by one into a pot full of water. If the three things unite then the proposed name is accepted. The baby is usually named after some older relatives usually grandmother or grandfather or after the day of the week the child is born. For example, who is born on Sunday is named as Robibari, who is borns on Monday is named as Sombari, etc. One may be called as Sikari (hunter) if he is born on the day of annual hunting.

No separate rice-giving ceremony is performed among them. When the child becomes capable to digest the starchy materials or foods he is given gruel of rice.

The *lutur-tukui* or ear boring ceremony of the baby is celebrated either in the first, second or third year. The *sakhi* or *mita,* after whom the baby has been named, plays the leading role. This is done on the first day of the month of *Magh* (January-February). At that time a fowl is sacrificed generally and the ear lobes of the child are bored through by means of a brass needle. This task is done by two persons of the village who are expert for this task. At the end the guests are entertained with food and drinks. With this ceremony the Munda society formally accepts the child.

Marriage is obligatory for the Mundas. As they believe the spirits and deities have their marriage partners, it plays an important role in the life of an individual. They consider the marriage as an affair between the groups of kin instead of two persons. Marriage by negotiation is the most common form of marriage. But for the changed socio-economic life of the tribe *sangai* (widow marriage) or marriage by mutual choice and elopement take place.

Marriage usually takes place outside one's clan. Most of the marriages are arranged usually with bride price, where parents take the initiative and the formal consent of the boys and girls is taken later.

To fix the date of marriage, after the preliminary talks of both sides, *dutam* visits from bridegroom's house to bride's house. The good or bad sign is aught and on that basis the negotiation breaks or continues. So, it is the major functionary to negotiate marriage among Mundas.

On an appointed day, the bride's party visits the bridegroom's house to settle up and to accept the bride price. This is called *bala* or betrothal which is celebrated by dancing and singing and guests are entertained with *handia* (homebrewn liquor). After returning with the payment of marriage two ceremonies, *pon-bhanga,* and *chuman* are performed in the bride's house. After that the date of marriage is fixed. The actual marriage ceremony which is called *arandi ara* is performed during the month of *Falgun* (February-March) or in *Vaisakh* (April-May).

Before the day of marriage *bairoar* ceremony is performed in which bride and bridegroom are ritually bathed in front of an antmound. A fowl is sacrificed on that occasion by the priest.

On the day of marriage the first ceremony is *abra-khawa* in which both the bride and bridegroom are given expensive food. Then bridegroom performs *uli-sakhi* by putting a thread around a tree before starting to the bride's house, and his mother smears a mango twig with *gur* (molasses) which is called *amkuljom.* After the arrival at bride's house *chaman* (benedictory) is performed by the female members.

Then bride and bridegroom are taken to the *mandea* (pulpit) for marriage. Two ceremonies are performed there. These are *sindra-dan* or *sindua-rakab* and *hat-gati.* In the *sindra-dan,* the bridegroom and bride stand on two *sal* leaves facing towards west and east respectively. The *hat-gati* is performed by the priest by making a knot with the corners of wrappers of the couples. After that *Khaigum* is performed in which puffed paddy (*Khai*) are dropped on fire by the bride.

Then the bride and bridegroom salute the elders and a feast is followed in which the bride serves rice and salt to the guests. Next day bridegroom returns to his house with the bride. In the village of bridegroom, the bride goes to a pond along with the others to perform *Kado-ghati* ceremonies. Then the bride carries a small pot full of water to the house and then washes the feet of her in-laws. At last a bride feast is followed.

Like birth, the death of any member in Munda community is followed by a number of rituals and purificatory ceremonies. After hearing the death-news of a person all the relatives and neighbours usually assemble at the house of the deceased. Female members cover the face of the dead with turmeric paste. Then the dead body is placed on a charpoy and is carried by the agnates to the *sasan*. The *sasan* is generally situated by the side of a river. At the *sasan*, the deadbody is placed on a pyre and there it is cremated. All the attending members return to the village throwing the chared bones in the river and after taking bath. The house of the deceased is purified with the sprinkling of cow-dung paste and water sanctified by *tulsi* leaf. Pollution period continues for seven or nine days. On the seventh or ninth day the purificatory ceremony is observed. Sometimes, nowadays, a Brahmin priest is employed to preform death rituals. The families which cannot afford to appoint Brahmin priest, appoint another ritual specialist called *gosain,* who is in the rank junior to the Brahmin. The barber is called to shave the beard and head of all the male members of the family of the deceased. The Brahmin and the *gosain* sometimes, both, come for the purification ceremony. The Brahmin chants *mantras* and uses copper coins and *tulsi* leaves for that purpose. The Brahmin sprinkles water three times on the person who has offered *pind* to his ancestors and then it is sprinkled on all his relatives. On their way back from the river where they go for mortuary rituals, all persons chant *Haribol.* The *gosain* gets one-half and the barber one-fourth of what the Brahmin gets as his fee. A feast of simple type is then arranged for all the relatives.

VI

The supernatural world of the Munda comprises of a number of deities and spirits which have a great impact on their life. The spirits are benevolent and manevolent in nature. They are recalled in times of prosperity as well as in times of danger. Each and every house has its own ancestral deity which is worshipped with due respect. Except familial deities they have also village deities which are worshipped by the community members as a whole. Now a days they accept many important deities of the Hindu pantheon as their gods and goddesses.

Singhbonga is the supreme deity of the Munda. He is worshipped before each and every religious function. There is no specific occasion of worshipping this deity. He is reverentially remembered by the Munda in their day to day life. As for example, before every meal a Munda puts down on the ground a few grains of rice from his plate as an offering. In serious natural calamities *Singhbonga* is specially worshipped with sacrificing a white fowl. He is believed to accept the offerings of white colour such as white *gulainchi* flowers, white hen, white goat, white cloth and milk etc.

In Munda society the village gods lie *Dasaulibonga, Jayarbongako* and *Devibonga* play an important role in their agricultural operations and hunting excursions. They are the benevolent gods who bring prosperity to the village and protect the villagers from diseases and other calamities. *Pahan* is their village priest and the sacred groves are known as *Sarna* where the *Pahan* worships those gods on behalf of the whole village.

The living place of *Dasaulibonga* is in a field. The village priest worships the *Dasaulibonga* with *Arua* rice and sometimes he is offered a black bullock for his sacrifice.

Sarna or *Jayar* is a protected place in each Munda village where *Jayarbongako* lives. This deity is worshipped by Sal flowers and by sacrificing hens for good crops and protection of the people and cattle from diseases, epidemics and other calamities.

The concept of *Devibonga* is borrowed from the Hindus. Once in every year and at the time of epidemics *Devi Mai (Devibonga)* along with *Burubonga* and *Ikirbonga* is worshipped. To propitiate these deities different types of sacrifices like goat, sheep and hen either he or she, red or black are offered.

The head of every Munda household worships the house gods in the *ading* of his house. These include *Haram Horoko* or ancestors of each family who are worshipped once a year; and a light reddish hen is sacrificed for the well-being of the family. *Marangbonga* is another house god which is synonymous with Lord Mahadeo of the Hindus. Only this deity is represented symbolically. *Urad* pulse and boiled rice are used as offering objects instead of hen or cattle. If *Marangbonga* becomes angry the fruit trees like karanj, mango and jack fruit do not bear fruit.

Gonrabonga is the name of another house god who looks after the welfare of the household cattle. *Gonrabonga* is known by four different names depending upon the method of worship. These are *Gonra Hankar, Hissi Hankar, Be-Hankar* and *Tundu Hankar.*

The Munda also believe in different supernatural spirits who are malevolent in nature. *Banitabongas* are such earth bound spirits of those persons who died an unnatural death. These malevolent spirits include *churibongas* (spirits of women who died in pregnancy), *harsulivadbongas* (spirits of those who committed suicide), *muabongas* (those who were killed with a weapon), *nagdavabongas* (those who died as a result of snake bite), *kulanchandi* (those killed by a tiger) and *nasanbongas*. The class of spirits is not only propitiated by the Munda household or by the village priest, but also by the ghost finder.

According to the Munda, nature gods possess supernatural powers. They are the *Burubonga, Ikirbonga, Naga Era, Chandibonga* and *Birbonga* etc. These nature gods are both benevolent and malevolent as they do good and bad for the people. These nature gods live in various places like, hill, rock, spring, forest or in any other natural surroundings.

Irrespective of their tribal deities and spirits the Munda accept different Hindu gods and goddesses from the Hindu pantheon. They consider themselves as the Hindu and as a result a variety of traits of Hindu culture are adopted by them. These are reflected through propitiation of different gods and goddesses. The most commonly observed Hindu *pujas* are offered to Goddesses Durga, Saraswati, Lakshmi,

Sitala, Manasa, Tusu, etc. Usually a Hindu Brahmin priest conduct these *pujas* for the tribal devotees. They also offer fowl, goat, etc., to these gods and goddesses for sacrifice.

The goddesses Sitala and Manasa are given special importance in their community, because *Sitala* protects them from small-pox and Manasa from snake-bites, Tusu worshipped by the female members and this worship is done on the last day of *Paus* (December-January). Tusu is the folk goddess of the Hindu inhabitants which represents Lakshmi. Parasura, another folk-god is worshipped by those who cultivate sugarcane, and who extract juice from *gur* (jaggery) preparation. In this worship an effigy of buffalo made of straw is placed near the hearth where *gur* is prepared, this effigy represents the Parasura. Also during first ploughing of sugarcane of the season this god is worshipped at the field.

Magical beliefs, practices and witchcrafts are very much evident in the daily life of the Munda. The magical practitioners are specialized in their field. The Munda distinguish also between benevolent (white) and malevolent (black) magic.

The practitioners of white magic are named as *sokha, mati, deonra, najo, vaidya* (medicine-man), *ojha* or *bhagat* (diviner), whereas the black magic practitioners are known as *dain* or witches and sorcerers. A *sokha* is believed to possess special power through which he is able to perform certain tasks which are beyond the capacity of ordinary people. Among the Munda only men can become sokhas. A woman who professes to have intimate relations with *bongas* is considered to be a witch and is persecuted.

The Munda also have belief in the potent evil powers of a witch. Most dreaded of magical effects result from witchcraft. It is believed that no medicine can cure diseases caused by spirits and witches. But usually a witch is not accepted by the Munda people. Munda people have developed remedial measures to cope with the witches' effects. Among the most potent remedies are white magic, omens and taboos.

Throughout the year the Munda observe different types of festivals with song and dance. The main festivals among the Munda are *Mage, Phagu, Ba, Honba, Batauli, Karam, Dasai* and *Sohrai.* These festivals associated with folk music are celebrated in specific period of the year.

Mage Parab is celebrated with great enthusiasm in the month of *Magh* which marks the end of the year and the beginning of the new year for the Munda. Food and drink are offered to the ancestors on that day. In the evening village priest offers them rice-beer. Late in the evening, the boys and girls dance in the village *akhara*.

Phagu is the festival which coincides with Holi festival of the Hindu. It is performed on Purnima (full moon) in the month of *Phalgun*. To get the blessings of *Chandibonga*, a black hen is sacrificed by the village priest. Bread made of rice flour is prepared in all the houses and the *Haram Horoko* are offered bread and rice-beer by the householder on this day.

Sarhul or *Ba* festival is celebrated in the month of *Chait* (at the end of March or in the beginning of April). It is one of the important festivals in their society.

The *Sal* flower is worshipped in this *Ba* festival. On *Ba Parab* a light red hen or *sukra sim* is sacrificed in every Munda household in the name of the ancestors. The festival is celebrated for three consecutive days. *Urd dal*, cooked rice and fish and leafy branches of *sal* are also offered to them. The head of the household performs the worship and sacrifices in the *ading*. After worship all the family members are offered *sal* and *gurul* flowers to put on their ears and hair.

Hon-ba is *Garhul* on a smaller scale. It is celebrated in every Munda household. The festival continues for two days. During the time of worship in those days fish, boiled rice and *Urd* dal are offered and a pink hen is sacrificed to the deity. In the evening young men and young girls drink rice-beer and enjoy the day with *Jadur* dance and song. In the evening of that day *Jadur* dance and song are performed by young men and young girls in the village *akhara*.

Batauli is celebrated in *Asarh* when the crops germinate. A pink hen is sacrificed to the ancestors to get better crops. The village priest (*Pahan*) prays to the *Singbonga* and other *bongas* and worships on behalf of the whole village. Women fast on the first half of the day before Batauli. Young men and women dance in the village *akhara* at night.

An important festival is celebrated on the eleventh day

of *Karam* festival. *Bhado* is known by the Munda. It is believed that one can achieve wealth, prosperity and joy in life by celebrating this festival. After a bath on the *Karam* day, a man goes to the forest with some unmarried girls to cut a *Karam* (branch). All of them fast and sing *Karam* songs to the accompaniment of musical instruments while going to the forest. The *pahan* of the village performs worship with the virgins and after worship he recites the *Karam* story. On that day all the villagers go door to door and are received with ricebeer.

The Hinduised Munda perform Durga Puja or *Desai* and goats are sacrificed at the Durga temple. The *pahan* acts as the ritual sacrificer.

The Munda like the Hindus celebrate *Sohrai* to protect the cattle from diseases. It is celebrated on the new moon day of October and November (*Kartik Amawasya*). Ploughing is stopped about a fortnight before the *Sohrai* festival to give rest to the cattle. People sing and request the cattle to forgive them for any kind of trouble they might have given them during the year and also to accept their offerings.

Generally the festivals of the Munda are incorporated with fairs and *Jatras* (indigenous theatre). The Munda and the Hindus share the common festivals and worship the common Hindu deities in their socio-religious life— where the little Hindu tradition merges with the greater Hindu tradition. One great *mela* where the Munda and the Hindu participate jointly is Rameshwar Mela (fair). This fair is held at Midnapore district of West Bengal during *Shivachaturdashi* in the month of March. The fair is arranged in propitiating the Lord Shiva. The Munda show immense interest in that Hindu festival and therefore assemble there from the surrounding villages.

During the festivals the people of Munda community like to observe *Jatras* (indigenous theatre) in merry-making which is an indispensible part of Munda festivals. All the villagers enjoy the jatra-play at night in open place after worshipping their deities at day time.

BHUMIJ

The Bhumij are one of the non-Aryan Hinduised tribes found in Manbhum, Singhbhum districts of Bihar and in Midnapur and Bankura districts of West Bengal. They are the original inhabitants of Dhalbhum, Barabhum, Patkum and Bagmundi estates of Bihar and still form the bulk of the population in those and adjoining estates. They are chiefly located in the area between the Kasai and Subarnarekha rivers. In the past they had possessed large settlements to the north of the Kasai river, but were dislodged by the Aryans. Like the Mundas and Hos, they are also Kolarian tribe. Though the Bhumij being an important branch of Mundari speaking race, lost their own language and speak in Bengali with regional accents.

The etymological meaning of the term 'Bhumij' or 'Bhumija' indicates one, born of the soil. The immigrant Hindus might have given the name Bhumija as they were found already in possession of the land.[9]

The Bhumij of the Jungle Mahals were the terror of the surrounding districts and were under the nick-name 'Chuar'. Their outbreaks were called 'Chaaris' and in those outbreaks they had very little interest. In most of the cases they were provoked by some chiefs, ambitious of obtaining power.

It is found that the Bhumij do not have any independent tradition of migration. Those who live in the vicinity of Chutia Nagpur hardly distinguish themselves from the Mundas. Actually the Bhumij community is very much close to that of the Munda and is considered as a branch of it. The Bhumij, in course of time, mingled with the Hindus, adopted many customs, religion of the Hindus. Linguistically and culturally they have come very close to the Hindu caste people and have accepted many of the in-cultural traits leaving aside many of their tribal traits and marks of culture. It is thought that in future the Bhumij would identify themselves with these Hindus and deny their tribal identity.

II

The Bhumij according to Risley (1891) are divided into six sub-tribes viz. (1) *Desi*, (2) *Tamaria*, (3) *Sikharya* or *Memo* (supposed to come from Manbhum), (4) *Putkumia*, (5) *Shelo* (iron-smelters), and (6) *Barabhumia* (Zamindar Bhumij). There are very little social intercourse and communications among the subgroups. Each of these subgroups is endogamous group. As the rules of endogamy do not permit the marriage outside the community, no Bhumij of one sub-group marries the Bhumij of other sub-group. Each of these subgroups again has exogamous units or septs known as

Kilis. Each of them is believed to have traditional ancestral village. For each *Kili* there is a symbol (of animal or bird or fish or tree) which they are not permitted to touch or kill or eat and it is known as totem. Few names of such septs are *Nag, Hasda, Kamal, Barda,* etc. Being exogamous the members of one sept are not permitted to marry within his or her sept. Even the persons having same ancestral village are prohibited to intermarry. The sept of Bhumij is patrilineal and it has no important economic or religious role. Nowadays, most of the Bhumij people cannot always remember their septs and totems accurately.

As the Bhumij family is patriarchal and patrilineal the tradition continues from father to son and the wife comes to live with husband in his father's house. In the social and political affairs of the family, the father is considered as head. He is the sole proprietor of the family property. Each and every member pays regard and love to him. Though he is the sole administrator of the family, his power passes to his sons when he becomes old.

Most of the Bhumij family consists of parents, daughters, sons and their wives and children. Married daughters live in their husbands' houses and visit occasionally to their paternal family. Though in some few cases married sons live separately, usually they do not leave the paternal roof during the lifetime of their father. After the death of father, brothers may live together but usually those who are married live independently in separate houses. One or two unmarried brothers or sisters may live with them. If the family consists of husband, wife and their unmarried children, it is known as unclear family. When the unmarried brother or unmarried sister live with the husband and wife is called intermediate family. A joint family consists of husband, wife and their married sons or married brothers. Usually these three family types are prominent among Bhumij.

III

The houses of the Bhumij are not built up following any definite plan. The houses are mostly built of mud with roofs generally made of straw. Two types of walls are found. One type of walls are made of pure mud, whereas other type are of twigs plastered with mud. In most cases, houses have no window, but for the purpose of ventilation some square space is left on the wall. Separate kitchens are found in some of the houses, but in the most of the houses cooking is done in the enclosed varandahs. Nearly in each and every house, there is a courtyard and some space is also used as kitchen-garden. Cow-sheds and poultry-sheds are also found in most of the Bhumij households. The cowsheds are usually built in the remote corner of the house.

Like the neighbouring tribes, the Bhumij are also settled agriculturists. They cultivate land with the plough and produce rice. But agriculture is not a major source for earning cash. Oil seeds and tobacco are the important cash crops. They also rear lac, resin on privately owned trees and this is their main regular source of earning.

The Bhumij being basically agriculturists have strong inclination to private cwnership of land. But those who are landless, work as agricultural labourers. The Bhumij also go for hunting and trapping wild games in the jungles.

IV

The Bhumij have their own traditional tribal panchayat. All adult members of their community became the members of the panchayat. Before the establishment of the three-tier system of panchayat, this tribal panchayat holds prestigious position and still it performs many important functions. These functions are categorised into two forms: Administrative and Socio-religious. The *Mukhia* is the administrative head and his post is hereditary. Being an administrator he looks after the law and order of village. Each and every villager shows respect to him. All petty disputes, conflict between husband and wife, widow remarriage, separations and divorce or any other problem of their day-to-day life are settled down by his decision taken in consultation with other officials. All meetings are presided by him. After the introduction of the gram panchayat the *Mukhia* has become a nominal head. All important household functions, ceremonies of his village are celebrated under the supervision of the *Mukhia*. Newly married couple visits first to his house for showing respect to him.

Socio-religious functions of the Bhumij are mainly performed by the *Laia* and the *Gunin*. The *Laia* is the priest and performs many important religious functions. The post of the *Laia* is also hereditary. He is duely paid and well-honoured by the members of his community. In their traditional village society the *Gunin* or *Ojha* performs many magico-religious functions. Spirits are controlled by him. Now a days they are decreasing in number due to increasing influence of modern science and technology.

V

Like others the Bhumij consider menstruation as a defilement period, especially the first one. The women are considered as totally polluted and are prohibited from doing any kind of domestic or ceremonial duties during such uncleanliness.

Pregnancy is highly appreciated in the Bhumij community. During pregnancy a woman is given nourishing food. She is not allowed to do heavy work. Various kinds of restrictions and regulations are also imposed on an expectant mother such as, not to kill any creature, not to attend any funeral ceremony, not to go to forest alone etc.

When a pregnant woman feels the labour pain, she informs to other elderly females of the family to prepare a lying-in-room and to contact a midwife or *dai* from the *Handi* or *Ghasi* community. Such lying-in-room is prepared generally in empty cowshed or in any other unoccupied hut.

At the time of delivery, the birth of a child is announced with the sound of a conch shell. The umbilical cord is cut by the midwife and after birth she buries it under the ground in one corner of the house. Like other tribes, the Bhumij believe that if the umbilical cord is exposed to the public, any kind of serious harm may cause to the mother and the baby.

The mother has to remain in the lying-in-room for eight to ten days. In this period with the mother and child, the whole family is considered as polluted. On the last day of this period, a washerman washes the clothes of the family and a barber comes, shaves the male members and pares the nails of all members including the newborn baby. On the final purificatory day a dinner is served to the invited relatives with rice, meat or fowl curry and *handia* (homebrewn liquor).

Among the Bhumij, name-giving ceremony is an important ceremony. Generally on the 21st day after the birth of the child it takes place. At the time of name-giving the members of the family becomes very cautious. If any kind of bad sound (like sneezing sound) comes at that moment the given name is cancelled and another is given. Such name-giving ceremony usually takes place in a cleaned courtyard decorated with *alpana* (designs made by rice-paste). The ceremony concludes with a feast, in which *handia* is a compulsory item.

In Bhumij community the first rice feeding ceremony is held in the seventh or ninth month after the birth of a child, which is known as *mukh jutna*. An auspicious day is fixed for this purpose by a priest. On that day, after the fortune test is performed for the child, the father-in-law or the mother-in-law of the father of the child feeds *payas* (a special preparation of rice with milk and molasses) to it. Among the well-off family a dinner is arranged for the guests.

Like all the people, marriage is considered as a very important event in the life of a Bhumij. Marriage proposals usually come from friends and relatives. Sometimes the *Mukhia* (headman) of the village may help in this matter. After getting the information the members of bridegroom visit the bride's family. If the bride is primarily selected, astrological calculations are performed. If the signs are found good the marriage is negotiated.

Then on a selected day bride's guardian comes to the bridegroom's house with other relatives for betrothal ceremony. They talk with the bridegroom. They have a meal of boiled rice, pulse and fowl curry and *handia*. Some betrothal takes place in bride's house also. Before three days of the actual marriage ceremony *lagon-bandha* ceremony takes place in which a knot is tied with the rope of hemp so that the rope contains the *durba* grass (a kind of grass known as holy) and a grain of paddy. Such rope smeared with turmeric paste is called *lagan*.

In the morning of the particular day, a barber comes and shaves the bridegroom and pares his nails. In this morning a rectangular mud platform is made in the courtyard known as *chhamra* in both the houses. Some rites are performed on this *chhamra* in the afternoon of the day of the marriage. Then the bridegroom starts a procession to the bride's house. After reaching there, he is carried to the *chhamra*. At first the priest utters some incantations and then the bridegroom takes vermilion with the help of a nut cracker (*janti*) and puts on the forehead of the bride. The bride in turn puts vermilion on the bridegroom's forehead.

This is the ceremony of *sindurdan.* After that bride's father or maternal or paternal uncle gives over her to the bridegroom. To do this bride's father or the maternal or paternal uncle repeats the incantations uttered by the priest undergoing a whole day fasting. At last bride's hand is placed on the hand of the bridegroom. Then the corners of the bridegroom's cloth and bride's cloth are knotted together. The bridegroom's party is entertained with the *handia,* sweet and meats. The bridal feast is arranged after the marriage ceremony. On this occassion the bridegroom's party is served cooked rice, meat curry and *handia* along with the bridegroom.

Like birth, the people of Bhumij community observe a number of rites and rituals after the death of a member of their families. Both the burial and cremation are practised by the Bhumij as socially sanctioned methods of removal of the dead bodies.

When death occurs at night, the members of the family sit near the dead body till morning. In the morning, before the funeral procession starts the dead body is bathed in water and smeared with turmeric paste and mustard oil. Then the dead body is placed on bier and is carried by the sons, brothers or any other relatives of the deceased. The name of *Hari* (God) is uttered during the whole procession.

For cremation, the dead body is placed on a funeral pyre in *sasan* (crematorium) which is prepared to the north-south direction. Then the rite of *mukhe-agun* or touching fire to the mouth of the dead body is performed by the eldest or the youngest son. In case of burial, the grave is generally three feet in depth. The grave is dug also in north-south direction and dead body is laid there facing its head to the north and legs to the south. The earth is put first on the grave by the eldest or the younger son. After cremation or burial, all participants take bath in the nearest pond, put some thorns on the road and cross them. It signifies that the way of return is closed forever for the deceased. After returning to the house of the deceased the participants touch fire and are served with fried rice and *handia.*

Next day few male members of the family visit the crematorium. There they pour water over the pyre and collect the bones. Putting these into an earthen pot, they bury it under a tree.

The people of Bhumij community observe mourning period usually for ten days. On the 11th day, the *sradh* ceremony is performed which ends the mourning period. During the mourning period, the Bhumij people face a number of prohibitions. They are prohibited to take fish, meat, egg, *musuri dal* (a kind of pulse) etc. and to use soap or soda for cleaning. They are not allowed to cut their beard, moustache, hair and to pare the nails.

Several rites are performed on the tenth day after the death. The relatives of the deceased assemble on *ghat* or beside a pond and the priest enchants the name of *Hari* (God) when musicians beat the drums. All assembled relatives at the *ghat* are called *ghat kutumbu* (relatives who can attend the rites of *ghat*). Then the barber shaves the male members and pares the nails of all the members of the family. Then everyone takes bath in the pond and put on new chothes. This rite is followed by *Pindadan* or oblation to the soul. All the participants of these rites take boiled pulses (except *musuri*) at night.

On the 11th day a place in the courtyard is chosen and is cleansed with cowdung paste for the *sradh* ceremony. A Brahmin is called again. All the members sit before the Brahmin. After uttering the incantations he offers oblation to the soul of the dead as well as to the other dead relatives. Then he sprinkles holy water to all. All the relatives are entertained with a feast.

VI

Like any other tribal people the Bhumij believe in certain supernatural powers. In this supernatural world, those powers believed to be good for the people are known as benevolent and those to be bad are known as malevolent. Both regulate the destiny of the Bhumij people. They worship the benevolent spirits to keep them satisfied. At the same time as they fear the malevolent spirits, they perform several rites and rituals to gratify them.

The Bhumij people have faith on magic and religion like other tribes. Both the magic and religion serve as the sources of security and confidence in the mind of the Bhumij people in time of crisis.

Barapahar is one deity mentioned in Bhumij pantheon, is believed to live on the peak of the mountain. Bhumij people worship *Barapahar* traditionally. There is no fixed date for worshipping. *Barapahar* is worshipped at the time of worshipping other deities.

Bhumij set apart a *jahirthan* (sacred shrine) generally at the foot of *Asan* or *Piasal* trees in the forest. *Jahir Buru* is believed to reside in this sacred shrine. She is believed to be a very benevolent deity who helps to grow good crops. But if she gets angry somewhow, all the crops damage. So, *Jahir Buru* occupies a very important position in Bhumij pantheon. But there is also no fixed date for worshipping *Jahir Buru*. They perform her worship at the time of the worship of other deities.

Bhumij people believe in the existence of various ghosts also who have the power to do mischiefs. The names of some such ghosts are *Kala Kundra, Dhana Kundra, Pretasun, Pretini, Sannashi Bhut, Daini Bhut* etc. Bhumij believe that jungles, big trees, big tanks are the permanent places for free spirits and ghosts. To resist their various kinds of mischief the Bhumij people believe in magic and magical performances. There are usually three kinds of magicians who possess the magical power. They are *gunin* (medicineman or sorcerer), *dain* (witch) and *ojha* (snake charmer who also have the power to drive away ghosts). Bhumij believe most on the power of *dains* or witches than the other two. The power of the witches is malevolent in nature and may cause harm to persons without any specific reasons.

The people of Bhumij community take part in a number of festivals throughout the year. Though these festivals differ from place to place, some important common festivals are as follows.

Bhumij worship *Garam* in a *jahir-than* (sacred shrine) in the jungles in the month of *Sravan* (July-August). They believe that, *Garam* is the presiding deity of the village. It is a communal worship which is performed by a Bhumij priest known as *naya* in some places or *deheri* in some other places. Though there is no actual image of *Garam,* he is represented usually by a piece of stone. The Bhumij priest pours milk over this stone and offers flowers, *bel* leaves (a kind of leaves which is considered holy), and sweet. He also offers a cock and a he-goat. Those who want to pray to the deity, perform their prayers with the priest. It is believed that without the priest such prayers cannot reach to the *Garam.* No incantation is used for this purpose.

Bhumij of some regions worship *Sitala* in the month of *Chaitra* (March-April) as a deity of cholera and small-pox. There is no scheduled date for *Sitala* worship but a date is fixed for worship in a meeting. In the morning of the day of worship, the sacred shrine is cleansed with water and cowdung. Sweets, milk etc., are offered by the Bhumij priest. Then sacrifice of a black goat is followed. But in some other regions Bhumij people believe that small-pox takes place for the evil workings of *Sitala* and there *Sitala* is not worshipped. In those places the Bhumij venerate goddess *Atra.* They believe that they get relief from small-pox for the blessings of goddess *Atra.* When small-pox spreads out, a black hen and a black she-goat is set free on a night by an old man.

The people of Bhumij community believe that if *Manasa* (who is regarded as the goddess of snakes) becomes angry the snakes cause serious harm to them. *Manasa* is worshipped generally in the month of *Sravana* (June-July). But the Bhumij of some other regions worship *Manasa* once more on the last day of the *Aswin* (August-September). Worshipping of *Manasa* sometimes takes place on community basis and sometimes family basis. For the community basis, worship is held on the *jahir than* (sacred shrine) and a cowdung-plastered courtyard is used when any family performs the worship. In both type an earthen pot filled with water and marked with vermilion is put on the sacred shrine or on the courtyard. Flowers, *bel* leaves and *tulsi* leaves (both leaves are considered as holy) are put there. The sweets, fruits, milk etc. are offered. The worship is ended with sacrifices of a goat and a pigeon.

The Bhumij people believe *Karam* (*Nauclea Parvifolia*) tree satisfies the desires if it is worshipped. So they worship *Karam* and on this occassion *Karam* festival takes place. This festival takes place in the month of *Bhadra* (August-September). In the morning of the day of worship the Bhumij priest goes to the jungle. He cuts *Karam* branches and carries to the courtyyard of his house where the worship takes place. In some other regions *Karam* worship takes place in such families, those who have *Karam* tree in their house. Like other worshippings, flowers, *bel* and *tulsi* leaves and sweets are offered. Sometimes a he-goat is sacrificed.

On the day of worship, the participants remain in fasting for the whole day. The whole worship is accompanied with dancing and singing. After the ceremonial performances the participants take bath in the next morning and then they break their fasting in the name of *Karam.*

The Bhumij also have many traditional gods and goddesses who reside in mountains, hills, sacred places, groves, plants etc. They believe that all these natural objects possess some supernatural powers which control the ways of their everyday life. Sometimes their fortune-unfortune, hope-despair, joy-sorow are regulated by their blessings or wrath. As the Bhumij community interacts with the people of the Hindu community, naturally many Hindu gods and goddesses of the greater Hindu pantheon are now worshipped by them. Due to their illiteracy they are not well aware of the origin and the all-mighty power of these gods and goddesses like Siva, Durga, Kali, Manasa, Saraswati, Lakshmi, Ram, Jagannath, Ganesa and Balaram. Nowadays Vaishnavism influences their community like other communities. A good number of Bhumij become the followers of this sect.

Reference

1. *Bodri*, 1972.
2. *Adhikary*, 1984.
3. *Roy*, 1925.
4. *Sahu*, 1995.
5. *Bhowmick*, 1963.
6. *Risely*, 1981.
7. *Roy and others*, 1982.
8. *Bhowmick*, 1991.
   (i) *Nandi Basu*, 1993.
   (ii) *Dalton*, 1872.
   (iii) *Sachchidananda*, 1979.
9. *Risley*, 1891.

4

Demographic Profile

This chapter portrays the detailed description and distribution of the respondents village wise. For each community, different villages selected for this purpose have been described in Table 2.2.

Number of villages is not uniform for each community considering its size and density of population.

In Table 4.1 the informants of the Birhor community in Purulia District of West Bengal have been categorised into five age groups '0-4', '5-14', '15-45', '46-60' and '61 +'. There are 9.76 per cent males and 9.21 per cent females in the age group of '0-4'. As compared to this there are more males and females in the age group of '5-14', i.e., 34.15 per cent males and 35.53 per cent females. Most of the males (39.01 per cent) and females (40.79 per cent) belong to the age group of '15-45'. 9.76 per cent males and 9.21 per cent females fall in the age group of '46-60' and there are 7.32 per cent males and 5.26 per cent females in the '61 +' age group.

From the Table it is evident that there are more males 53. 17 per cent than females 46.83 per cent in the village of Bhupatipalli. The village Mangaltaur has more females (53.12 per cent) than males (46.88 per cent).

The respondents of the Birhor families have been categorised into five age groups. In case of Birhor community of Hazaribagh of Bihar 14.29 per cent males and 12,24 per cent females are in the age group of '0-4' followed by 26.53 per cent males and 29.59 per cent females in the age group of '5-14'. Most of the males (46.43 per cent) and females (50.00 per cent) of the total population belong to the age group

TABLE 4.1
POPULATION STRUCTURE: BLRHOR
WEST BENGAL AND BIHAR

State	*District*	*Village*	*No. of family*	*Age group in Years* 0 - 4 *M*	*F*	5 - 14 *M*	*F*
	Purulia	Mang-	8	1	2	5	8
		altaur		(6.67)	(11.76)	(33.33)	(47.06)
West		Bhupatipalli	29	7	5	23	19
Bengal				(10.45)	(08.47)	(34.33)	(32.20)
		Total	37	8	7	28	27
				(9.76)	(09.21)	(34.15)	(35.55)
	Hazari-	Tantijharia	3	3	-	1	1
	bagh			(42.86)	-	(14.29)	(25.00)
		Gobindapur	5	4	1	5	6
				(12.05)	(06.67)	(26.32)	(40.00)
		Janga	5	3	-	5	3
				(23.08)	-	(38.46)	(33.33)
Bihar		Baladoh-	6	3	2	7	5
		aratola		(18.75)	(15.38)	(43.75)	(38.46)
		Jhumri-	6	-	3	2	4
		Mohua Colony		-	(23.08)	(20.00)	(30.77)
		Daru	9	2	2	2	5
				(12.50)	(10.00)	(12.50)	(25.00)
		Khijura	11	2	2	6	10
				(09.09)	(09.09)	(27.27)	(45.77)
		Tilra	21	5	9	17	8
				(11.36)	(21.95)	(38.64)	(19.51)
		Banchitao	34	6	5	7	16
				(12.24)	(08.47)	(14.29)	(27.12)
		Total	100	28	24	52	58
				(14.29)	(12.24)	(26.53)	(29.59)

15 - 45		*46 - 60*		*61 +*		*Total*			
M	*F*	*M*	*F*	*M*	*F*	*M*	*%*	*M*	*%*
6	5	2	2	1		15	46.88	17	53.12
(40.00)	(29.41)	(13.33)	(11.76)	(6.67)	(00.00)	(100.00)		(100.00)	
26	26	6	5	5	4	67	53.17	59	46.83
(38.80)	(44.07)	(08.95)	(08.47)	(07.46)	(06.78)	(100.00)		(100.00)	
32	31	8	7	6	4	82	51.90	76	48.10
(39.01)	(40.79)	(09.76)	(09.21)	(7.32)	(05.26)	(100.00)		(100.00)	
2	2	-	1	1	-	7	63.64	4	36.36
(28.57)	(50.00)	-	(25.00)	(14.29)	-	(100.00)		(100.00)	
10	8	-	-	-	-	19	55.88	15	44.12
(52.63)	(53.33)	-	-	-	-	(100.00)		(100.00)	
4	6	1	-	-	-	13	59.09	9	40.91
(30.77)	(66.67)	(07.69)	-	-	-	(100.00)		(100.00)	
5	5	-	1	1	-	16	55.17	13	44.83
(31.25)	(38.46)	-	(07.69)	(06.25)	-	(100.00)		(100.00)	
7	5	-	-	1	1	10	43.48	13	56.52
(70.00)	(38.46)	-	-	(10.00)	(07.69)	(100.00)		(100.00)	
10	11	-	-	2	2	16	44.44	20	55.56
(62.50)	(55.00)	-	-	(12.50)	(10.00)	(100.00)		(100.00)	
7	6	3	1	4	3	22	50.00	22	50.00
(31.82)	(27.27)	(13.64)	(04.55)	(18.18)	(13.64)	(100.00)		(100.00)	
19	22	1	2	2	-	44	51.76	41	48.24
(43.18)	(53.66)	(02.27)	(04.88)	(04.55)	-	(100.00)		(100.00)	
27	33	7	5	2	-	49	45.37	59	54.63
(55.10)	(55.93)	(14.29)	(08.47)	(04.08)	-	(100.00)		(100.00)	
91	98	12	10	13	6	196	50.00	196	50.00
(46.43)	(50.00)	(06.12)	(05.10)	(06.63)	(03.07)	(100.00)		(100.00)	

of '15-45'. 6.12 per cent males and 5.10 per cent females fall in the age group of '46-60' whereas 6.63 per cent males and 3.07 per cent females belong to the age group of '61 +'.

From the Table it is also evident that out of 9 villages majority (5) have more males than females. The number of aged females are less than the number of aged males (61 +).

The respondents of the Lodha families of both the districts, namely Midnapur in West Bengal and Mayurbhanj in Orissa, have been classified into five age groups— '0-4', '5-14', '15-45', '46-60' and '61 +' in years (Table 4.2). In case of the Lodha in West Bengal 15.94 per cent males and 11.86 per cent females are in the age group of '0-4' years followed by 25.90 per cent males and 25.85 per cent females in the age group of '5-14' years. Most of the males (41.82 per cent) and females (45.76 per cent) belong to the age group of '15-45' years. There are 7.97 per cent males and 12.72 per cent females who belong to the '46-60' years age group. The Table shows a few number of males (8.37 per cent) and females (3.81 per cent) in the age group of '61 +' years.

Considering the age distribution of the respondents of each village separately it can be said that villages Kukai (54.13 per cent male and 45.87 per cent female), Kajla (57.50 per cent male and 42.50 per cent female), Bardai (51.54 per cent male and 48.46 per cent female), Maliara (60.00 per cent male and 40.00 per cent female) and Parulia (52.38 per cent male and 47.62 per cent female) are male dominated. Only one village Padampur (male 50.00 per cent and female 50.00 per cent) has an equal percentage of male and female, and the remaining 3 villages are female-dominated. These are Panchrol (46.67 per cent male and 53.33 per cent female), Shakharidanga (47.92 per cent male and 52.08 per cent female) and Daharpur (47.06 per cent male and 52.94 per cent female).

From the Table it is clear that the Lodha community of Orissa has 15.09 per cent males and 13.21 per cent females belonging to the age group of '0-4' years followed by 30.19 per cent males and 27.36 per cent females in the age group of '5-14' years. Comparatively there are more males 39.62 per cent and more females 44.34 per cent in the age group of '15-45' years. The Table also depicts that 9.43 per cent males and 11.32 per cent females of the total population belong to

TABLE 4.2
POPULATION STRUCTURE : LODHA
WEST BENGAL AND ORISSA

State	*District*	*Village*	*No. of family*	*Age group in Years*										*Total*			
				0 - 4		*5 - 14*		*15 - 45*		*46 - 60*		*61 +*					
				M	*F*	*M*	*F*	*M*	*F*	*M*	*F*	*M*	*F*	*M*	*%*	*F*	*%*
Bengal West	Midnapur	Padampur	2	1	-	2	3	2	2	-	-	-	-	5	50.00	5	50.00
				(20.00)	-	(40.00)	(60.00)	(40.00)	(40.00)	-	-	-			(100.00)		(100.00)
		Maliara	5	-	-	3	1	6	5	2	2	1	-	12	60.00	8	40.00
				-	-	(25.00)	(12.50)	(50.00)	(62.00)	(17.00)	(25.00)	(08.00)	-		(100.00)		(100.00)
		Parulia	5	3	1	3	2	5	6	-	-	-	1	11	52.38	10	47.62
				(27.00)	(10.00)	(27.00)	(20.00)	(45.00)	(60.00)	-	-	-	(10.00)		(100.00)		(100.00)
		Danarpur	8	2	1	3	3	7	8	-	5	4	1	16	47.06	18	52.94
				(13.00)	(05.56)	(19.00)	(16.00)	(44.00)	(44.00)	-	(27.00)	((25.00)	(05.00)		(100.00)		(100.00)
		Kajla	9	3	2	9	4	8	9	1	2	2	-	23	57.50	17	42.50
				(13.00)	(12.00)	(39.00)	(24.00)	(35.00)	(53.00)	(04.00)	(12.00)	(09.00)	-		(100.00)		(100.00)

(Contd.)

West Bengal	Shakhari-danga	9	2	3	5	5	10	10	3	5	3	2	23	47.9	25	52.08
			(08.69)	(12.00)	(22.00)	(20.00)	(43.00)	(40.00)	(13.00)	(20.00)	(13.00)	(08.00)	(100.00)		(100.00)	
	Panchrol	15	7	4	10	14	14	15	1	5	3	2	35	46.6740		53.33
			(20.00)	(10.00)	(28.57)	(35.00)	(40.00)	(37.50)	(02.86)	(12.50)	(08.57)	(05.00)	(100.00)		(100.00)	
	Kuka	21	13	7	12	13	22	22	9	5	3	3	5954.13		50	45.87
			(22.03)	(14.00)	(20.33)	(26.00)	(37.28)	(44.00)	(15.25)	(10.00)	(05.18)	(06.00)	(100.00)		(100.00)	
	Barda	26	9	10	18	16	31	31	4	6	5	-	6751.54		63	48.46
			(13.00)	(16.00)	(27.00)	(25.00)	(46.00)	(49.00)	(06.00)	(10.00)	(08.00)	-	(100.00)		(100.00)	
	Total	100	40	28	65	61	105	108	20	30	21	9	251	51.54	236	48.46
			(15.94)	(11.86)	(25.90)	(25.85)	(41.82)	(45.76)	(07.97)	(12.72)	(08.37)	(03.81)	(100.00)		(100.00)	
Orissa	Mayurbhanj															
	Chittamatiya	50	16	14	32	29	42	47	10	12	6	4	106	50.00	106	50.00
			(15.09)	(13.21)	(13.19)	(27.35)	(39.62)	(44.34)	(09.43)	(11.32)	(05.66)	(03.77)	(100.00)		(100.00)	

N.B. *Figures in the Parentheses indicate percentages.*

the age group of '46-60' years whereas 5.67 per cent males and 3.77 per cent females of the total population are in '61 +' years age group.

In this Table (4.3) the respondents of the Mahali families of both the districts of Midnapur in West Bengal and Singbhum in Bihar have been categorised into five age groups. From the Table it is evident that in case of the Mahali in West Bengal 12.45 per cent males and 9.33 per cent females are in the age group of '0-4' years, 28.22 per cent males and 28.00 per cent females are in '5-14' years age group and most of the males (42.32 per cent) and females (45.78 per cent) fall in the age group of '15-45' years. It also shows that 11.20 per cent males and 9.33 per cent females are in the age group of '46-60' years and in the age group of '61 +' years are few males (5.81 per cent) and females (7.56 per cent).

From the Table it can also be seen that out of 8 villages 4 villages are female dominated. These are Sarisaraiidihi (male 46.15 per cent and female 53.85 per cent), Chotamatkatpur (male 41.67 per cent and female 58.33 per cent), Maghalmari (43.75 per cent male and 56.25 per cent female) and Maynapara (40.00 per cent male and 60.00 per cent female). Only one village (Saorapich 50.00 per cent male and 50.00 per cent female) has an equal number of males and females. The remaining 3 villages have more males than females. These are Kotaigarh (male 51.35 per cent and female 48.65 per cent), Ektal (50.78 per cent male and 49.22 per cent female) and Jayrampur (55.56 per cent male and 44.44 per cent female).

In case of the Mahali community of Bihar it is observed that the percentage of male members is higher than the percentage of female members in all the three villages. The majority of the population both male and female lie in the age group of '15-45' years where the female (50.00 per cent) predominate over the male (37.10 per cent). A few of the population male (4.03 per cent) and female (3.19 per cent) belong to the age group of '61 +' years. So the age distributions of the Mahali population in Bihar and West Bengal do not reveal any special trend.

TABLE 4.3
POPULATION STRUCTURE : MAHALI WEST BENGALAND BIHAR

State	District	Village	No. of family	Age group in Years 0 - 4 M	F	5 - 14 M	F	15 - 45 M	F
	Midna-pur	Mayna-para	1	-	1	-	-	1	1
				-	(33.33)	-	-	(50.00)	(33.33)
		Shaorapich	1	-	1	1	-	1	2
				-	(33.33)	(33.33)	-	(33.33)	(66.67)
		Chotamatka-pur	3	-	-	-	3	4	2
				-	-	-	(42.86)	(80.00)	(28.57)
West Bengal		Maghalmari	4	-	1	2	2	4	4
				-	(11.11)	(28.57)	(22.22)	(57.14)	(44.44)
		Sarisasaral-dihl	7	1	1	2	4	5	5
				(08.33)	(07.14)	(16.67)	(28.57)	(41.67)	(35.71)
		Kotaigarh	23	6	2	20	23	23	21
				(10.53)	(03.70)	(35.09)	(42.59)	(40.35)	(38.89)
		Ektal	27	4	6	21	17	29	30
				(06.15)	(09.52)	(32.31)	(26.98)	(44.62)	(47.62)
		Jayrampur	34	19	9	22	14	35	38
				(21.11)	(12.50)	(24.44)	(19.44)	(39.89)	(52.78)
		Total	100	30	21	68	63	102	103
				(12.45)	(09.33)	(28.22)	(28.00)	(43.32)	(45.78)
		Old Potamda	8	4	-	6	3	5	6
				(18.18)	-	(27.27)	(23.10)	(22.73)	(46.15)
Bihar		Bidra	15	8	3	7	5	15	14
				(22.86)	(10.34)	(20.00)	(17.24)	(42.86)	(48.28)
		New Potamda	27	9	9	20	8	26	27
				(13.43)	(17.31)	(29.85)	(15.38)	(38.81)	(51.92)
		Total	50	21	12	33	16	46	47
				(16.94)	(12.77)	(26.61)	(17.02)	(37.10)	(50.00)

(Contd.)

Age group in years				*Total*			
46 - 60		*61 +*					
M	*F*	*M*	*F*	*M*	*%*	*F*	*%*
-	1	1	-	2	40.00	3	60.00
-	(33.33)	(50.00)	-	(100.00)		(100.00)	
1	-	-	-	3	50.00	3	50.00
(33.33)	-	-	-	(100.00)		(100.00)	
1	1	-	1	5	41.67	7	58.33
(20.00)	(14.29)	-	(14.29)	(100.00)		(100.00)	
1	1	-	1	7	43.75	9	56.25
(14.29)	(11.11)	-	(11.11)	(100.00)		(100.00)	
2	2	2	2	12	46.15	14	53.85
(16.67)	(14.29)	(16.67)	(14.29)	(100.00)		(100.00)	
4	5	4	3	57	51.35	54	48.65
(07.72)	(09.26)	(07.02)	(05.56)	(100.00)		(100.00)	
8	4	3	6	65	50.78	63	43.22
(12.31)	(06.35)	(04.62)	(09.52)	(100.00)		(100.00)	
10	7	4	4	90	55.56	72	44.44
(11.11)	(09.72)	(04.44)	(05.56)	(100.00)		(100.00)	
27	21	14	17	241	51.72	225	48.28
(11.20)	(09.33)	(05.81)	(07.56)	(100.00)		(100.00)	
4	2	3	2	22	62.86	13	37.14
(18.18)	(18.38)	(13.64)	(15.38)	(100.00)		(100.00)	
4	7	1	-	35	54.69	29	45.31
(11.43)	(24.14)	(02.84)	-	(100.00)		(100.00)	
11	7	1	1	67	56.30	52	43.70
(16.42)	(13.46)	(1.49)	(01.92)	(100.00)		(100.00)	
19	16	5	3	124	56.88	94	43.12
(15.32)	(17.02)	(04.03)	(03.19)	(100.00)		(100.00)	

N.B. *Figres in the Parentheses indicate percentages.*

The respondents of the Santal families (Table 4.4) of both the districts of West Bengal and Orissa have been divided into five age groups. In case of the Santal in the district of Midnapur (W.B.) 17.01 per cent males and 13.55 per cent females are in the age groups of '0-4' years, followed by 26.97 per cent males and 27.11 per cent females are in the age group of '5-14' years. Maximum number of males (41.49 per cent) and females (45.05 per cent) are in the age group of '15-45' years, 10.79 per cent males and 8.42 per cent females are in the age group of '46-60' years. In this tribal community the percentages of males (3.73 per cent) and females (5.86 per cent) in the age group of '61 +' years are not high.

From the Table it is evident that out of 15 villages 10 villages have more female members than the male members. These are Kharika (48.00 per cent male and 52.00 per cent female), Susinda (42.55 per cent male and 57.45 per cent female), Dakshinkhatnagar (47.5 per cent male and 52.50 per cent female), Subujpalli (44.12 per cent male and 55.88 per cent female), Deuli (46.67 per cent male and 53.33 per cent female), Haldia (40.91 per cent male and 59.09 per cent female), Baganshahi (46.27 per cent male and 53.73 per cent female), Chotamatkarpur (25.00 per cent male and 75.00 per cent female), Bahna (45.45 per cent male and 54.55 per cent female) and Belda (41.67 per cent male and 58.33 per cent female). Only in two villages (Maynapara and Kalabani the percentages of male and female are the same (50.00 per cent). The remaining 3 villages (Babalpur, Maghlmori and Chotomatkatpur) have more males than females.

The Santal community in Mayurbhanj district of Orissa shows that 13.29 per cent males and 6.82 per cent females fall in the age group of '0-4' years, followed by 35.67 per cent males and 37.12 per cent females in the age group of '5-14' years. There are 37.06 per cent males and 41.67 per cent females in the '15-45' years age group whereas 7.69 per cent males and 9.84 per cent females belong to the age group of '46-60' years. The Table shows that there are only 6.29 per cent males and 4.55 per cent females in the age group of '61 +' years.

Considering the age distribution of two villages of Orissa separately it can be said that the village Sannyasi has more (52.56 per cent) males than females (47.44 per cent). But it is just the opposite in case of Ghorabandha village where there are more females (51.22 per cent) than the males (48.78 per cent).

Table 4.5 depicts the age distribution of the Munda respondents of two States. There are 10.51 per cent males and 14.00 per cent females in the age group of '0-4' years. Compared to this there are more males (28.40 per cent) and females (26.00 per cent) in the age group of '5-14' years. Most of the males (45.91 per cent) and females (46.80 per cent) belong to the age group of '15-45' years. Males (7.00 per cent) and females (8.00 per cent) lie in the age group of '46-60' years, and in the '61 +' age group there are 8.17 per cent males and 5.20 per cent females.

From the above Table it is evident that most of the villages (5 out of 8) have more males than females. These villages are Daharpur (51.67 per cent males and 48.33 per cent females), Abhirampur (51.19 per cent males and 48.81 per cent females), Gaganeswar (51.79 per cent males and 48.21 per cent females), Gobindapur (53.57 per cent males and 46.43 per cent females) and Hirapari (55.36 per cent males and 44.64 per cent females). There are two villages (Deulchak and Kotaigarh) where the number of females is more than that of males.

Considering the age distribution of the Munda community in Bihar it can be said that there are 14.06 per cent male and 18.05 per cent female in the age group of '0-4' years, followed by 32.03 per cent males and 24.86 per cent females in the age group of '5-14' years, 42.19 per cent males and 45.86 per cent females in the age group of '15-45' years, 7.81 per cent males and 9.02 per cent females in the age group of '46-60' years and there are 3.91 per cent males and 3.01 per cent females who are aged '61' years and above.

TABLE 4.4
POPULATION STRUCTURE : SANTAL
WEST BENGAL AND ORISSA

State	*District*	*Village*	*No. of family*	*Age group in Years* 0 - 4 *M*	0 - 4 *F*	5 - 14 *M*	5 - 14 *F*	15 - 45 *M*	15 - 45 *F*
	Midn-apur	Chakmakr-ampur	1	-	-	-	-	1	-
				-	-	-	-	(50.00)	-
		Belda	3	1	-	1	3	2	4
				(20.00)	-	(20.00)	(42.86)	(40.00)	(57.14)
		Chotamatka-tpur	3	-	4	1	1	2	4
				-	(44.44)	(33.33)	(11.11)	(66.67)	(44.44)
		Kalabani	3	-	1	1	2	5	3
				-	(11.11)	(11.11)	(22.22)	(55.55)	(33.33)
West		Kharika	3	2	4	5	4	4	3
Bengal				(16.67)	(30.77)	(41.67)	(30.77)	(33.33)	(23.08)
		Bahna	6	2	1	3	7	5	10
				(13.33)	(05.56)	(20.00)	(38.89)	(33.33)	(55.56)
		Dakshin Khatnager	6	2	3	3	7	11	10
				(10.53)	(14.29)	(15.79)	(33.33)	(57.89)	(47.62)
		Sabujpalli	6	4	4	5	6	4	6
				(26.67)	(21.05)	(33.33)	(31.58)	(26.67)	(31.58)
		Babalpur	7	5	-	7	4	5	7
				(27.78)	-	(38.89)	(30.77)	(27.78)	(53.85)
		Deuli	9	2	2	10	9	8	10
				(09.52)	(08.33)	(47.62)	(37.50)	(38.10)	(41.67)
	Midna-pur	Haldia	9	-	-	3	4	12	16
				-	-	(16.67)	(15.38)	(66.67)	(61.54)
		Maghalmari	9	8	3	7	4	7	9
				(32.00)	(13.64)	(28.00)	(18.18)	(28.00)	(40.91)
		Susinda	9	6	6	5	7	8	12
West				(30.00)	(22.22)	(25.00)	(25.93)	(40.00)	(44.44)
Bengal		Baganshahi	12	5	6	6	8	14	14
				(16.13)	(16.67)	(19.35)	(22.22)	(45.16)	(38.89)
		Maynapara	14	4	3	8	8	12	15
				(14.29)	(10.71)	(28.57)	(28.57)	(42.86)	(53.57)
		Total	100	41	37	65	74	100	23
				(17.01)	(13.55)	(26.97)	(27.11)	(41.49)	(45.05)
	Mayur-bhanj	Ghorab-andha	9	2	1	8	10	5	5
				(10.00)	(04.76)	(40.00)	(47.61)	(25.00)	(23.80)
Orissa		Sannyasi	41	17	8	43	39	48	50
				(13.82)	(07.20)	(34.95)	(35.13)	(39.02)	(45.04)
		Total	50	19	9	51	49	53	55
				(13.29)	(06.82)	(35.67)	(37.12)	(37.06)	(41.67)

Age group in years				*Total*			
46 - 60		*61 +*					
M	*F*	*M*	*F*	*M*	*%*	*F*	*%*
-	1	1	-	2	66.67	1	33.33
-	(100.00)	(50.00)	-	(100.00)		(100.00)	
1	-	-	-	5	41.67	7	58.33
(20.00)	-	-	-	(100.00)		(100.00)	
-	-	-	-	3	25.00	9	75.00
-	-	-	-	(100.00)		(100.00)	
3	2	-	1	9	50.00	8	50.00
(33.33)	(22.22)	-	(11.11)	(100.00)		(100.00)	
-	1	1	1	12	48.00	13	52.00
-	(07.69)	(08.33)	(07.69)	(100.00)		(100.00)	
5	-	-	-	15	45.45	18	54.55
(33.33)	-	-	-	(100.00)		(100.00)	
3	1	-	-	19	47.50	21	52.50
(15.79)	(04.76)	-	-	(100.00)		(100.00)	
1	2	1	1	15	44.12	19	55.88
(06.67)	(10.53)	(06.67)	(05.26)	(100.00)		(100.00)	
1	2	-	-	18	58.06	13	41.94
(05.56)	(15.38)	-	-	(100.00)		(100.00)	
1	1	-	2	21	46.67	24	53.33
(04.76)	(04.17)	-	(08.33)	(100.00)		(100.00)	
3	4	-	2	18	40.91	26	59.09
(16.67)	(15.38)		(07.69)	(100.00)		(100.00)	
-	2	3	4	25	53.19	22	46.81
-	(09.09)	(12.00)	(18.18)	(100.00)		(100.00)	
1	2	-	-	20	42.55	27	57.45
(05.00)	(07.41)	-	-	(100.00)		(100.00)	
4	4	2	4	31	46.27	36	53.73
(12.90)	(11.11)	(06.45)	(11.11)	(100.00)		(100.00)	
3	1	1	1	28	50.00	28	50.00
(10.71)	(03.57)	(03.57)	(03.57)	(100.00)		(100.00)	
26	23	9	16	241	46.89	273	53.11
(10.79)	(08.42)	(03.73)	(05.86)	(100.00)		(100.00)	
2	2	3	3	20	48.78	21	51.22
(10.00)	(09.52)	(15.00)	(14.28)	(100.00)		(100.00)	
9	11	6	3	123	52.56	111	47.44
(07.31)	(09.09)	(04.87)	(02.70)	(100.00)		(100.00)	
11	13	9	6	143	52.00	132	48.00
(07.69)	(09.84)	(06.29)	(04.55)	(100.00)		(100.00)	

N.B. *Figures in the Parentheses indicate percentages.*

TABLE 4.5
POPULATION STRUCTURE : MUNDA
WEST BENGAL AND BIHAR

State	District	Village	No. of family	Age group in Years 0 - 4 M	0 - 4 F	5 - 14 M	5 - 14 F	15 - 45 M	15 - 45 F
West Bengal	Midna-pur	Kotaig-arh	1	-	-	1	1	1	1
				-	-	(33.33)	(33.33)	(33.33)	(33.33)
		Deulchak	10	3	9	5	6	13	13
				(12.50)	(29.03)	(20.83)	(19.35)	(54.17)	(41.94)
		Gobindapur	10	3	-	9	8	12	15
				(10.00)	-	(30.00)	(30.77)	(40.00)	(57.69)
		Hirapari	11	1	3	13	7	13	15
				(03.23)	(12.00)	(41.93)	(28.00)	(41.93)	(60.00)
		Daharpur	13	3	3	6	5	15	14
				(09.68)	(10.34)	(19.35)	(17.24)	(48.39)	(48.28)
		Pichabani	15	5	7	8	11	17	15
				(13.51)	(17.07)	(21.62)	(26.83)	(45.94)	(36.59)
		Abhirampur	16	4	8	19	11	17	17
				(09.30)	(19.51)	(44.19)	(26.83)	(39.53)	(41.46)
		Gaganeswar	24	8	5	12	16	30	27
				(13.79)	(09.26)	(20.69)	(29.63)	(51.72)	(50.00)
		Total	100	27	35	73	65	118	117
				(10.51)	(14.00)	(28.40)	(26.00)	(45.91)	(46.80)
Bihar	Sing-bhum	Pagla-bera	50	18	24	41	32	54	61
				(14.06)	(18.05)	(32.03)	(24.06)	(42.19)	(45.86)

Age group in years							
46 - 60		61 +		Total			
M	F	M	F	M	%	F	%
-	1	1	-	3	50.00	3	50.00
-	(33.33)	(33.33)	-	(100.00)		(100.00)	
2	3	1	-	24	43.64	31	56.36
(08.33)	(09.68)	(04.17)	-	(100.00)		(100.00)	
3	1	3	2	30	53.57	26	46.43
(10.00)	(03.85)	(10.00)	(07.69)	(100.00)		(100.00)	
4	-	-	-	31	55.36	25	44.64
(12.90)	-	-	-	(100.00)		(100.00)	
2	2	5	5	31	51.67	29	48.33
(06.45)	(06.90)	(16.13)	(17.24)	(100.00)		(100.00)	
1	6	6	2	37	47.44	41	52.56
(02.70)	(14.63)	(16.21)	(04.88)	(100.00)		(100.00)	
1	2	2	3	43	51.19	41	48.81
(02.33)	(04.88)	(04.65)	(07.32)	(100.00)		(100.00)	
5	5	3	1	58	51.79	54	48.21
(08.62)	(09.26)	(05.17)	(01.85)	(100.00)		(100.00)	
18	20	21	13	257	50.69	250	49.31
(07.00)	(08.00)	(08.17)	(05.20)	(100.00)		(100.00)	
10	12	5	4	128	49.04	133	50.96
(07.81)	(09.02)	(03.91)	(03.01)	(100.00)		(100.00)	

N.B. *Figures in the Parentheses indicate percentages.*

TABLE 4.6
POPULATION STRUCTURE: BHUMIJ WEST BENGAL AND BIHAR

State	District	Village	No. of family	Age group in Years 0-4 M	0-4 F	5-14 M	5-14 F	15-45 M	15-45 F
	Midna-pur	Abhira-mpur	1	-	-	-	3	1	1
				-	-	-	(60.00)	(50.00)	(20.00)
		Kanchanpur	5	-	-	5	7	4	6
				-	-	(45.45)	(50.10)	(36.36)	(42.86)
		Manoharpur	6	-	1	3	-	7	8
				-	(11.11)	(27.27)	-	(63.64)	(888.89)
West Bengal		Deuli	10	2	4	3	7	12	13
				(10.53)	(14.29)	(15.79)	(25.00)	(63.16)	(46.43)
		Gan-Belda	17	5	4	11	11	15	18
				(13.51)	(10.81)	(29.73)	(29.73)	(40.54)	(48.65)
		Vinodpur	29	10	12	30	20	36	32
				(12.20)	(17.30)	(36.59)	(28.99)	(43.90)	(46.38)
		Shikharpari	32	7	12	16	23	39	34
				(10.14)	(15.38)	(23.19)	(29.49)	(56.52)	(43.59)
		Total	100	24	33	68	71	114	112
				(10.39)	(13.75)	(29.44)	(29.58)	(49.34)	(46.67)
Bihar	Singhbhum	Gadi-gram	50	14	15	34	28	80	56
				(09.33)	(12.93)	(22.67)	(24.14)	(53.33)	(48.28)

Age group in years							
46 - 60		*61 +*		*Total*			
M	*F*	*M*	*F*	*M*	*%*	*F*	*%*
1	1	-	-	2	28.57	5	71.43
(50.00)	(20.00)	-	-	(100.00)		(100.00)	
1	-	1	1	11	44.00	14	56.00
(09.09)	-	(09.09)	(07.14)	(100.00)		(100.00)	
1	-	-	-	11	55.00	9	45.00
(09.09)	-	-	-	(100.00)		(100.00)	
-	2	2	2	19	40.43	28	59.57
-	(07.14)	(10.53)	(07.14)	(100.00)		(100.00)	
5	2	1	2	37	50.00	37	50.00
(13.51)	(05.41)	(02.70)	(05.41)	(100.00)		(100.00)	
3	2	3	3	82	54.30	69	45.70
(03.66)	(02.90)	(03.66)	(04.35)	(100.00)		(100.00)	
5	5	2	4	69	46.94	78	53.06
(07.25)	(06.41)	(02.90)	(05.13)	(100.00)		(100.00)	
16	12	9	12	231	49.04	240	50.96
(06.93)	(05.00)	(03.90)	(05.00)	(100.00)		(100.00)	
20	14	2	3	150	56.39	116	43.61
(13.33)	(12.07)	(01.33)	(02.59)	(100.00)		(100.00)	

N.B. *Figures in the Parentheses indicate percentages.*

The sample Bhumij families of West Bengal and Bihar have been classified into five age groups. In West Bengal there are 10.39 per cent males and 13.75 per cent females in the age group of '0-4' years, 29.44 per cent males and 29.58 per cent females belong to the age group of '5-14' years. The males (49.34 per cent) and females (46.67 per cent) are more in the age group of '15-45' years. In the age group of '46-60' years there are 6.93 per cent males and 5 per cent females. Table also shows that only 3.90 per cent males and 5.00 per cent females lie in the age group '61 +' years (Table 4.6).

Considering the sex distribution of all the villages separately it can be said that out of 7 villages 2 villages are male-dominated, another 4 villages are female-dominated and one village has equal percentages of male and female. Male-dominated villages are Vinodpur and Monoharpur. There are 54.30 per cent male and 45.70 per cent female in Vinodpur and 55.00 per cent male and 45.00 per cent female are in the village Monoharpur. Female-dominated villages are Deuli (40.43 per cent males and 59.57 per cent females), Shikharpari (46.94 per cent males) and 53.06 per cent females), Kanchanpur (44.00 per cent males and 56.00 per cent females) and Abhirampur (28.57 per cent males and 71.43 per cent females). The equal percentages (50.00 per cent male and 50 per cent females) of males and females have been found in Gan belda village too.

In the Bhumij community of Bihar, one village Gadigram shows 9.33 per cent male and 12.93 per cent female belonging to the age group of '0-4' years followed by 22.67 per cent male and 24.14 per cent female belonging to the age group of '5-14' years, 53.33 per cent male and 48.28 per cent females to the age group of '15-45' years, 13.33 per cent male and 12.07 per cent female to the age group of '46-60' years. Only 1.33 per cent male and 2.59 per cent female belong to the age group of '61 +' years.

Table 4.7 represents that the overall sex-ratio of the Birhor families of Purulia in West Bengal is 927. It shows that the sex-ratio (1133) of the village Mangaltour is higher than the sex-ratio (881) of the village Bhupatpalli.

From the Table it is evident that overall sex-ratio of the Birhor community of Hazaribagh in Bihar is 1000. The highest sex-ratio (1300) belongs to the village of Jhumri Mahua Colony and Tantijharia village has the lowest sex-ratio (571). Only one village (Khijura) has perfect sex-ratio (1000). The average family size of the respondents of West Bengal and Bihar is 4.

TABLE 4.7
SEX RATLO OF BIRHAR WEST BENGAL AND BIHAR

Tribe	*State*	*Village*	*No. of family*	*Male*	*Female*	*Total*	*Sex Ratio*	*Average family member*
Birhor	West Bengal	Mangaltaur	8	15	17	32	1133	4
		Bhupati-palli	29	67	59	126	881	4
		Total	37	82	76	158	927	4
		Tanti Jharia	3	7	4	11	571	4
		Gobindapur	5	19	15	34	789	7
		Jarga	5	13	9	22	692	4
		Baladohar-atola	6	16	13	29	1250	5
Birhor	Bihar	Jhumri-Mahua Colony	6	10	13	23	1300	4
		Daru	9	16	20	36	1250	4
		Khijura	11	22	22	44	1000	4
		Tilra	21	44	41	85	932	4
		Banchitao	34	49	59	108	1204	3
		Total	100	196	196	392	1000	4

From the Table it is evident that the overall sex-ratio of the Lodha families in West Bengal is 940. The highest sex-ratio (1143) belongs to the village Panchrol. But the sex-ratio of Maliara village is very low (667). The village Padampur has perfect sex-ratio (1000).

But in the case of the Lodha village, Chittamatiya, situated in the district of Mayurbhanj (Orissa), it has observed that the number of male-female population is equal. So the sex-ratio is 1000. The average size of the Lodha in West Bengal (5) is higher than that of the Lodha in Orissa (4) Table 4.8.

The overall sex-ratio of the sample Mahali families of Midnapur district is 934. From the Table 4.9 it is found that the highest sex-ratio is exhibited (1500) in the village Maynapara and the lowest sex-ratio (800) in the village Jayrampur. It is also observed that the village Shaorapich has sex-ratio (1000). The overall average size of the family is 5. On the other hand, the overall sex-ratio of the Mahali community in district Singbhum (Bihar) is 758. So the sex-ratio of this community is lower than that of the Mahali community in West Bengal. The average number of family size is lower in Bihar than the Mahali community in West Bengal.

From Table 4.10 it is observed that the overall sex-ratio of the Santal families in West Bengal is 1133. The highest sex-ratio (1625) is exhibited in village Babalpur. But the sex-ratio of Chakmakrampur village is extremely low (500). Villages Maynapara and Kalabani have perfect sex-ratios (1000).

TABLE 4.8
SEX RATIO OF THE LODHA WEST BENGAL AND ORISSA

Tribe	*State*	*Village*	*No. of family*	*Male*	*Female*	*Total*	*Sex Ratio*	*A.F.M.*
		Padampur	2	5	5	10	1000	5
		Mallara	5	12	8	20	667	4
		Parulla	5	11	10	21	999	4
		Daharpur	8	16	18	34	1125	4
Lodha	W.B.							
		Kajla Shakhar	9	23	17	40	739	4
		Idanga	9	23	25	48	1087	5
		Panchrol	15	35	40	75	1143	5
		Kukai	21	59	50	109	848	5
		Bardai	26	67	63	130	940	5
		Total	100	251	236	487	940	5
Lodha	Orissa							
		Chittamatiya	50	106	106	212	1000	4

Note :- A = (Average), F= (Family), M= (Member)

TABLE 4.9
SEX RATIO OF MAHALI WEST BENGAL AND BIHAR

Tribe	State	Village	No. of family	Male	Female	Total	Sex Ratio	A.F.M.
Mahali	W.B.	Maynapara	1	2	3	5	1500	5
		Shaorapich	1	3	3	6	1000	6
		Chotamat-katpur	3	5	7	12	1400	4
		Maghalmari	4	7	9	16	1285	4
		Sarisasar-aidihi	7	12	14	26	1166	4
		Kotalgarh	23	57	54	111	947	5
		Ektal	27	65	63	128	969	5
		Jayrampur	34	90	72	162	800	5
		Total	100	241	225	466	934	5
Mahali	Bihar	Old Potomda	8	22	13	35	591	4
		Bidra	15	35	29	64	829	4
		New Potomda	27	67	52	119	776	4
		Total	50	124	94	218	758	4

Note :- A = (Average), F= (Family), M= (Member)

TABLE 4.10
SEX RATIO OF SANTAL WEST BENGAL AND ORISSA

Tribe	State	Village	No. of family	Male	Female	Total	Sex Ratio	A.F.M.
		Chakmak-rampur	1	2	1	3	500	3
		Belda	3	5	7	12	1400	4
		Chotamat-katpur	3	3	9	12	3000	4
		Kalabani	3	9	9	18	1000	6
		Kharika	3	12	13	25	1083	8
		Bahna	6	15	18	33	1200	6
		Dakshin Khatnagar (Ranisarai)	6	19	21	40	1105	7
		Sabujpali	6	15	19	34	1266	6

Santal West	Bengal						
	Babalpur	7	18	13	31	1625	4
	Deuli	9	21	24	45	1142	5
	Haldia	9	18	26	44	1444	5
	Maghalmari	9	25	22	47	880	5
	Susinda	9	20	27	47	1350	5
	Baganshahi	12	31	36	67	1161	6
	Maynapara	14	28	28	56	1000	4
	Total	100	241	273	514	1133	5
	Ghorabandha	9	20	21	41	1050	5
Santal Orissa							
	Sannyasi	41	123	111	234	902	6
	Total	50	143	132	275	923	6

Note :- A = (Average), F= (Family), M= (Member)

Table 4.10 also depicts that the overall sex-ratio of the Santal families in Orissa is 923. The sex-ratio of Ghorabandha village (1050) is higher than that existing in the village of Sannyasi (902). So the sex-ratio of Santal in the Midnapur district in West Bengal is relatively higher than that of Orissa. The average family size of West Bengal is 5 which is lower than that of Orissa which is 6.

From the Table 4.11 it is evident that the overall sex-ratio of the Munda families in Midnapur district is 973. The highest sex-ratio (1292) is exhibited in village Deulchak and the lowest sex-ratio (807) in the village Hirapari. The village Kotaigarh represents sex-ratio 1000.

But on the other hand, the sample families of Munda community in the district Singbhum of the State of Bihar show the sex-ratio 1039. The average family size (5) is the same in both states.

Table 4.12 represents that the overall sex-ratio of the Bhumij families in West Bengal is 1039. Among the seven villages, the village Abhirampur has very high sex-ratio (2500) and the lowest sex-ratio (818) is found in village Monoharpur. The village Gan-Belda has perfect sex-ratio (1000). The sex-ratio of the Bhumij community in the district of Singbhum, Bihar is tremendously low (773). The average family size of this community in West Bengal and Bihar is equal (5).

Table 4.13 depicts state-wise distribution of age and sex composition of six tribal communities of the Birhor, Lodha, Mahali, Santal, Munda and Bhumij from the State of West Bengal, the Lodha and Santal from Orissa and Birhor, Mahali, Munda and Bhumij from the State of Bihar.

The age of the sample has been categorised into five age groups. '0-4' years age group is generally considered as the 'pre-school age' for the children. The Munda and Bhumij community of the States of West Bengal and Bihar reveal the same trend of male-female distribution belonging to '0-4' year age group where the percentage of female is higher than that of male members. But the rest of the tribal communities in all other states show that the males out-number the females.

TABLE 4.11
SEX RATIO OF MUNDA WEST BENGAL AND BIHAR

Tribe	*State*	*Village*	*No. of family*	*Male*	*Female*	*Total*	*Sex Ratio*	*A.F.M.*
Munda	W.B.	Kotaigarh	1	3	3	6	1000	6
		Deulchak	10	24	31	55	1292	6
		Gabindapur	10	30	26	56	867	6
		Hirapari	11	31	25	56	807	5
		Daharpur	13	31	29	60	936	5
		Pichabani	15	37	41	78	1108	5
		Abhirampur	16	43	41	84	954	5
		Gaganeswar	24	58	54	112	931	5
		Total	100	257	250	507	973	5
Munda	Bihar	Paglabera	50	128	133	261	1039	5

Note :- A = (Average), F= (Family), M= (Member)

TABLE 4.12
SEX RATIO OF BHUMIJ WEST BENGAL AND BIHAR

Tribe	*State*	*Village*	*No. of family*	*Male*	*Female*	*Total*	*Sex Ratio*	*A.F.M.*
		Abhirampur	1	2	5	7	2500	7
		Kanchanpur	5	11	14	25	1272	5
		Monoharpur	6	11	9	20	818	3
		Deuli	10	19	28	47	1473	5
Bhumij	W.B.							
		Gan-Belda	17	37	37	74	1000	4
		Vinodpur	29	82	69	151	841	5
		Shikharpari	32	69	78	147	1130	5
		Total	100	231	240	471	1039	5
Bhumij	Bihar	Gadigram	50	150	116	266	773	5

Note :- A = (Average), F= (Family), M= (Member)

Considering the nature of the distribution in the age group of '5-14' years, i.e., the age for school-going children —it has been observed that the male and female distribution of the tribal population like the Birhor, Lodha, Mahali, Santal, Bhumij and Munda in the State of West Bengal, the Lodha and Santal in the State of Orissa and Birhor in Bihar show a similar picture. But a different picture is observed among the three tribal communities viz., the Mahali, Munda and Bhumij of Bihar where the percentage of female members is remarkably lower than that of the males.

The '15-45' year age group is considered as one of the important age groups that assumes the character of a working force for the tribal population, where in maximum cases—the majority of the samples (male and female) lie. The percentage of male population of all the states varies from 37.06 (Santal of Orissa) to 53.33 (Bhumij of Bihar), whereas the percentage of the female members in all the states is more than 45.00 per cent except the Birhor of Purulia, West Bengal (40.79 per cent) and the Santal of Orissa (41.67 per cent). In this age group '15-45' years the number of female members is higher than that of the male except Bhumij in Bihar and West Bengal.

TABLE 4.13
STATE-WISE SEX AND AGE GROUP COMPOSITION

State	Tribe	No. of family	Age group in Years 0 - 4 M	0 - 4 F	5 - 14 M	5 - 14 F	15 - 45 M	15 - 45 F	46 - 60 M	46 - 60 F	61 + M	61 + F	Total M	Total F
	Birhor	37	8	7	28	27	32	31	8	7	6	4	82	76
			(09.76)	(09.21)	(34.15)	(35.53)	(39.02)	(40.79)	(09.76)	(09.21)	(07.32)	(05.26)	(100.00)	(100.00)
	Lodha	100	40	28	65	61	195	108	20	30	21	9	251	236
			(15.94)	(11.86)	(25.90)	(25.85)	(41.83)	(45.76)	(07.97)	(12.71)	(08.37)	(03.81)	(100.00)	(100.00)
	Mahali	100	30	21	68	63	102	103	27	21	14	17	241	225
			(12.45)	(09.33)	(28.22)	(28.00)	(42.32)	(45.78)	(11.20)	(09.31)	(05.81)	(07.56)	(100.00)	(100.00)
W.B	Santal	100	41	37	65	74	100	123	26	23	9	16	241	273
			(17.01)	(13.55)	(26.97)	(27.11)	(41.50)	(45.05)	(10.79)	(08.42)	(03.73)	(05.86)	(100.00)	(100.00)
	Munda	100	27	35	73	65	118	117	18	20	21	13	257	250
			(10.51)	(14.00)	(28.40)	(26.00)	(45.91)	(46.80)	(07.00)	(08.00)	(08.17)	(05.20)	(100.00)	(100.00)
	Bhumij	100	24	33	68	71	114	112	16	12	9	12	231	240
			(10.39)	(13.75)	(29.44)	(29.58)	(49.35)	(46.67)	(6.93)	(5.00)	(3.90)	(5.00)	(100.00)	(100.00)

(Contd.)

	Lodha	50	16	14	32	29	42	47	10	12	6	4	106	106
			(15.09)	(13.21)	(30.19)	(27.36)	(39.62)	(44.34)	(09.43)	(11.32)	(05.66)	(03.77)	(100.00)	(100.00)
Orissa														
	Santal	50	19	9	51	49	53	55	11	13	9	6	143	132
			(13.29)	(06.82)	(35.66)	(37.12)	(37.06)	(41.67)	(07.69)	(09.85)	(06.29)	(04.55)	(100.00)	(100.00)
	Birhor	100	28	24	52	58	91	98	12	10	13	6	196	196
			(14.29)	(12.24)	(26.53)	(29.59)	(46.43)	(50.00)	(06.12)	(05.10)	(06.63)	(03.06)	(100.00)	(100.00)
	Mahali	50	21	11	34	16	48	47	17	17	4	3	124	94
			(16.94)	(11.70)	(27.42)	(17.02)	(38.71)	(50.00)	(13.71)	(18.09)	(03.23)	(03.19)	(100.00)	(100.00)
Bihar														
	Munda	50	18	24	41	32	54	61	10	12	5	4	128	133
			(14.06)	(18.05)	(32.03)	(24.06)	(42.19)	(45.19)	(07.81)	(09.02)	(03.91)	(03.01)	(100.00)	(100.00)
	Bhumij	50	14	15	34	28	80	56	20	14	2	3	150	116
			(09.33)	(12.93)	(22.67)	(24.14)	(53.33)	(48.28)	(13.33)	(12.07)	(01.33)	(02.59)	(100.00)	(100.00)

N.B. *Figures in the Parentheses indicate percentages.*

In the age group of '46-60' years, maximum number of male and female in all tribal communities irrespective of all the state associations vary more or less from 7.00 per cent to 12.00 per cent except a few cases where male-female population is sharply declined or inclined.

The '61 +' year age group is considered for aged population where the percentage of both male and female members is less and varies more or less from 4.00 per cent to 8.00 per cent. Only some exceptions are found among the male (1.33 per cent) and female (2.59 per cent) population of the Bhumij in Bihar, male population (8.37 per cent) of the Lodha and female population (7.56 per cent) of the Mahali in West Bengal.

Considering the distribution of population under labour force (15-60 years) and non-labour force (below 15 years and above 60 years) it has been observed from Table 4.14 that majority of the population including both male and female (more than 50 per cent) belong to the labour force category, though the percentage does not highlight any strong positive statement regarding the population distribution under labour force or non-labour force. Actually the total output of the community depends on the size of the labour force and generally a healthy society indicates greater increase in the size of labour force than in non-labour forces. Irrespective of the state and district, the sample communities of the study reveal that relatively the population below 15 years and above are lower than the population under 15 to 60 years. So the population composition is not totally deviated from the prevailing mode of a normal society.

TABLE 4.14
STATE-WISE LABOUR FORCE AND NON-LABOUR FORCE

District	Tribe	No. of family	Total		Non-Labour Population				Labour Population	
					0-14 (years)		61 + (years)		15-60 (years)	
			M	F	M	F	M	F	M	F
Purulia (W.B.)	Birhor	37	82	76	36 (43.90)	34 (44.74)	6 (07.32)	4 (05.26)	40 (48.78)	38 (50.00)
	Lodha	100	251	236	105 (41.83)	89 (37.71)	21 (08.37)	9 (03.81)	125 (49.80)	138 (58.47)
	Mahall	100	241	225	98 (40.66)	84 (37.33)	14 (05.81)	17 (07.56)	129 (53.53)	124 (55.11)
Midnapore (W.B.)	Santal	100	241	273	106 (43.98)	111 (40.66)	9 (03.73)	16 (05.86)	126 (52.28)	146 (53.48)
	Munda	100	257	250	100 (38.91)	100 (40.00)	21 (08.17)	13 (05.20)	136 (52.92)	137 (54.80)
	Bhumij	100	231	240	92 (39.83)	104 (43.33)	9 (03.90)	12 (05.00)	130 (56.28)	124 (51.67)

(Contd.)

	Lodha	50	106	106	48	43	6	4	52	59
					(45.28)	(40.57)	(05.66)	(03.77)	(49.06)	(55.66)
Mayur-bhanj										
(Orissa)	Santal	50	143	132	70	58	9	6	64	68
					(48.95)	(43.94)	(06.29)	(04.55)	(44.76)	(51.52)
Hazari-bagh										
(Bihar)	Birhar	100	196	196	80	82	13	6	103	108
					(40.82)	(41.84)	(06.63)	(03.06)	(52.55)	(55.10)
	Mahali	50	124	94	55	27	4	3	65	64
					(44.35)	(28.72)	(03.23)	(03.19)	(52.42)	(68.09)
Singbhum (Bihar)										
	Munda	50	128 (46.09)	133 (42.11)	59 (03.91)	56 (03.01)	5 (50.00)	4 (54.89)	64	73
	Bhumij	50	150	116	48	43	2	3	100	70
					(32.00)	(37.07)	(01.33)	(02.59)	(66.67)	(60.34)

N.B. *Figures in the Parentheses indicate percentages.*

5

Occupation

In this chapter the occupational status of the tribal women with their different occupational roles, familial income and expenditure patterns, nature of indebtedness etc., are illuminated with the respective tables and discussions.

Generally, in tribal societies most of the women assume the main role in economy, along with their indispensable role in child care and rearing and family maintenance. Status of the women also depends on the economic activity on which the living conditions of the family hangs down. But in our country the socio-economic conditions of the tribal communities, particularly in Bengal, Orissa and Bihar are deplorable. Through this project an attempt has been made to find out the nature of occupations which are followed by the tribal women and also the nature of domestic work they perform in their day to day life. The study reveals their poor insufficient income leading to poverty, indebtedness and many other associated problems which are not ignorable in their daily life.

This work also tries to study their awareness for better income along with various steps taken by them to increase their annual income level. The study reveals the awareness of the tribal women who have demanded occupational training through restoring their traditional occupational cultural traits by which they may earn more without destroying their traditional cultural heritage.

Table 5.1 depicts the occupational distribution of the respondents (women) of six tribal communities viz. the Birhor, Lodha, Mahali, Santal, Munda and Bhumij of West Bengal, Orissa and Bihar.

TABLE 5.1
OCCUPATION PATTERN

Type of Occupation	*Birhor*	*Lodha*	*Mahali*	*Santal*	*Munda*	*Bhumij*
Cultivation Daily labour and Rope making	W.B. 7 (18.92) Bihar 84 (84.00)	-	-	-	-	-
Cultivation and Rope making	W.B. 13 (35.14)	-	-	Orissa 2 (4.00)	-	-
Daily labour and Rope making	W.B. 16 (43.25) Bihar 16 (16.00)	Orissa 20 (40.00)	-	-	-	-
Cultivation	-	W.B. 5 (5.00)	-	W.B. 1 (1.00) Orissa 7 (14.0)	W.B. 6 (6.0) Bihar 8 (16.0)	W.B. 13 (13.0) Bihar 14 (28.0)
Agricultural Labour	-	W.B. 15 (15.00)	W.B. 1 (1.00)	W.B. 30 (30.00) Orissa 32 (64.0)	W.B. 8 (8.0) Bihar 2 (4.0)	W.B. 34 (34.0) Bihar 5 (10.0)
Cultivation and Agricultural Labour	-	W.B. 77 (77.00)	W.B. 1 (1.00)	W.B. 46 (46.00) W.B. 75 (75.0)	Bihar 37 (74.0)	W.B. 38 (38.0) Bihar 29 (58.0)

(*Contd.*)

Type of Occupation	*Birhor*	*Lodha*	*Mahali*	*Santal*		*Munda*	*Bhumij*	
Industrial Labour	-	-	-	W.B. 3 (3.00)		-	W.B. 4 (4.00	
Basket making	-	-	W.B. 38 (38.00)	Bihar 43 (86.00)	W.B. 3 (3.00)	-	-	
Service	-	W.B. 1 (1.00)	-	W.B. 3 (3.00)	W.B. 2 (2.00)		W.B. 1 (1.00)	
Cultivation and Basket making	-	W.B. 1 (1.00)	W.B. 59 (59.00)	Bihar 7 (14.00)	-	W.B. 1 (1.00)	-	
Cultivation and Service	-	-	-		Orissa 1 (2.00)	W.B. 1 (1.00)	W.B. 1 (1.00)	
Dally Labour and Leat making	-	Orissa 6 (12.00)	- -	- W.B.		- -	- -	---
Business	1 (1.00)							
Cultivation Rope making	-	Orissa 19	-	-		-	-	

(*Contd.*)

Type of Occupation	Birhor		Lodha	Mahali	Santal		Munda		Bhumij	
and Leaf making			(38.00)							
Cultivation	-		Orissa	-	-		-		-	
Rope making			1							
& Business			(2.00)							
Tailoring &	-		-		-	Orissa	-	-		
Cultivation						1				
						(2.00)				
Rope making	-		Orissa	-	Orissa		-	-		
Leaf making &			3		7					
Daily Labour			(6.00)		(14.00)					
Daily Labour	-				(14.00)					
Daily Labour	-		Orissa	-		-	-	-		
and			1							
Carpentry			(2.00)							
Household	-	-	W.B.		W.B.	W.B.	Bihar	W.B.		Bihar
worker			1		13	7	3	9		2
			(1.00)		(13.00)	(7.00)	(3.00)	(9.00)		(4.00)
Others	-		-	-	-	W.B.	-	-		
						1				
						(1.00)				

N.B. *Figures in the parentheses indicate percentages.*

In West Bengal 18.92 per cent Birhor women are engaged in cultivation, daily labour and rope making according to the availability of works whereas the occupations of 35.14 per cent respondents are cultivation and rope making. Table also shows that 43.25 per cent respondents are engaged in daily labour and rope making. So it is evident that all the Birhor families are directly involved in rope-making a traditional occupation. On the other hand, majority of the respondents, 84.00 per cent in Bihar, are engaged in cultivation, daily labour and rope making, whereas the occupations of 16.00 per cent respondents are daily labour and rope making.

The women of the Birhor community of West Bengal and Bihar are engaged in leaf making and carpentry besides rope making and their household work. All women in Birhor community in West Bengal and Bihar are directly attached to their traditional occupation, rope making, but due to the problem of collecting raw materials from the forest, now-a days they have to remain engaged with other available agricultural work (seasonal).

Majority of the respondents of the Lodha (98.00 per cent) in West Bengal are associated with agricultural work whereas 78.00 per cent of the Lodha women in Orissa are making rope from the bark of the trees and they also produce various products of leaf. Besides this, they also work as casual agricultural labourers. So it is clear from Table 5.1 that the women of the Lodha community of Orissa are still maintaining their forest based occupation because they have not enough agricultural land.

In case of the Mahali in West Bengal 97.00 per cent women of this community are engaged in their traditional occupation of basket making; of them 38.00 per cent solely depend on basket making and 59.00 per cent are engaged in this occupation as well as in cultivation. In case of the Mahali community in Bihar it is observed that 86.00 per cent respondents are engaged in basket making and 14.00 per cent in cultivation and basket making both.

Except the Mahali and Birhor communities majority of the respondents of the remaining four communities are engaged in cultivation and/or agricultural work. In most of the cases they work as agricultural labourers in others' fields.

In West Bengal 77.00 per cent Santals are engaged in agricultural work, 13.00 per cent in household activities and the remaining respondents are in different types of occupation.

Majority of the Santal women in Orissa 64.00 per cent are engaged in agricultural work and 14.00 per cent are cultivating their own land. 22.00 per cent of them are engaged in different occupations such as rope making and leaf working, tailoring and service along with cultivation.

In case of the Munda community of West Bengal, it is observed that the majority (89.00 per cent) of women are engaged in agricultural work and cultivation. Only 7.00 per cent women are housewives. None of the Munda woman is engaged in basket making. On the other hand in Bihar majority of the Munda women 94.00 per cent are associated with agricultural activities.

In the Bhumij community of West Bengal and Bihar a few responded are housewives—9.00 per cent and 4.00 per cent respectively. Most of the rest (85.00 per cent in West Bengal and 96 per cent in Bihar) are engaged in agricultural activities.

Table 5.2 represents income distribution of six selected tribal communities of West Bengal. The daily income of the respondents is categorised into four groups, viz : (a) Rs. 15.00 to Rs. 30.00, (b) Rs. 31.00 to Rs. 45.00, (c) Rs. 46.00 to Rs. 60.00 (d) Rs. 61.00 and above.

Among the Birhor community of Purulia district, majority (78.37 per cent) are not satisfied with their job and 91.89 per cent women are dissatisfied regarding income. Majority (91.89 per cent) of them earn Rs. 15.00 to Rs. 30.00 per day.

Among the Lodha community of West Bengal the income of 92.00 per cent women is between Rs. 15.00 to Rs. 30.00 only, 2.00 per cent respondents can earn more than Rs. 61.00 per day. 65.00 per cent women are satisfied regarding job and 31.00 per cent women are satisfied regarding income.

In case of the Mahali community of West Bengal 74.00 per cent women are satisfied with their jobs but only 18.00 per cent women are satisfied with their income. The daily income of the majority of women (96.00 per cent) is in the range of Rs. 15.00 to Rs. 30.00.

Among the Santal respondents of West Bengal, 12.00

TABLE 5.2
JOB AND INCOME NATURE OF SATISFACTION

Tribe	No. of respon-dent	No. of house-wife	Working woman	Job satisfa-ction Yes	Job satisfa-ction No	Daily Income (in Rs.) 15-30	31-45	46-60	61 +	Mode of satisfa-ction regarding Income Yes	No	No. of students
WEST BENGAL												
Birhor	37	-	37	8	29	34	3	-	-	3	34	-
			(100.00)	(21.62)	(78.37)	(91.89)	(8.11)			(8.11)	(91.89)	
Lodha	100	-	100	65	35	92	4	2	2	31	69	-
			(100.00)	(65.00)	(35.00)	(92.00)	(4.00)	(2.00)	(2.00)	(31.00)	(69.00)	
Mahali	100	1	99	74	25	96	3	-	-	18	81	-
		(1.00)	(99.00)	(74.75)	(25.25)	(96.97)	(3.03)			(18.18)	(81.82)	
Santal	100	12	87	53	34	81	5	-	1	44	43	1
		(12.00)	(87.00)	(60.92)	(39.08)	(93.10)	(5.75)		(1.15)	(50.57)	(49.43)	(1.00)
Munda	100	2	93	73	20	86	6	-	1	37	56	5
		(2.00)	(93.00)	(78.49)	(21.51)	(92.47)	(6.45)		(1.08)	(39.78)	(60.22)	(5.00)

(Contd.)

Bhumij	100	9	91	66	25	86	3	1	1	46	45	-
		(9.00)	(91.00)	(72.53)	(27.47)	(94.51)	(3.30)	(1.09)	(1.09)	(50.55)	(49.45)	
						ORISSA						
Lodha	50	-	50	14	36	44	5	-	1	12	38	-
			(100.00)	(28.00)	(72.00)	(88.00)	(10.00)		(2.00)	(24.00)	(76.00)	
Santal	50	-	50	24	26	27	19	2	2	19	31	
			(100.00)	(48.00)	(52.00)	(54.00)	(38.00)	(4.00)	(4.00)	(38.00)	(62.00)	
						BIHAR						
Birhor	100	-	100	40	60	100	-	-	-	35	65	-
			(100.00)	(40.00)	(60.00)	(100.00)				(35.00)	(65.00)	
Mahali	50	-	50	23	27	50	-	-	-	5	45	-
			(100.00)	(46.00)	(54.00)	(100.00)				(10.00)	(90.00)	
Munda	50	3	47	23	24	47	-	-	-	6	41	-
		(6.00)	(94.00)	(48.94)	(51.06)	(100.00)				(12.77)	(85.42)	
Bhumij	50	2	48	21	27	48	-	-	-	5	43	-
		(4.00)	(96.00)	(43.75)	(56.25)	(100.00)				(10.42)	(89.58)	

N.B. *Figures in the parentheses indicate percentages.*

per cent are housewives and 1.00 per cent belongs to the student community; regarding their job 53.00 per cent women are satisfied and 35.00 per cent are not and with respect to income 44.00 per cent women are satisfied and 43.00 per cent are not. The daily income of 81.00 per cent women is in the range of Rs. 15.00 to Rs. 30.00, 5.00 per cent women are between Rs. 31.00 and Rs. 45.00 and only 1.00 per cent respondents earn more than Rs. 61.00.

In the Munda community of West Bengal 2.00 per cent are housewives, 5.00 per cent are students; while 73.00 per cent are satisfied with their jobs and 37.00 per cent are satisfied with their income. The daily income of 86.00 per cent women is between Rs. 15.00 and Rs. 30.00 and of 6.00 per cent women is between Rs. 31.00 and Rs. 45.00.

9.00 per cent Bhumij respondents of West Bengal are housewives, 66.00 per cent are satisfied regarding job whereas 46.00 per cent are satisfied regarding income. The income for 86.00 per cent respondents is between Rs. 15.00 and Rs. 30.00 and for 3.00 per cent women it is Rs. 31.00 to Rs. 45.00; only 1.00 per cent women earns more than Rs. 61.00

Table 5.2 also describes the occupation and income distribution of the Santal and Lodha tribal women of Mayurbhanj district of Orissa. Among the Santal 52.00 per cent are satisfied with the job and 38.00 per cent women are satisfied with their income. The daily income of 54.00 per cent women is between Rs. 15.00 and Rs. 30.00, of 38.00 per cent between Rs. 31.00 and Rs. 45.00 and of 4.00 per cent between Rs. 46.00 and Rs. 60.00. Only 4.00 per cent respondents earn more than Rs. 61.00 per day.

In case of the Lodha community, 28.00 per cent women are satisfied with their job and 24.00 per cent with their income. It is observed that maximum number of women (88.00 per cent) earn Rs. 15.00 to Rs. 30.00.

The majority of the tribal women in Bihar are satisfied neither with their jobs nor with their income. The satisfied women regarding job for the Birhor community are 38.00 per cent, for the Mahali 46.00 per cent, for the Munda 51.06 per cent and in case of the Bhumij 43.75 per cent. The respondents of all these four communities earn Rs. 15 to 30 daily. So the majority of women of the Mahali, Munda and Bhumij communities are not satisfied regarding their income, but in the Birhor community the number of satisfied women regarding income is higher than that of other three communities.

As to occupational contentment maximum number (more than 60.00 per cent) of tribal communities of West Bengal except the Birhors are satisfied. The Lodhas of Orissa are less satisfied than the Santals of Orissa regarding their jobs and comparatively both of these communities are less satisfied with them in West Bengal. But in Bihar the number of dissatisfied women (except the Munda) is more than that of the satisfied women regarding their job. Especially in the case of the Birhor community, both the states show that the number of dissatisfied women is greater regarding their jobs.

Maximum number of tribal women in all cases have daily earning between Rs. 15.00 and Rs. 30.00 but in Bihar 100.00 per cent women's daily earning is Rs. 15.00 to Rs. 30.00, and majority of them are dissatisfied with their income.

Table 5.3 depicts the nature of work done by the respondents of six tribal communities of West Bengal. In case of the Birhor it is noticed that 91.89 per cent respondents are engaged in rearing domestic animals and cent per cent respondents have to be engaged in collecting fuel, bringing water, cleaning clothes and cooking. From the table it is also found that 75.68 per cent of them are engaged in other economic activities also.

39.00 per cent Lodha respondents are engaged in rearing domestic animals, 20.00 per cent in fishing, 81.00 per cent in collecting fuel whereas all of them are engaged in bringing water, cleaning clothes, cooking and other household works. The table also shows that 85.00 per cent respondents are in religious activities.

Among the Mahali respondents 23.00 per cent are engaged in rearing domestic animals, 3.00 per cent in fishing, 66.00 per cent respondents in collecting fuel whereas all of them are engaged in bringing water, cleaning clothes, cooking and other household works. There are 83.00 per cent respondents who are engaged in different economic activities followed by 13.00 per cent and 4.00 per cent respondents who are engaged in religious and political activities respectively.

TABLE 5.3
PATTERN OF WORK

Tribe	No. of respon-dent	Rearing Domestic animals	Fishing	Bringing fuel	Bringing water, cleaning clothes and cooking	Other economic activities	Religious activities	Political activities
				WEST BENGAL				
Birhor	37	34		37	37	28		-
		(91.89)		(100.00)	(100.00)	(75.68)		
Lodha	100	39	20	81	100	85	16	-
		(39.00)	(20.00)	(81.00)	(100.00)	(85.00)	(16.00)	
Mahali	100	23	3	66	100	83	13	4
		(23.00)	(3.00)	(66.00)	(100.00)	(85.00)	(13.00)	(4.00)
Santal	100	16		60	100	22	12	4
		(16.00)		(60.00)	(100.00)	(22.00)	(12.00)	(4.00)
Munda	100	33	10	62	100	71	16	2
		(33.00)	(10.00)	(62.00)	(100.00)	(71.00)	(16.00)	(2.00)

(Contd.)

Bhumij	100	23 (23.00)	6 (6.00)	59 (59.00)	100 (100.00)	58 (58.00)	24 (24.00)
ORISSA							
Lodha	50	31 (62.00)	24 (48.00)	50 (100.00)	50 (100.00)	33 (66.00)	-
Santal	50	27 (54.00)	21 (42.00)	48 (96.00)	50 (100.00)	15 (30.00)	-
BIHAR							
Birhor	100	28 (28.00)	13 (13.00)	100 (100.00)	100 (100.00)	23 (23.00)	-
Mahali	50	36 (72.00)	5 (10.00)	41 (82.00)	50 (100.00)	36 (72.00)	-
Munda	50	36 (72.00)	9 (18.00)	49 (98.00)	50 (100.00)	-	-
Bhumij	50	40 (80.00)	3 (6.00)	47 (94.00)	50 (100.00)	-	-

N.B. *Figures in the parentheses indicate percentages.*

In case of the Santal it has been observed that cent per cent respondents are engaged in bringing water, cleaning clothes and cooking. 16.00 per cent and 60.00 per cent respondents are engaged in the rearing of domestic animals and in bringing fuel respectively. It is also seen that 22.00 per cent of them are engaged in economic pursuits and 4.00 per cent are in political activities.

33.00 per cent Munda are engaged in rearing domestic animals, 10.00 per cent are in fishing, 62.00 per cent are in bringing fuel and all of them are engaged in bringing water, cleaning clothes and cooking. It is also seen that 71.00 per cent and 16.00 per cent respondents are engaged in other economic and religious activites respectively whereas only 2.00 per cent of them are engaged in political activities.

In case of the Bhumij 23.00 per cent are engaged in rearing of domestic animals, 6.00 per cent are in fishing and 59.00 per cent of them are in bringing fuel whereas all of them are engaged in bringing water, cleaning clothes and cooking. 58.00 per cent and 24.00 per cent of them are engaged in other economic and religious activities respectively.

Data regarding the nature of domestic work done by the two tribal communities (Lodha and the Santal) of Orissa are shown in Table 5.3. 62.00 per cent Lodha are engaged in rearing domestic animals. All are engaged in fishing, bringing fuel and water, cleaning clothes and cooking, whereas 66.00 per cent of them are engaged in other economic activities.

In case of the Santal 54.00 per cent are engaged in rearing domestic animals, 42.00 per cent in fishing, 96.00 per cent in bringing fuel, all of them are engaged in bringing water for cleaning clothes, cooking, etc. It also shows that 30.00 per cent of them are engaged in other economic activities.

Table 5.3 also depicts the picture about the nature of work done by the female respondents of four tribal communities of Bihar. In case of the Birhor it is evident that 28.00 per cent are engaged in rearing domestic animals whereas all of them are engaged in bringing fuel, bringing water, cleaning clothes and cooking. It is also found that besides these 23.00 per cent of them are engaged in other economic activities.

In case of the Mahali it is found that 72.00 per cent respondents are engaged in rearing domestic animals whereas all of them are engaged in bringing water, cleaning clothes and cooking. Along with these 72.00 per cent of them are also engaged in other economic activities.

98.00 per cent Mundas are engaged in bringing fuel whereas all of them are engaged in bringing water, cleaning clothes and cooking. Regarding the Bhumij it has been observed that 80.00 per cent and 94.00 per cent respondents are engaged in rearing domestic animals and bringing fuel respectively. It is also evident that all the respondents are engaged in bringing water, cleaning clothes and cooking and other household activities.

Considering the four tribes of Bihar together we may conclude that the nature of domestic work of these respondents is more or less same but the womenfolk of the Mahali and Birhor are engaged in some other economic activities also.

Table 5.4 represents the data on annual pattern of the selected tribal communities of West Bengal, Orissa and Bihar.

In case of the Birhor 81.00 per cent households have their annual family income between Rs. 5001 and Rs. 15000 whereas 18.90 per cent of them have their income Rs. 5,000 or less than that.

The majority of the Lodha (75.00 per cent) belong to the income group of Rs. 5001-15000 followed by 18.00 per cent to the income group of Rs. 15001-25000 whereas only 4.00 per cent and 3.00 per cent of them belong to the income group of Rs. 25001 - Rs. 35000 and below Rs. 5000.00 respectively.

TABLE 5.4
APPROXIMATE ANNUAL INCOME (FAMILY WISE)

Tribe	*No. of family*	*Income (in Rs.)*					
		Below 5000	*5001-15000*	*15001-25000*	*25001-35000*	*35001-45000*	*45001 and above*
		WEST BENGAL					
Birhor	37	7 (18.90)	30 (81.17)	-	-	-	-
Lodha	100	3 (3.00)	75 (75.00)	18 (18.00)	4 (4.00)	-	-
Mahali	100	3 (3.00)	78 (78.00)	15 (15.00)	3 (3.00)	1 (1.00)	-
Santal	100	6 (6.00)	56 (56.00)	28 (28.00)	7 (7.00)	2 (2.00)	1 (1.00)
Munda	100	-	70 (70.00)	21 (21.00)	6 (6.00)	2 (2.00)	1 (1.00)
Bhumij	100	1 (1.00)	74 (74.00)	9 (9.00)	8 (8.00)	6 (6.00)	2 (2.00)
		ORISSA					
Lodha	50	3 (6.00)	45 (90.00)	1 (2.00)	1 (2.00)	-	-
Santal	50	-	47 (94.00)	1 (2.00)	2 (4.00)	- -	- -
		BIHAR					
Birhor	100	2 (2.00)	98 (98.00)	-	-	-	-
Mahali	50	2 (4.00)	47 (94.00)	1 (2.00)	-	-	-
Munda	50	-	49 (98.00)	1 (2.00)	-	-	-
Bhumij	50	-	39 (78.00)	6 (12.00)	2 (4.00)	3 (6.00)	-

N.B. *Figures in the parentheses indicate percentages.*

In is noticed that the majority (78.00 per cent) of the Mahali belong to income grou of Rs. 5001-1500 followed by 14.00 per cent to the income group of Rs. 15001-25000 and no one belongs to the income group of Rs. 45001 and above.

In case of the Santal 56.00 per cent have annual family income of Rs. 5001-15000 followed by 28.00 per cent having their income of Rs. 15001-25000. There are only 6.00 per cent whose family income is Rs. 5000.00 or less than that and only 1.00 per cent has their annual family income of Rs. 45001 and above.

It is seen that the majority (70.00 per cent) of the Munda community fall in the income group Rs. 5001-15000 followed by 21.00% belonging to the income group of Rs. 15001-25000 whereas only 1.00 per cent of them belongs to the income group of Rs. 45001.00 and above and no one belongs to the income group of Rs. 5001.00 or less than that.

74.00 per cent Bhumij have their annual family income Rs. 5001-15000 followed by 9.00 per cent having their income Rs. 15000-25000 whereas 2.00 per cent of them are in the income group of Rs. 45001.00 and above.

Considering the distribution of annual income of six tribal group in West Bengal it is evident that majority of them belong to the annual family income of Rs. 5001-15000.

90.00 per cent Lodha of Orissa belong to the income group of Rs. 5001-15000 follwed by 2.00 per cent to the income group of Rs. 15001-25000 and 2.00 per cent to the income group of Rs. 25001-35000. There are 6.00 per cent whose annual family income is Rs. 5000.00 or less than that.

In case of the Santal of Orissa it is noticed that 94.00 per cent have their annual family income of Rs. 5001-15000 followed by 2.00 per cent having their income of Rs. 15001-25000 and 4.00 per cent having their income of Rs. 25001-35000.

In Bihar, in case of the Birhor, it is seen that 98.00 per cent have their annual income of Rs. 5001-15000 whereas only 2.00 per cent of them belong to the income group of Rs. 5000.00 or less than that.

In case of the Mahali of the said state it has been noticed that 94.00 per cent belong to the income group of Rs. 5001-15000 and most of the Mundas (98.00 per cent) also fall under the same income group.

It is found, that 78.00 per cent Bhumij have their annual family income of Rs. 5001-15000 whereas only 6.00 per cent have their family income of Rs. 35001-45000.

Comparing the annual income of the four tribal groups in Bihar, it can be said that the Bhumij is the only tribal community where 4.00 per cent and 6.00 per cent families have their annual family income of Rs. 25001-35000 and

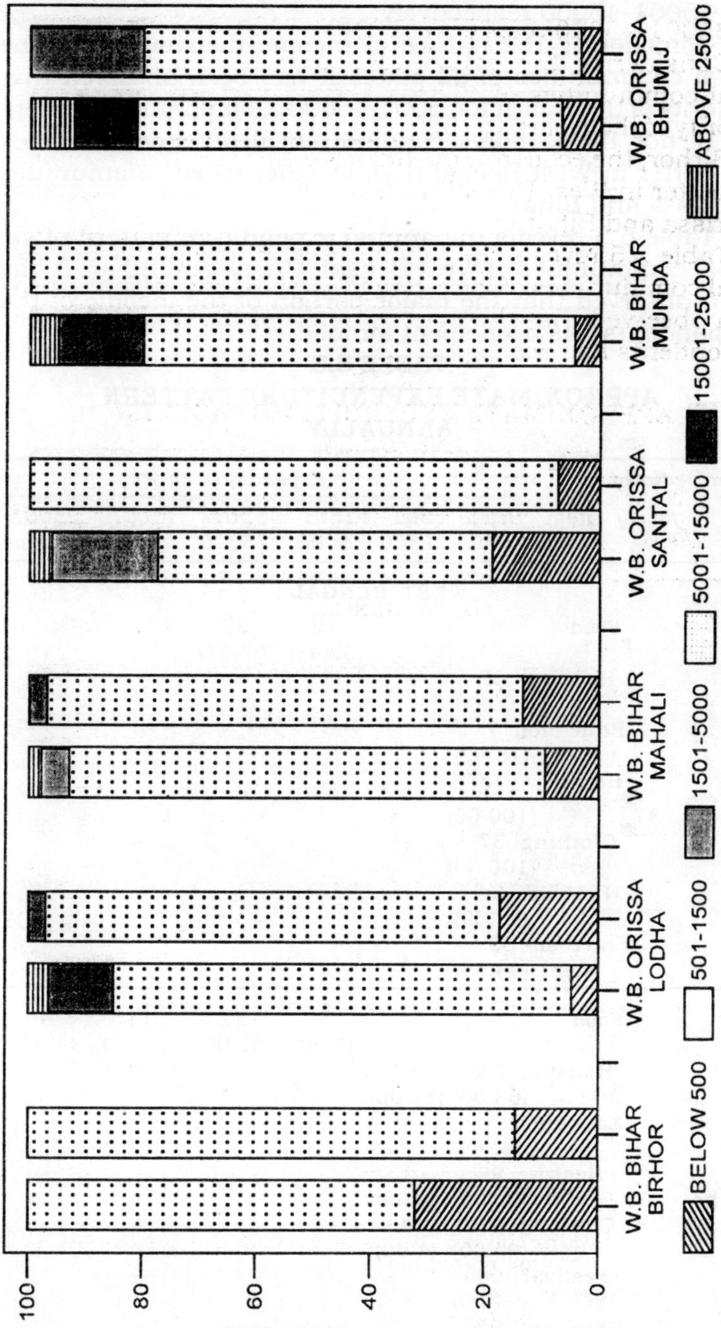

AVERAGE EXPENDITURE ON FOOD
COMMUNITY AND STATE WISE

Rs. 35001-45000 respectively.

Considering the nature of income distribution of the tribal communities of all states it has been observed that majority of them earn Rs. 5001-15000. Comparatively, except the Birhor, the economic conditions of all other communities are better in West Bengal than in other tribal communities of Orissa and Bihar.

Table 5.5 reveals the annual expenditure pattern of six tribal communities of West Bengal, Orissa and Bihar. It has been observed that the major portion of the income of the respondents has been spent for food.

TABLE 5.5

APPROXIMATE EXPENDITURE PATTERN ANNUALLY

Tribe	*No. of family*	*Item*	*Expenditure (in Rs.)* Below 500	501-1500	1501-5000	5001-15000	15001-25000	25001 and above
			WEST BENGAL					
		Food	-	-	12 (32.43)	25 (67.57)	-	-
		Housing	37 (100.00)	-	-	-	-	-
		Education	7 (18.92)	-	-	-	-	-
Birhor	37	Health	37 (100.00)	-	-	-	-	-
		Clothing	37 (100.00)	-	-	-	-	-
		Festival	34 (91.89)	-	-	-	-	-
		Entertain-ment	35 (94.59)	-	-	-	-	-
		Food	-	-	3 (3.00)	82 (82.00)	11 (11.00)	4 (4.00)
		Housing	63 (63.00)	37 (37.00)	-	-	-	-
		Education	5 (5.00)	-	-	-	-	-
Lodha	100	Health	99 (99.00)	1 (1.00)	-	-	-	-
		Clothing	96 (96.00)	4 (4.00)	-	-	-	-
		Festival	94 (94.00)	-	-	-	-	-
		Entertain-ment	95 (95.00)	-	-	-	-	-

(*Contd.*)

Tribe	*No. of family*	*Item*	*Expenditure (in Rs.)* Below 500	501-1500	1501-5000	5001-15000	15001-25000	25001 and above
Mahali	100	Food	-	-	7 (7.00)	86 (86.00)	5 (5.00)	2 (2.00)
		Housing	52 (52.00)	48 (48.00)	-	-	-	-
		Education	20 (20.00)	1 (1.00)	1 (1.00)	-	-	-
		Health	100 (100.00)	-	-	-	-	-
		Clothing	96 (96.00)	4 (4.00)	-	-	-	-
		Festival	94 (94.00)	-	-	-	-	-
		Entertain-ment	95 (95.00)	-	-	-	-	-
Santal	100	Food	-	-	15 (15.00)	59 (59.00)	21 (21.00)	5 (5.00)
		Housing	58 (58.00)	42 (42.00)	-	-	-	-
		Education	12 (12.00)	-	3 (3.00)	-	-	-
		Health	100 (100.00)	-	-	-	-	-
		Clothing	88 (88.00)	11 (11.00)	3 (3.00)	-	-	-
		Festival	90 (90.00)	-	-	-	-	-
		Entertain-ment	93 (93.00)	-	-	-	-	-
Munda	100	Food	-	-	2 (2.00)	75 (75.00)	17 (17.00)	6 (6.00)
		Housing	65 (65.00)	35 (35.00)	-	-	-	-
		Education	23 (23.00)	-	2 (2.00)	-	-	-
		Health	100 (100.00)	-	-	-	-	-
		Clothing	94 (94.00)	6 (6.00)	-	-	-	-
		Festival	94 (94.00)	-	-	-	-	-
		Entertain-ment	95 (95.00)	-	-	-	-	-

(Contd.)

Tribe	No. of family	Item	Expenditure (in Rs.) Below 500	501-1500	1501-5000	5001-15000	15001-25000	25001 and above
Bhumij	100	Food	-	-	4 (4.00)	80 (80.00)	9 (9.00)	7 (7.00)
		Housing	43 (43.00)	57 (57.00)	1 (1.00)	-	-	-
		Education	24 (24.00)	-	2 (2.00)	-	-	-
		Health	89 (89.00)	13 (13.00)	-	-	-	-
		Clothing	80 (80.00)	22 (22.00)	-	-	-	-
		Festival	93 (93.00)	-	-	-	-	-
		Entertainment	96 (96.00)	-	-	-	-	-
ORISSA								
Lodha	50	Food	-	-	8 (16.00)	41 (82.00)	1 (2.00)	-
		Housing	49 (98.00)	1 (2.00)	-	-	-	-
		Education	3 (6.00)	-	-	-	-	-
		Health	50 (100.00)	-	-	-	-	-
		Clothing	49 (98.00)	1 (2.00)	-	-	-	-
		Festival	46 (92.00)	-	-	-	-	-
		Entertainment	47 (94.00)	-	-	-	-	-
Santal	50	Food	-	-	3 (6.00)	47 (94.00)	-	-
		Housing	47 (94.00)	3 (6.00)	-	-	-	-
		Education	1 (2.00)	1 (2.00)	1 (2.00)	-	-	-
		Health	50 (100.00)	-	-	-	-	-
		Clothing	48 (96.00)	2 (4.00)	-	-	-	-
		Festival	46 (92.00)	-	-	-	-	-
		Entertainment	45 (90.00)	-	-	-	-	-

(Contd.)

Tribe	*No. of family*	*Item*	*Expenditure (in Rs.)* Below 500	501-1500	1501-5000	5001-15000	15001-25000	25001 and above
				BIHAR				
Birhor	100	Food		-	12 (12.00)	88 (88.00)	-	-
		Housing	100 (100.00)	-	-	-	-	-
		Education	7 (7.00)	-	-	-	-	-
		Health	100 (100.00)	-	-	-	-	-
		Clothing	100 (100.00)	-	-	-	-	-
		Festival	95 (94.00)	-	-	-	-	-
		Entertainment	95 (95.00)	-	-	-	-	-
Mahali	50	Food	-	-	5 (10.00)	44 (88.00)	1 (2.00)	-
		Housing	50 (100.00)	-	-	-	-	-
		Education	6 (12.00)	-	-	-	-	-
		Health	50 (100.00)	-	-	-	-	-
		Clothing	50 (100.00)	-	-	-	-	-
		Festival	47 (94.00)	-	-	-	-	-
		Entertainment	48 (96.00)	-	-	-	-	-
Munda	50	Food	-		-	50 (100.00)	-	-
		Housing	50 (100.00)	-	-	-	-	-
		Education	7 (14.00)	-	-	-	-	-
		Health	50 (100.00)	-	-	-	-	-
		Clothing	50 (100.00)	-	-	-	-	-
		Festival	44 (88.00)	-	-	-	-	-
		Entertainment	47 (94.00)	-	-	-	-	-

(*Contd.*)

Tribe	*No. of family*	*Item*	*Expenditure (in Rs.)* Below 500	501-1500	1501-5000	5001-15000	15001-25000	25001 and above
Bhumij	50	Food	-		1 (2.00)	40 (80.00)	9 (18.00)	-
		Housing	40 (80.00)	10 (20.00)				-
		Education	12 (24.00)	-	-			-
		Health	50 (100.00)	-	-			-
		Clothing	46 (92.00)	4 (8.00)	-			-
		Festival	47 (94.00)	-	-			-
		Entertain-ment	48 (96.00)	-	-			-

N.B. *Figures in the parentheses indicate percentages.*

In West Bengal majority (67.57 per cent) of the Birhor families spend Rs. 5001-15000 annually for food, followed by 32.43 Rs. 1501-5000. Major part of the income is mostly spent for food and except it, the rest of the income has been spent for housing, education, clothing, festive occasions and other entertainments (less than Rs. 500.00) only 18.92 per cent spend less than Rs. 500.00 for education.

82.00 per cent Lodha families spend Rs. 5001-15000 for food whereas only 4.00 per cent of them spend Rs. 25001.00 and above for this purpose. Maximum number of families expend Rs. 500.00 or less against housing (63.00 per cent), health (99.00 per cent), clothing (96.00 per cent), festival (94.00 per cent) and entertainmemt (95.00 per cent). Except food they have very little amount of money to spend for other important items (less than Rs. 500.00 for each item annually).

The picture is same among all the remaining tribal communities. Among the Mahali, it has been noticed that the majority (86.00 per cent) of the families' expenditure on food is Rs. 5001 to Rs. 15000 whereas only 7.00% of them spend Rs. 1501 to Rs. 5000 for food annually. In each of the item viz. housing, health, clothing, festive occasions and entertainment, majority of them spend Rs. 500.00 or less. Only 22.00 per cent of them give education to their children where as 20.00 per cent spend Rs. 500.00 or less on educational purposes yearly.

In case of the Santal majority (59.00 per cent) of the families' annual expenditure for food is Rs. 5001-15000 followed by 21.00 per cent whose expenditure is Rs. 15001-25000 and above. Here it has also been observed that majority of them spend Rs. 500.00 or less for each item like housing (58.00 per cent), health (100.00 per cent), clothing (86.00 per cent), festive occasions (90.00 per cent) and entertainment (93.00 per cent).

In case of the Bhumij 80.00 per cent families spend Rs. 5001-15000 on food and the picture of expenditure pattern against housing is different from the former three tribal communities, that is 57.00 per cent families spend Rs. 501-1500 for this purpose. But in the remaining cases the picture is same.

The above mentioned of annual expenditure pattern is also found among the Munda. Like other communities most of the amount of income is spent for food than the rest of the item.

From the above spend it can be concluded that majority of the families of all tribal communities in West Bengal spend Rs. 5001-15000 for food whereas for each item like health, clothing, festive occasions and entertainment the majority of the families spend Rs. 500.00 or less than that.

In Orissa, among the Lodha the picture is more or less same. 82.00 per cent families spend yearly Rs. 5001-15000 for food followed by 2.00 per cent Rs. 15001-25000. For each item like housing, clothing, festive occasions and entertainment their expenditure is Rs. 500.00 or less than that.

In case of the Santal it is noticed that 94.00 per cent families spend Rs. 5001-15000 for food whereas only 6.00 per cent of them spend Rs. 1501-15000 annually. It has been observed that majority of them spend Rs. 500.00 or less than that for each item like housing (94.00 per cent), health (100.00), clothing (96.00 per cent), festive occasions (92.00 per cent) and entertainment (90.00).

Table 5.5 also delineates the picture of annual expenditure pattern of four tribal communities (the Birhor, Mahali, Munda and Bhumij) of Bihar. In case of the Birhor it has been observed that out of 100 families 88 (88.00%) families spend Rs. 5001-15000 for food whereas the remaining 12.00 per cent families spend Rs. 1501-15000 for food. It has been observed that about all of them spend Rs. 500.00 or less for the items like housing (100.00 per cent), health (100.00 per cent), clothing (100.00 per cent). A good number of families also spent Rs. 500 or less for festive occasions (94.00 per cent) and entertainments (95.00 per cent) annually.

In case of the Mahali 88.00 per cent families spend Rs. 5001-15000 for food. Majority of them spend Rs. 500.00 or less than that annually for each item like, housing, health, clothing, festive occasions and entertainment.

Among the Munda it is evident that all the families spend Rs. 5001-15000 for food and here also majority of them spend Rs. 500.00 or less than that for each housing, health, clothing etc.

Majority of the Bhumij families spend Rs. 5001-15000 for food whereas only 18.00 per cent families spend Rs. 15001-25000 for the said purpose. The pattern of expenditure for other items is the same in nature like other communities.

The problem of indebtedness can be studied through the nature of personal loan, its sources and payment (Table 5.6). Except the Birhor in West Bengal the other sample communities like the Lodha, Mahali, Santal, Munda and Bhumij take loan (more than 50.00 per cent) from various sources. Except the Birhor the rest of the sample communities of Bihar, and the sample communities of Orissa take loan (12.00 per cent or less). The important reason behind is that the socio-economic conditions of the tribal communities in Bihar and Orissa are not very good and more or less majority of them belong to the same stratum. Variation in their income is not clearly observable. Naturally, very few persons or organizations are there to give loan. For this reason very few persons in emergency are not habituated to take loan. On the other hand, in case of West Bengal most of the tribal villages are multi-ethnic groups and many higher caste people are exploiting these poor sections by giving loan to them. Socio-economically the society is also stratified. Considering this factor it has been observed that the Lodha (Orissa), Mahali (Bihar), Santal (Orissa), Bhumij and Munda (Bihar) belong to poor villages than that of West Bengal. But in case of the Birhor it can be observed that in West Bengal there are very few families who are taking

TABLE 5.6
INDEBTEDNESS

Tribe	State	No. of family	No. of family taken Personal loan	No. of family not taken loan	Sources of personal loan: Money-lenders	Sources of personal loan: Friends and relatives	Annual rate of interest (%) Rs: No interest	Annual rate of interest (%) Rs: 60-120	Annual rate of interest (%) Rs: 121-180	In kind: Paddy
Birhor	West Bengal	37	7 (18.92)	30 (81.08)	-	7 (100.00)	7 (100.00)	-	-	-
	Bihar	100	50 (50.00)	50 (50.00)	6 (12.00)	44 (88.00)	44 (88.00)	6 (12.00)	-	-
Lodha	West Bengal	100	88 (88.00)	12 (12.00)	30 (34.09)	58 (65.91)	38 (43.18)	42 (47.73)	1 (1.14)	7 (7.95)
	Orissa	50	6 (12.00)	44 (84.00)	-	6 (100.00)	5 (83.33)	1 (16.67)	-	-
Mahali	West Bengal	100	82 (82.00)	18 (18.00)	35 (42.68)	47 (57.32)	36 (43.90)	26 (31.71)	11 (13.41)	9 (10.98)

	Bihar	50	6 (12.00)	44 (88.00)	-	6 (100.00)	6 (100.00)	-	-	-
Santal	West Bengal	100	54 (54.00)	46 (46.00)	14 (25.93)	40 (74.07)	33 (61.11)	18 (33.33)	1 (1.85)	2 (3.70)
	Orissa	50	5 (10.00)	45 (90.00)	-	5 (100.00)	5 (100.00)	-	-	-
Munda	West Bengal	100	74 (74.00)	26 (26.00)	38 (51.35)	36 (48.65)	22 (29.73)	19 (25.68)	13 (17.57)	20 (27.03)
	Bihar	50	4 (8.00)	46 (92.00)	-	4 (100.00)	4 (100.00)	-	-	-
Bhumij	West Bengal	100	56 (56.00)	44 (44.00)	33 (58.93)	23 (41.07)	19 (33.93)	22 (39.29)	4 (7.14)	11 (19.64)
	Bihar	50	3 (6.00)	47 (94.00)	-	3 (100.00)	3 (100.00)	-	-	-

N.B. *Figures in the parentheses indicate percentages.*

loan (18.92 per cent). But in Bihar 50.00 per cent Birhor families are taking loan.

Regarding the sources of loan it has been observed that in maximum cases the tribal families in all states are taking loan from their friends and relatives without giving any interest. But in few cases they have to take loan from money-lenders where the rate of interest is tremendously high— 60.00 per cent to 180.00 per cent and sometimes they have to pay the interest not in cash but by the agricultural crops which they produce.

Table 5.7 depicts different steps which are taken by the respondents of the six tribal communities of West Bengal, Orissa and Bihar to improve their economic condition.

Maximum number of tribal communities in Bihar are taking various steps to improve their economic condition of which the name of the Mahali and Bhumij are worth mentioning. Maximum members of the Bhumij (90.00 per cent) followed by the Mahali (74.00 per cent) of Bihar are taking only Government loan. On the other hand, majority of the Birhor of both the states are not getting Government loan for the upliftment of their statuses. In West Bengal five tribal communities have attempted to take various steps for changing their social position. Number of attempted persons are highest among the Lodha (56.00 per cent) and lowest among the Mahali (34.00 per cent). Maximum number of respondents of the Santal community (26.00 per cent) are taking Government loan followed by the Lodha (34.00 per cent). The Lodha and Santal in Orissa and the Birhor in the state of West Bengal and Bihar are trying to improve their economic status by selling their extra labour sometimes without getting minimum help from the government.

It is noticed from the Table 5.8 that in first five selected tribal communities of West Bengal maximum number of respondents do not want to take any training regarding occupation. But in the Birhor community (West Bengal) all are interested to train themselves in rope making.

Out of 100 Lodha respondents only 35 are interested in different training programmes. Among them 24 (68.57 per

TABLE 5.7
ATTEMPT TO INCREASE INCOME

(Contd.)

Tribe	*State*	*No. of family*	*Never attempted*	*Attempted*	*Government help*	*Other Steps taken*
Birhor	West Bengal	37	1 (2.07)	36 (97.30)	8 (21.62)	28 (75.68)
	Bihar	100	35 (35.00)	65 (65.00)	19 (19.00)	46 (46.00)
Lodha	West Bengal	100	44 (44.00)	56 (56.00)	34 (34.00)	22 (22.00)
	Orissa	50	17 (34.00)	33 (66.00)	7 (14.00)	26 (52.00)
Mahali	West Bengal	100	66 (66.00)	34 (34.00)	23 (23.00)	11 (11.00)
	Bihar	50	-	50 (100.00)	37 (74.00)	13 (26.00)
Santal	West Bengal	100	57 (57.00)	43 (43.00)	26 (26.00)	17 (17.00)
	Orissa	50	21 (42.00)	29 (58.00)	12 (24.00)	17 (34.00)
Munda	West Bengal	100	48 (48.00)	52 (52.00)	25 (25.00)	27 (27.00)
	Bihar	50	10 (20.00)	40 (80.00)	27 (54.00)	13 (26.00)
Bhumij	West Bengal	100	60 (60.00)	40 (40.00)	19 (19.00)	21 (21.00)
	Bihar	50	-	50 (100.00)	45 (90.00)	5 (10.00)

N.B. *Figures in the parentheses indicate percentages.*

cent) like basket making and 10 (28.57 per cent) like tailoring only 1 (2.86 per cent) likes to learn rope making.

In the Mahali community all 23 respondents (who are willing to learn something) prefer tailoring.

In the Santal community only 37 respondents are interested in occupational training programme. Out of 37 respondents, 21 (56.76 per cent) women want to learn basket making. 15 (40.54 per cent) women are interested in tailoring.

It is observed in the Munda community that out of 100 selected women 59 are not interested in training and 41 are interested to take training of which (48.78 per cent) respondents are in the basket making, 19 (46.34 per cent) in tailoring and 2 (4.88 per cent) in rope making.

In the Bhumij community out of 32 respondents, 18 (56.25 per cent) women want to learn basket making and 14 (43.75 per cent) like tailoring.

From the above table it can be observed that out of 50 respondents of the Santal community of Orissa 45 respondents want to take training regarding occupation whereas it is cent per cent in the Lodha community. Out of 45 Santal women 29 (64.44 per cent) want to take training in rope making and 16 (35.56 per cent) want to take training both in rope making and leaf work, whereas in case of the Lodha 26 (52.00 per cent) want to take training in rope making and 24 (48.00 per cent) in leaf work.

In Bihar all the Birhor respondents (100) want to take training in rope making. Among the Mahalis of this state, all the respondents (50) want to take training in basket making. In case of the Munda all the respondents do not (50) want to take any training regarding occupation. Among the Bhumij it is evident that out of 50 respondents 34 respondents want to take training and all of them (100.00 per cent) want to be trained in basket making.

Table 5.9 depicts the preference of tribal women's occupation. Majority of the tribal women of the sample belonging to all states and districts prefer to cling to their traditional occupation.

Particularly in case of the Birhor (both the states) all have shown their positive inclineness to their traditional occupation. So they are more conservative regarding restoring their traditional occupation.

TABLE 5.8

DEMAND FOR BETTER OCCUPATION THROUGH TRAINING

Tribe	*No. of respondent*	*Training*		*Preferred Occupational Training*			
		Not Demanded	*Demanded*	*Basket making*	*Tailoring*	*Rope making*	*Rope making and leaf work*
			WEST BENGAL				
Birhor	37	-	37 (100.00)	-	-	37 (100.00)	-
Lodha	100	65 (65.00)	35 (35.00)	24 (68.57)	10 (28.57)	1 (2.86)	-
Mahali	100	77 (77.00)	23 (23.00)	-	23 (100.00)	-	-
Santal	100	63 (63.00)	37 (37.00)	21 (56.76)	15 (40.54)	1 (2.70)	-
Munda	100	59 (59.00)	41 (41.00)	20 (48.78)	19 (46.34)	2 (4.88)	-

(Contd.)

Bhumij	100	68 (68.00)	32 (32.00)	18 (56.25)	14 (43.75)	-	-
ORISSA							
Lodha	50	-	50 (100.00)	-	-	26 (52.00)	24 (48.00)
Santal	50	5 (10.00)	45 (90.00)	-	-	29 (64.44)	16 (35.56)
BIHAR							
Birhor	100	-	100 (100.00)	-	-	100 (100.00)	-
Mahali	50	-	50 (100.00)	50 (100.00)	-	-	-
Munda	50	50 (100.00)	-	-	-	-	-
Bhumij	50	16 (32.00)	34 (68.00)	34 (100.00)	-	-	-

N.B. *Figures in the parentheses indicate percentages.*

The Lodha, Mahali, Santal, Munda and Bhumij in West Bengal, show their less conservative outlook regarding preferring traditional occupation than the tribal people in Orissa (Lodha, and Santal) and in Bihar (Mahali, Munda and Bhumij).

TABLE 5.9
OCUUPATION PREFERRED

Tribe	*No. of respondents*	*Type of occupation*		
		Traditional	*Modern*	*Both*
		WEST BENGAL		
Birhor	37	37 (100.00)	-	-
Lodha	100	71 (71.00)	14 (14.00)	15 (15.00)
Mahali	100	67 (67.00)	9 (9.00)	24 (24.00)
Santal	100	55 (55.00)	33 (33.00)	12 (12.00)
Munda	100	63 (63.00)	26 (26.00)	11 (11.00)
Bhumij	100	63 (63.00)	25 (25.00)	12 (12.00)
		ORISSA		
Lodha	50	50 (100.00)	-	-
Santal	50	47 (94.00)	3 (6.00)	-
		BIHAR		
Birhor	100	100 (100.00)	-	-
Mahali	50	44 (88.00)	4 (8.00)	2 (4.00)
Munda	50	39 (78.00)	7 (14.00)	4 (8.00)
Bhumij	50	28 (56.00)	21 (42.00)	1 (2.00)

N.B. *Figures in the parentheses indicate percentages.*

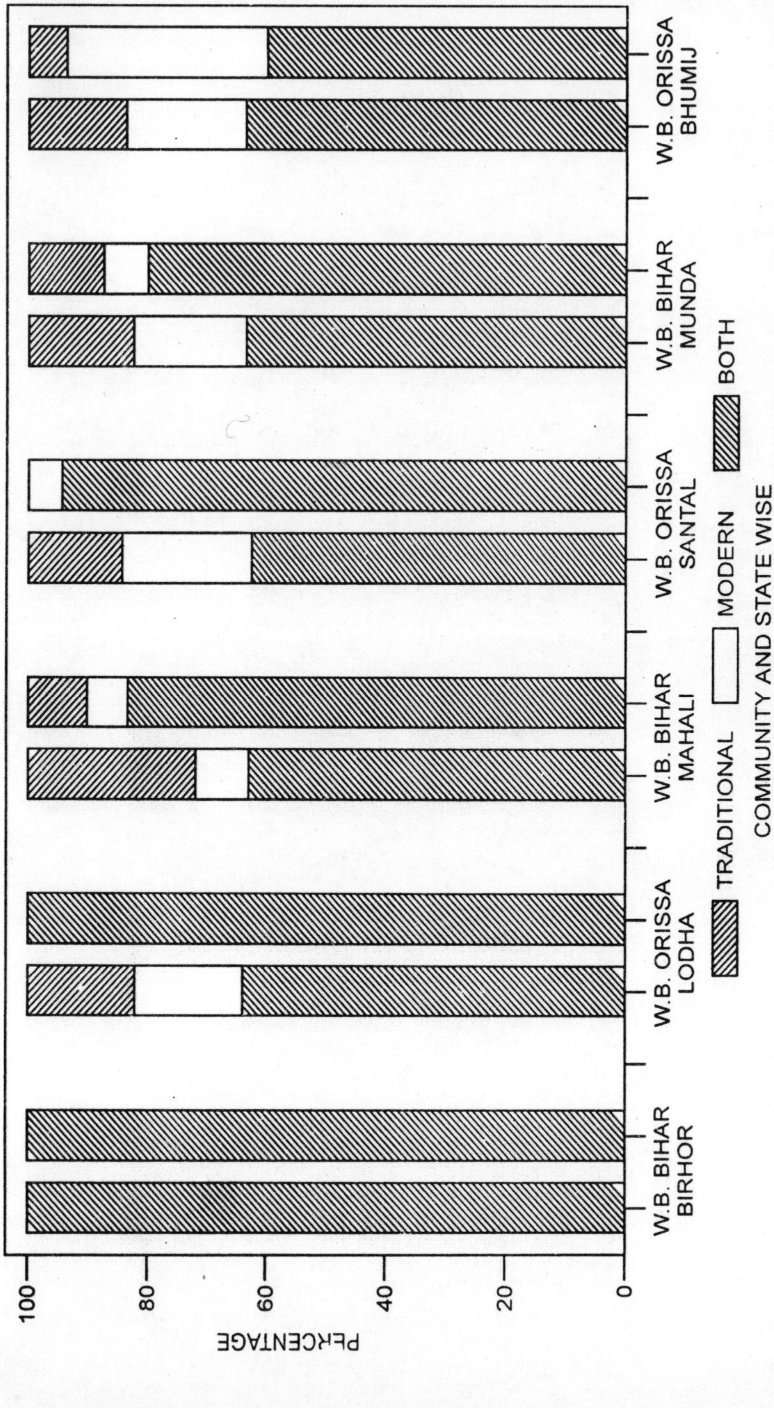
PERCENTAGE
100
80
60
40
20
0
W.B. BIHAR
BIRHOR
W.B. ORISSA
LODHA
W.B. BIHAR
MAHALI
W.B. ORISSA
SANTAL
W.B. BIHAR
MUNDA
W.B. ORISSA
BHUMIJ
TRADITIONAL
MODERN
BOTH
COMMUNITY AND STATE WISE

6

Education

"Education is key to Development"—This statement is well accepted by all planners, administrators, scholars and developmental agencies throughout the world. Illiteracy is one of the important criteria of scheduled tribe population. Among the tribal communities a conservative attitude can be observed towards the education of female and consequently female literacy level is lower than that of the male in their society.

The literate persons are those who are functionally literates having knowledge of reading and writing either through formal, non-formal and informal way of attaining various educational qualifications "read and write" to "graduate and above". In this chapter the various aspects of their education—their success and failure, changing attitudes towards children's education, problems related to educational attainments for the betterment of tribal life are studied in detail.

Table 6.1 depicts the educational status of the members of the tribal families who have been selected from three states—West Bengal, Orissa and Bihar. Total population have been categorised in two groups, literates and illiterates.

Considering the level of literacy it has been observed that all tribal families show a similar sorrowful picture regarding their education. The number of literate males is higher than the number of literate females. Majority of the females in all age groups of six tribal communities are illiterate.

The rate of literacy varies from tribe to tribe. Literacy level is very poor (male and female both) among the Birhors in Bihar where only 8.16 per cent males and 6.12 per cent females are literates. Literacy level of the Birhor in West Bengal is also low in comparison to the level of education of other tribal communities. On the other hand, the literacy rate is highest among the Munda in West Bengal both in case of male and female.

Examining the nature of literacy level among the three states it has been observed that the literacy rate is high in all sample tribal (Birhor, Lodha, Mahali, Santal, Munda and Bhumij) in West Bengal than in the other states.

Table 6.1 also reveals in detail the education of the literates and illiterates according to different age groups. Age of the people has been categorized into four important groups—'0-14' to '61+' years. In all these groups the number of male literates is higher than that of female literates. On the other hand, an illiterate group is again divided into four categories according to age and sex. It is also observed in all cases that the number of female illiterates is higher than that of male illiterates.

Table 6.2 shows the educational level of the respondents of three states (West Bengal, Orissa and Bihar). It is observed from the table that among six selected tribal communities of West Bengal, highest women literacy rate (53.00 per cent) is found in the Munda community and lowest (nil) in the Birhor community. Except in Birhor, in all tribal communities, maximum women have functional level of literacy and only a few have middle level of education and in the Santal community alone it is found that 2.00 per cent women have Higher Secondary level of education and 1.00 per cent has become a graduate.

In the state of Orissa, both among the Lodha and the Santal communities only 2.00 per cent women are literate.

TABLE 6.1
EDUCATION AND AGE WISE DISTRIBUTION

Tribe	State	Total Population		Educational Status with Age (in years) — Lites rate								Illiterate								Total			
				0-14		15-45		46-60		61+		0-14		15-45		46-60		61+		Literate		Illiterate	
		M	F	M	F	M	F	M	F	M	F	M	F	M	F	M	F	M	F	M	F	M	F
Birhor	West Bengal	82	76	20 (24.40)	17 (22.37)	18 (21.95)	1 (01.31)	-	-	-	-	16 (19.51)	17 (22.37)	14 (17.07)	30 (39.47)	8 (09.75)	7 (09.21)	6 (07.32)	4 (05.26)	38 (46.34)	18 (23.68)	44 (53.66)	58 (76.32)
	Bihar	196	196	9 (4.59)	10 (05.10)	7 (03.57)	2 (01.02)	-	-	-	-	71 (36.22)	72 (36.74)	84 (42.86)	96 (48.98)	12 (06.12)	10 (05.10)	13 (06.63)	6 (03.06)	16 (08.16)	12 (06.12)	180 (91.84)	184 (93.88)
Lodha	West Bengal	251	236	44 (17.53)	29 (12.29)	65 (25.90)	27 (11.44)	8 (03.19)	3 (01.27)	9 (03.59)	2 (00.85)	61 (24.30)	60 (25.42)	40 (15.94)	81 (34.32)	12 (04.78)	27 (11.44)	12 (04.78)	7 (02.97)	126 (50.20)	61 (25.85)	125 (49.80)	175 (74.15)
	Orissa	106	106 (18.87)	20 (12.29)	13 (15.09)	16 (01.89)	2	- (01.89)	2	-	-	28 (26.42)	30 (28.30)	26 (24.53)	45 (42.45)	10 (09.43)	10 (09.43)	6 (05.66)	4 (03.47)	36 (33.96)	17 (16.04)	70 (66.04)	88 (83.02)
Mahali	West Bengal	241	225	47 (19.50)	41 (18.22)	72 (19.88)	31 (13.78)	13 (05.39)	1 (00.44)	5 (02.07)	-	51 (21.16)	43 (19.11)	30 (12.45)	72 (32.00)	14 (05.21)	20 (08.89)	9 (03.73)	17 (07.56)	137 (56.85)	73 (32.44)	104 (43.15)	152 (67.56)
	Bihar	124	94 (20.16)	25 (10.64)	10 (20.16)	25 (08.51)	8 (03.23)	4 (01.06)	1	-	-	30 (24.19)	17 (18.09)	23 (18.55)	39 (41.49)	13 (10.48)	16 (17.02)	4 (03.23)	3 (03.19)	54 (43.55)	19 (20.21)	70 (56.45)	75 (79.79)
Santal	West Bengal	241	273 (19.50)	47 (11.36)	31 (29.04)	70 (19.41)	53 (04.98)	12 (01.47)	4 (01.24)	3 (01.10)	3	59 (24.48)	80 (29.30)	30 (12.44)	70 (25.64)	14 (05.81)	19 (06.96)	6 (02.49)	13 (04.76)	132 (54.77)	91 (33.33)	109 (45.23)	182 (66.67)
	Orissa	143	132 (11.19)	16 (09.10)	12 (11.89)	17 (03.79)	5 (01.40)	2	- (01.40)	2	-	54 (37.76)	46 (34.85)	36 (25.17)	50 (37.88)	9 (06.29)	13 (09.85)	7 (04.89)	6 (04.55)	37 (25.87)	17 (12.88)	106 (74.13)	115 (87.12)
Munda	West Bengal	257	250	58 (22.57)	52 (20.80)	108 (42.02)	72 (28.80)	14 (05.45)	4 (01.60)	10 (03.89)	2 (00.80)	42 (16.34)	48 (19.20)	10 (03.89)	45 (18.00)	4 (01.56)	16 (06.40)	11 (04.28)	11 (04.40)	190 (73.93)	130 (52.00)	67 (26.07)	120 (48.00)
	Bihar	128	133 (23.44)	30 (17.29)	23 (28.91)	37 (13.53)	18 (01.56)	2	-	-	-	29 (22.66)	33 (24.81)	17 (13.28)	43 (32.33)	8 (06.25)	12 (09.02)	5 (03.91)	4 (03.00)	69 (53.91)	41 (30.83)	59 (46.09)	92 (69.17)
Bhumij	West Bengal	231	240	53 (22.94)	41 (17.08)	91 (39.39)	49 (20.42)	11 (04.76)	2 (00.83)	4 (01.73)	1 (00.42)	39 (16.96)	63 (26.25)	23 (09.96)	63 (26.25)	5 (02.16)	10 (04.17)	5 (02.16)	11 (04.58)	159 (68.83)	93 (38.75)	72 (31.17)	147 (61.25)
	Bihar	150	116	27	20 (18.00)	51 (17.24)	11 (34.00)	10 (09.48)	1 (06.67)	- (00.86)	-	21 (14.00)	23 (19.83)	29 (19.33)	45 (38.79)	10 (06.67)	13 (11.21)	2 (01.32)	3 (02.58)	88 (58.67)	32 (27.59)	62 (41.33)	84 (72.41)

TABLE 6.2

EDUCATIONAL LEVEL OF THE RESPONDENTS

Tribe	No. of illiterate	Education									
		Can sing	Can read	Can read and write	Primary	Middle	IX-X	S.F.	H.S.	Graduate	Total
WEST BENGAL											
Birhor	37 (100.00)	-	-	-	-	-	-	-	-	-	37 (100.00)
Lodha	81 (81.00)	15 (15.00)	-	-	1 (1.00)	3 (3.00)	-	-	-	-	100 (100.00)
Mahali	82 (82.00)	8 (8.00)	4 (4.00)	-	5 (5.00)	1 (1.00)	-	-	-	-	100 (100.00)
Santal	73 (73.00)	10 (10.00)	4 (4.00)	-	5 (5.00)	2 (2.00)	3 (3.00)	-	2 (2.00)	1 (1.00)	100 (100.00)
Munda	47 (47.00)	34 (34.00)	-	-	11 (11.00)	7 (7.00)	1 (1.00)	-	-	-	100 (100.00)
Bhumiji	66 (66.00)	19 (19.00)	-	-	8 (8.00)	7 (7.00)	-	-	-	-	100 (100.00)
ORISSA											
Lodha	49 (98.00)	1 (2.00)	-	-	-	-	-	-	-	-	50 (100.00)
Santal	49 (98.00)	-	-	-	1 (2.00)	-	-	-	-	-	50 (100.00)
BIHAR											
Birhor	100 (100.00)	-	-	-	-	-	-	-	-	-	100 (100.00)
Mahali	45 (90.00)	-	-	-	4 (8.00)	-	1 (2.00)	-	-	-	50 (100.00)
Munda	39 (78.00)	-	-	-	10 (20.00)	1 (2.00)	-	-	-	-	50 (100.00)
Bhumiji	45 (90.00)	-	-	-	2 (4.00)	2 (4.00)	1 (2.00)	-	-	-	50 (100.00)

N.B. *Figures in the parentheses indicate percentage.*

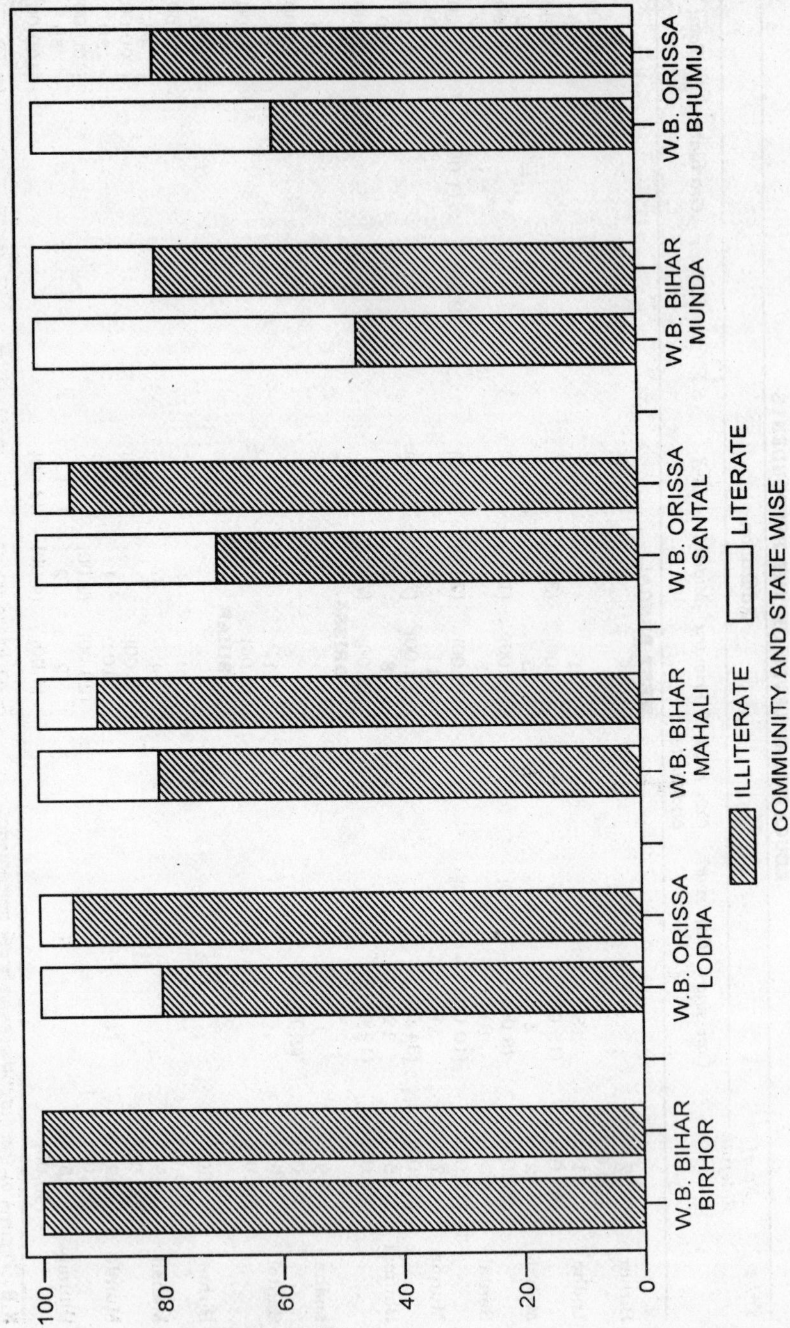
PERCENTAGE
100
80
60
40
20
0
W.B. BIHAR
BIRHOR
W.B. ORISSA
LODHA
W.B. BIHAR
MAHALI
W.B. ORISSA
SANTAL
W.B. BIHAR
MUNDA
W.B. ORISSA
BHUMIJ
ILLITERATE
LITERATE
COMMUNITY AND STATE WISE

In Bihar, except the Birhor (where literacy rate is nil) the rate of women literacy is higher in the Munda (22.00 per cent) than in the two communities—the Mahali and Bhumij.

Table 6.3 portrays the causes of illiteracy and discontinuity of education of tribal women (respondents), most of the tribal women under study are illiterate in all states. Among them, the high rate of illiteracy is prevalent in the Birhor and the literacy level is high in the Munda in both the states.

Four important causes are considered for their illiteracy. Among these causes of illiteracy, maximum number of women in all communities have mentioned ignorance of parents, poor economic condition, less emphasis on women's education and inadequacy of schools.

Searching for the causes of discontinuity of the education of respondents (though very few women belong to this category) it is observed that the following factors like poor economic condition, early marriage, negative apathetic cooperation from the caste students and involvement in domestic work are responsible for those dropouts.

Table 6.4 describes the participation of tribal women in the Adult Education Programme. Data reveal that except the tribal women of Midnapur district (West Bengal) the other women respondents who are in the district Purulia (West Bengal) and Mayurbhanj (Orissa), Singbhum and Hazaribagh (Bihar) could not join in the Adult Education Programme as the programme had not yet been implemented in those districts for mass enlightenment.

Even in Midnapur district (West Bengal) the large number of illiterates are among the Lodha (81.00 per cent) and Mahali (82.00 per cent), whereas the less number of illiterates (47.00 per cent) are visible among the Munda in West Bengal. Though the programme had already been implemented in those areas yet the number of participants to the programme is not satisfactory. Only the Munda participants to this programme is 70.21 per centper cent (maximum).

TABLE 6.3

ILLITERACY AND DISCONTINUITY OF EDUCATION

Tribe	Level of literacy		Not at all			Causes to stop learning					
	Literate	*Illiterate*	*Ignorance of parents*	*Education considered unimportant*	*Poor economic condition*	*Inadequacy of school*	*Econonic hurdles*	*Early marriage*	*Lack of adjustment*	*To earn money*	*Involvment in household work*
					WEST BENGAL						
Birhor	-	37	37	37	37	-	-	-	-	-	-
(37)				(100.00)	(100.00)						
Lodha	19	81	63	33	79	14	1	5	-	-	-
(100)	(19.00)	(81.00)	(77.78)	(44.74)	(97.53)	(17.28)	(5.26)	(26.32)			
Mahali	18	82	48	60	77	30	5	8	1	5	1
(100)	(18.00)	(82.00)	(58.54)	(73.17)	(93.90)	(36.59)	(67.78)	(44.44)	(05.56)	(27.78)	(05.56)
Santal	27	73	64	44	67	15	7	9	2	2	3
(100)	(27.00)	(73.00)	(87.67)	(60.27)	(91.78)	(20.55)	(25.93)	(33.33)	(07.41)	(07.41)	(11.11)
Munda	53	47	46	29	35	11	13	7	2	3	6
(100)	(53.00)	(47.00)	(97.87)	(61.70)	(74.47)	(23.40)	(24.53)	(13.21)	(03.77)	(05.66)	(11.32)

(*Contd.*)

Bhumij	34	66	44	35	45	7	13	15	-	3	2
(100)	(34.00)	(66.00)	(66.67)	(53.03)	(68.18)	(10.61)	(38.24)	(44.00)		(08.82)	(05.88)
ORISSA											
Lodha	1	49	49	49	49	20	-	-	-	-	-
(50)	(2.00)	(98.00)	(100.00)	(100.00)	(100.00)	(48.82)					
Santal	1	49	49	49	49	16	1	1	-	1	1
(50)	(2.00)	(98.00)	(100.00)	(100.00)	(100.00)	(32.65)	(100.00)	(100.00)		(100.00)	(100.00)
BIHAR											
Birhor	-	100	99	99	77	-	-	-	-	-	-
(100)		(100.00)	(99.00)	(99.00)	(77.00)						
Mahali	5	45	30	28	36	9	5	1	5	4	-
(50)	(10.00)	(90.00)	(66.67)	(62.22)	(78.26)	(20.00)	(100.00)	(20.00)	(100.00)	(80.00)	
Munda	11	39	37	39	36	8	6	2	-	4	3
(50)	(22.00)	(78.00)	(94.87)	(100.00)	(92.31)	(20.31)	(54.05)	(18.18)		(36.36)	(27.27)
Bhumij	5	45	38	37	41	9	3	2	-	3	4
(50)	(10.00)	(90.00)	(84.44)	(82.00)	(91.11)	(20.00)	(60.00)	(40.00)		(60.00)	(80.00)

N.B. *Figures in the parentheses indicate percentages.*

TABLE 6.4
ADULT EDUCATION PROGRAMME: PARTICIPATION AND NON-PARTICIPATION

Tribe	No. of Illiterate	No. of Partici-pant to	Achievement				No. of non Partici-pant
			No to ement	learn to read	learn to sign	learn to calculate	
Lodha	81	32	10	9	4	10	49
		(39.51)	(31.25)	(28.12)	(12.50)	(31.25)	(60.49)
Mahali	82	24	11	8	10	7	58
		(29.27)	(45.83)	(33.33)	(41.67)	(29.17)	(70.73)
Santal	73	18	4	7	8	6	55
		(24.66)	(22.22)	(38.89)	(44.44)	(33.33)	(75.34)
Munda	47	33	-	12	21	22	14
		(70.21)		(36.36)	(63.64)	(66.67)	(29.79)
Bhumij	66	32	-	10	10	9	34
		(48.48)		(31.25)	(31.25)	(28.12)	(51.52)

(Contd.)

Reasons for non-participation							
Lack of time	*Lack of energy*	*Inefficient teacher*	*Irregular administ-ration of centre*	*Due to long distance*	*Lack of prac-tice*	*Lack of education alienent*	*Lack of encoura-gement*
35	47	12	45	7	10	12	8
(71.43)	(95.92)	(24.49)	(91.84)	(14.29)	(20.41)	(24.49)	(16.33)
40	50	17	30	-	-	12	4
(68.97)	(86.21)	(29.31)	(51.72)			(20.69)	(06.90)
25	50	13	16	2	-	11	2
(45.45)	(90.91)	(23.64)	(29.09)	(03.64)		(20.00)	(03.64)
3	8	5	7	3	4	7	9
(21.43)	(57.14)	(35.71)	(50.00)	(21.43)	(28.51)	(50.00)	(64.29)
14	13	16	6	4	-	6	8
(41.18)	(38.23)	(47.06)	(17.65)	(11.76)		(17.65)	(23.53)

N.B. *Figures in the Parentheses indicate percentages.*

In most of the cases the Adult Education Programme has failed to attend its goal. The achievement level of some participants is zero. But among other participants, it has been observed that some have achieved the level to 'learn to read'; 'learn to sign'; 'learn to calculate'. But most of the achievements are observed among the Munda and Bhumij.

It has also been studied from the non-participant respondents the reasons for their non-participation. Maximum number of respondents mention lack of time, and energy, due to hard work, irregularities within the administration as different reasons for their non-participation.

From the Table 6.5 it is observed that the percentage of male school going children is always higher than that of the female school going children in the tribal communities.

Among the six tribal communities—the Birhor, Lodha, Mahali, Santal, Munda and Bhumij of West Bengal, the per cent age of male school going children is highest (71.43 per cent) in the Mahali community and the percentage of female school going children is lowest (26.87 per cent) in the Lodha.

The Birhor community of Purulia district is an exception. In this community the percentage of female school going children (60.71 per cent) is higher than that of the male school going children.

In the Lodha community in Orissa the percentage of male school going children (62.50 per cent) is higher than the percentage of female (29.03 per cent) school going children.

In the Santal of Mayurbhanj district in Orissa, 36.21 per cent males are school going and 63.79 per cent are non-school going children and among female 28.81 per cent are school going and 71.19 per cent are non-school going children.

Table 6.5 represents the percentage of school going and non-school going children of the four tribal communities (Birhor, Mahali, Munda and Bhumij) of Bihar.

In case of the Birhor in Bihar it has been observed that the 77.97 per cent of the male children and 82.61 per cent female are non-school going children. Among the Mahali 48.39 per cent male and 38.71 per cent female children are school going. In the Munda it is observed that majority (53.85 per cent) of the male children are school going where-as 64.41 per cent female are non-school going. Regarding the Bhumij it has been observed that the majority (55.00 per cent) of the male children are school going whereas the majority (52.38 per cent) of the female children are non school going.

TABLE 6.5

INFORMATION IN RESPECT OF SCHOOL GOING CHILDREN

Tribes	*No. of Families*	*No. of Childless Families*	*Total No. of Children*		*No. of School Going Children*		*No. of Non-School Going Children*	
			Male	*Female*	*Male*	*Female*	*Male*	*Female*
				WEST BENGAL				
Birhor	37	2	33	28	18 (54.55)	17 (60.71)	15 (45.45)	11 (39.29)
Lodha	100	9	73	67	45 (61.64)	18 (26.87)	28 (38.36)	49 (73.13)
Mahall	100	6	77	71	55 (71.43)	30 (42.25)	22 (26.19)	41 (57.75)
Santal	100	9	84	92	54 (64.29)	34 (36.96)	30 (35.71)	58 (57.18)
Munda	100	5	92	68	63 (68.48)	45 (66.18)	29 ((31.52)	23 (33.82)

(*Contd.*)

Bhumij	100	8	78	84	54 (69.23)	37 (44.05)	24 (30.77)	47 (55.95)
ORISSA								
Lodha	50	8	32	31	20 (62.50)	9 (29.03)	12 (37.50)	22 (70.97)
Santal	50	1	58	59	21 (36.21)	17 (28.81)	37 (63.79)	42 (71.19)
BIHAR								
Birhor	100	8	59	69	13 (22.03)	12 (17.39)	46 (77.97)	57 (82.61)
Mahali	50	5	62	31	30 (48.39)	12 (38.71)	32 (51.61)	19 (61.29)
Munda	50	-	65	59	35 (53.85)	21 (35.59)	30 (46.15)	38 (64.41)
Bhumij	50	-	60	42	33 (55.00)	20 (47.62)	27 (45.00)	22 (52.38)

N.B. *Figures in the parentheses indicate percentages.*

TABLE 6.6

MOTHER'S AWARENESS REGARDING CHILDREN' SEDUCATION

Tribes	No. of family	No. of child-less family	No. of family with adult population	Prefer education		Reason for education			
				Yes	No	They will know everything	Their mentality will be changed	They will be economically strong	They will lead their society
WEST BENGAL									
Birhor	37	3	1	31	2	30	1	25	4
				(93.94)	(6.06)	(96.77)	(3.23)	(80.65)	(12.90)
Lodha	100	9	9	74	8	65	16	58	8
				(90.24)	(9.76)	(87.84)	(21.62)	(78.38)	(10.81)
Mahali	100	4	19	77	-	76	5	74	13
				(100.00)		(98.70)	(6.49)	(96.10)	(16.88)
Santal	100	9	14	74	3	67	12	63	12
				(96.10)	(3.90)	(90.54)	(16.22)	(85.14)	(16.22)
Munda	100	3	2	92	3	70	9	74	16
				(96.84)	(3.26)	(76.09)	(9.78)	(80.43)	(17.39)

(*Contd.*)

Bhumij	100	9	-	87	4	71	25	61	7
				(95.06)	(4.40)	(81.61)	(28.74)	(70.11)	(8.05)
					ORISSA				
Lodha	50	8	3	31	8	31	14	31	14
				(79.49)	(20.51)	(100.00)	(45.16)	(100.00)	(45.16)
Santal	50	1	7	22	20	22	13	21	14
				(52.38)	(47.62)	(100.00)	(59.09)	(95.45)	(63.64)
					BIHAR				
Birhor	100	8	-	14	78	14	4	9	9
				(15.22)	(84.78)	(100.00)	(28.57)	(64.29)	(64.29)
Mahali	50	5	8	29	8	29	6	25	11
				(78.38)	(21.62)	(100.00)	(20.69)	(86.21)	(37.93)
Munda	50	-	2	41	7	41	6	28	19
				(85.42)	(14.58)	(100.00)	(14.63)	(68.29)	(46.34)
Bhumij	50	-	4	41	5	39	7	29	17
				(89.13)	(12.20)	(95.12)	(17.07)	(70.73)	(41.46)

N.B. *Figures in the parentheses indicate percentages.*

Considering all the tribes together it is evident that in all the cases the percentage of male school going children is higher than that of the female school going children.

Table 6.6 shows the tribal mothers' awareness regarding the education of their children. The study reveals two groups of women:

(1) those who want to educate their children and

(2) those who do not want to educate their children.

In this perspective, the former are high in number among all tribal respondents in all states, except the Birhor in Bihar where 84.78 per cent women are not willing to educate their children.

Four reasons considered as important for educating their children among these tribal societies are depicted in Table 6.6. Maximum number of women want to educate their children because through education:

(1) they will be able to acquire adequate knowledge for proper understanding of their socio-economic environment and

(2) their children will be able to improve their economic condition. (Apart from these two important factors a few residents also remark that)

(3) education helps to change the mental condition of the children and

(4) creates good members of their community for prosperity and better living.

Rate of willing mothers to educate their children is mostly prevalent in West Bengal than in the other two states, Bihar (except the Birhor) and Orissa.

Table 6.7 describes the willingness of tribal women to educate their girl children. In the state of West Bengal among the six sample tribal groups more than 50 per cent tribal mothers express their willingness to educate their daughters upto school level.

But in Orissa both the two groups, the Lodha and Santal, express their unwillingness (in majority of the cases) for giving education to their daughters.

But in case of Bihar, except the Birhor community, more than 50.00 per cent of all other tribal mothers of different communities (Mahali, M nda and Bhumij) express that they are eager to educate their girl children upto school level if the opportunity comes.

Data regarding facilities and problems related with children's education of different tribal communities of three states are shown in Table 6.8.

Except the Birhor in Bihar, all sample tribal communities of three states, have shown higher percentages of school going children than non-school going children though the later type is not very few. There are also few families that have no children and few families that have only adult population. Naturally they are not facing any problem or enjoying any facilities of education.

It has also been observed from the study that all children are not equally willing to go to school. The school going children in all the three states are getting different educational facilities for continuing their education. Every student is not getting the facility of free education. In Orissa and Bihar almost all students are getting free books and tiffins but in West Bengal majority of them are getting books and tiffins.

In this table it is found that a good number of children are not going to school. Studies are also going on to find out its causes which may be the poor socio-economic condition and/or engagement in the field from their early childhood days and/or lack of awareness of parents and/or, in a few cases teachers negligence to teach them.

TABLE 6.7
WOMEN INSPIRING DAUGHTER'S EDUCATION

Tribe	*No. of family*	*No. of daughter less family*	*No. of unmarried women*	*Not wanted*	*Wanted*					
					I - IV	*V - X*	*XI - XII*	*XII+*	*Up to the limitation*	*Total wanted*
WEST BENGAL										
Birhor	37	7	-	13	2	11	-	-	4	17
				(43.33)	(11.76)	(64.71)			(23.53)	(100.00)
Lodha	100	29	-	24	2	11	-	-	34	47
				(33.80)	(04.26)	(23.40)			(72.34)	(100.00)
Mahali	100	31	2	12	14	15	-	-	26	55
				(13.39)	(25.45)	(27.27)			(47.27)	(100.00)
Santal	100	20	6	21	3	11	1	2	36	53
				(26.25)	(05.66)	(20.75)	(1.89)	(3.77)	(67.92)	(100.00)
Munda	100	18	1	20	9	19	2	2	29	61
				(24.39)	(14.75)	(31.15)	(3.28)	(3.28)	(47.54)	(100.00)
Bhumij	100	21	6	11	12	30	1	3	16	62
				(13.92)	(19.35)	(48.39)	(1.61)	(4.84)	(25.81)	(100.00)

(Contd.)

						ORISSA				
Lodha	50	19	-	19	3	4	-	-	5	12
				(61.29)	(25.00)	(33.33)			(41.67)	(100.00)
Santal	50	15	-	19	-	7	3	1	5	16
				(54.29)		(43.75)	(18.75)	(6.25)	(31.25)	(100.00)
						BIHAR				
Birhor	100	11	-	75	-	10	-	-	4	14
				(84.27)		(71.43)			(28.57)	(100.00)
Mahali	50	22	-	7	1	5	-	-	15	21
				(25.00)	(4.76)	(23.81)			(71.43)	(100.00)
Munda	50	12	-	7	8	14	-	-	9	31
				(18.42)	(25.81)	(45.16)			(29.03)	(100.00)
Bhumij	50	16	1	6	4	10	4	-	9	27
				(17.65)	(14.81)	(37.04)	(14.81)		(33.33)	(100.00)

N.B. *Figures in the parentheses indicate percentages.*

TABLE 6.8
FACILITIES AND PROBLEMS RELATED WITH CHILDREN'S EDUCATION

Tribes	No. of family	No.of Child-less family	No. of family with adult population	Facilities			No. of family with school going chidren	No.of family with non-school going children	Problems			
				Free Tution	Free Books	Free Tiffin			Econo-mic	Chil-dren have to work in field	Neglig-ence of parents	Teachers do not teach well
WEST BENGAL												
Birhor	37	3	1	21	21	21	21	12	21	4	19	10
				(100.00)	(100.00)	(100.00)			(100.00)	(19.05)	(90.48)	(47.62)
Lodha	100	9	9	43	33	22	43	39	43	9	12	1
				(100.00)	(76.74)	(51.16)			(100.00)	(20.93)	(27.91)	(02.33)
Mahali	100	4	19	48	47	33	48	29	48	26	19	-
				(100.00)	(97.92)	(68.75)			(100.00)	(54.17)	(39.58)	
Santal	100	9	14	49	39	13	49	28	49	25	26	2
				(100.00)	(79.59)	(26.53)			(100.00)	(51.02)	(53.06)	(04.00)
Munda	100	3	2	59	50	33	59	36	53	12	20	2
				(100.00)	(84.75)	(55.93)			(89.83)	(20.34)	(33.90)	(03.39)

(Contd.)

Bhumij	100	9	-	51	45	24	51	40	43	14	16	1
				(100.00)	(88.24)	(47.06)			(84.31)	(27.45)	(31.37)	(01.96)
ORISSA												
Lodha	50	8	3	20	20	20	20	19	20	17	6	8
				(100.00)	(100.00)	(100.00)			(100.00)	(85.00)	(30.00)	(40.00)
Santal	50	1	7	21	19	19	21	20	21	15	4	2
				(100.00)	(90.48)	(90.48)			(100.00)	(71.43)	(19.05)	(09.52)
BIHAR												
Birhor	100	8	-	14	14	14	14	78	14	1	3	1
				(100.00)	(100.00)	(100.00)			(100.00)	(07.14)	(21.43)	(07.14)
Mahali	50	5	8	22	19	19	22	15	22	14	13	-
				(100.00)	(86.36)	(86.36)			(100.00)	(63.64)	(59.09)	
Munda	50	-	2	33	26	26	33	15	33	24	23	-
				(100.00)	(78.79)	(78.79)			(100.00)	(72.73)	(69.70)	
Bhumij	50	-	4	32	28	26	32	14	28	19	18	-
				(100.00)	(87.50)	(81.25)			(87.50)	(59.38)	(56.25)	

N.B. *Figures in the parentheses indicate percentages.*

7

General Problems

Problems of tribal people are many and of varied nature. Immense poverty creates many concurrent problems and blockages that hinder their social development. Since Independence successive governments have been trying to improve their socio-economic condition by implementing many developmental schemes. Except governmental efforts there are many voluntary organizations which are also working with that aim. But actually all are in vain. Tribal people are still in a precarious condition. Sometimes, due to their own traditional backward mentality, laziness, superstitious ideas, they like to stay in isolation. This segregated life often creates more problems and they feel unhappy and the others, who are working for them are also dissatisfied.

Table 7.1 describes various problems of tribal communities in Midnapur district of West Bengal. The problems, reported by them, are—Economic, Housing, Land, Fuel, Clothes, Water, Hygiene, Social, Educational and Food.

In the Birhor community of Purulia, all the families live in a poor economic condition, 10.81 per cent families face water problem, 29.73 per cent have hygienic problem. In the Lodha community, 78.00 per cent families have poor economic condition, 35.00 per cent household face fuel problem, 10.00 per cent families face social problems. In the Mahali community, 86.00 per cent families face economic problem, 31.00 per cent face land problem due to their infertile land, 12.00 per cent households face educational problem for their children. It is observed in the

Santal community that 16.00 per cent families have no problem, 68.00 per cent families face economic problem, 20.00 per cent families face housing problem and 39.00 per cent of them have land problem. Like other tribal communities, the Mundas also suffer from economic problems, 25.00 per cent Munda families face fuel problem. 20.00 per cent Bhumij families have mentioned that they have no specific problem, 54.00 per cent families have poor economic condition, 13.00 per cent have housing and 5.00 per cent families suffer from water problem.

It is observed that both the Lodhas and Santals of Orissa have reported that their economic problems are their main problems (100.00 per cent in each). Besides their acute economic problems 18.00 per cent Santal respondents have mentioned educational problems and 16.00 per cent Lodha have reported their food problem.

In the Birhor community of Bihar 100.00 per cent have mentioned that they have economic problem. It is remarkable that the majority of the surveyed families of other tribal communities (Mahali, Munda and Bhumij) are also suffering from economic problem. In comparison to other communities the Mahali community face the housing problem in a higher degree. The percentage of families that suffer from land and hygiene problem, is also high in the Mahali community.

Varied natures of houses of the tribal people of different states have been depicted in Table 7.2. From this table it has been observed that there are three categories of houses; *Katcha* house—built with mud wall and straw or tiled roof, mixed house—where the wall is made up of bricks but the roof is shaded with tins or tiles, and *pacca* house—completely brick built house.

TABLE 7.1

Perceived Problems

Tribe	*No. of family*	*No. of family who has no problem*	*Problems*									
			Economic	*Housing*	*Land*	*Fuel*	*Clothes*	*Water*	*Hygiene*	*Social/ familial*	*Educa- tional*	*Food*
WEST BENGAL												
Birhor	37	-	37	-	-	-	-	4	11	2	1	-
			(100.00)					(10.81)	(29.73)	(5.41)	(2.70)	
Lodha	100	5	78	21	19	35	2	6	4	10	2	1
		(5.00)	(78.00)	(21.00)	(19.00)	(35.00)	(2.00)	(6.00)	(4.00)	(10.00)	(2.00)	(1.00)
Mahali	100	2	86	21	31	4	1	2	11	6	12	3
		(2.00)	(86.00)	(21.00)	(31.00)	(4.00)	(1.00)	(2.00)	(11.00)	(6.00)	(12.00)	(3.00)
Santal	100	16	68	20	39	5	1	4	8	6	7	1
		(16.00)	(68.00)	(20.00)	(39.00)	(5.00)	(1.00)	(4.00)	(8.00)	(6.00)	(7.00)	(1.00)
Munda	100	15	71	12	24	25	1	3	6	13	2	-
		(15.00)	(71.00)	(12.00)	(24.00)	(25.00)	(1.00)	(3.00)	(6.00)	(13.00)	(2.00)	

(Contd.)

Bhumij	100	20 (20.00)	54 (54.00)	13 (13.00)	30 (30.00)	27 (27.00)	3 (3.00)	5 (5.00)	3 (3.00)	9 (9.00)	4 (4.00)	2 (2.00)
ORISSA												
Lodha	50	-	50 (100.00)	-	-	-	-	-	-	3 (6.00)	2 (4.00)	8 (16.00)
Santal	50	-	50 (100.00)	-	-	-	-	-	-	-	9 (18.00)	1 (2.00)
BIHAR												
Bihor	100	-	100 (100.00)	13 (13.00)	-	-	-	-	-	2 (2.00)	6 (6.00)	-
Mahali	50	4 (8.00)	46 (92.00)	35 (70.00)	16 (32.00)	-	4 (8.00)	-	10 (20.00)	-	-	-
Munda	50	7 (14.00)	43 (86.00)	17 (34.00)	13 (26.00)	-	1 (2.00)	-	4 (8.00)	-	-	-
Bhumij	50	9 (18.00)	41 (82.00)	11 (22.00)	7 (14.00)	-	-	-	5 (10.00)	-	5 (10.00)	-

N.B. *Figures in the parentheses indicate percentages.*

Most of the tribal families in all states, except the Lodha in Orissa, live in *katcha* house having only one room. On the other hand, in case of the Santal community, in the state of West Bengal, only 5.00 per cent families who are converted to Christianity and employees of Christian Hospital at Nekurshini live in the quarters of the Hospital. 54.00 per cent Lodha families of Orissa at Mayurbhanj district and 18.92 per cent Birhor families of West Bengal at Purulia live in mixed houses. All these houses are made by the Government.

Considering the nature of house and their way of living, it is very clear that except a very limited percentage of tribal families, their housing condition is not good. In most of the cases the houses are made for them by different government agencies with the help of the Housing Development Scheme but they are unable to maintain the houses. Often they have to sell the doors and windows due to their financial hardship.

Generally the tribal people prepare very simple food. Kitchen is a place where cooking takes place. But most of the tribal people have accommodation problem and they have no separate place for preparing food. One corner of the room is generally used by them as a kitchen. Mostly they prefer an outside open place for cooking purpose. But exception is found only among the Birhors. Table 7.3 describes the nature of kitchen of six tribal communities.

It has been observed from the table that not a single Birhor family used the courtyard for cooking purpose in both the states. They generally prefer to cook in a kitchen or in absence of a kitchen they cook inside the room or on a verandah by the side of a room.

20.00 per cent Lodha families of West Bengal and 72.00 per cent Lodha families in Orissa cook inside the house. Maximum Lodha households of West Bengal (71.00 per cent) use both inside and outside of their houses for cooking purposes.

In West Bengal, the Mahali families use outside (23.00 per cent), inside (17.00 per cent) and both outside and inside (60.00 per cent) of their rooms as cooking places, whereas in Bihar all the Mahali families cook both inside and outside of their houses.

TABLE 7.2
PATTERN OF RESIDENTIAL HOUSE

Tribe	State	No. of family	Type of House											
			Kutcha					Pucca				Mixed		
			No. of Rooms					No. of Rooms				No. of Rooms		
			1	2	3	4	4+	1	2	3	3+	1	2	3
	W.B.	37 (100.00)	24 (64.86)	3 (8.12)	1 (2.70)	-	-	-	2 (5.41)	-	-	-	5 (13.51)	2 (5.41)
Birhor														
	Bihar	100 (100.00)	59 (59.00)	40 (40.00)	-	-	-	1 (1.00)	-	-	-	-	-	-
	W.B.	100 (100.00)	68 (68.00)	26 (26.00)	6 (6.00)	-	-	-	-	-	-	-	-	-
Lodha														
	Orissa	50 (100.00)	3 (6.00)	1 (2.00)	-	-	-	10 (20.00)	9 (18.00)	-	-	21 (42.00)	6 (12.00)	-
	W.B.	100 (100.00)	60 (60.00)	30 (30.00)	9 (9.00)	1 (1.00)	-	-	-	-	-	-	-	-

(Contd.)

Mahali													
Bihar	50	22	14	9	5	-	-	-	-	-	-	-	-
	(100.00)	(44.00)	(28.00)	(18.00)	(10.00)								
W.B.	100	63	23	6	2	-	1	3	1	-	-	1	-
	(100.00)	(63.00)	(23.00)	(6.00)	(2.00)		(1.00)	(3.00)	(1.00)			(1.00)	
Santal													
Orissa	50	38	11	-	-	-	-	-	-	-	1	-	-
	(100.00)	(76.00)	(22.00)								(2.00)		
W.B.	100	51	37	10	2	-	-	-	-	-	-	-	-
	(100.00)	(51.00)	(37.00)	(10.00)	(2.00)								
Munda													
Bihar	50	21	16	7	6	-	-	-	-	-	-	-	-
	(100.00)	(42.00)	(32.00)	(14.00)	(12.00)								
W.B.	100	65	24	7	-	3	-	1	-	-	-	-	
	(100.00)	(65.00)	(24.00)	(7.00)		(3.00)		(1.00)					
Bhumij													
Bihar	50	15	20	7	4	4	-	-	-	-	-	-	-
	(100.00)	(30.00)	(40.00)	(14.00)	(8.00)	(8.00)							

N.B. *Figures in the parentheses indicate percentages.*

TABLE 7.3
KITCHEN PARTICULARS

Tribe	*State*	*No. of family*	*Nature of kitchen*		
			Outside	*Inside*	*Both*
Birhor	W.B.	37	-	35 (94.59)	2 (5.41)
	Bihar	100	-	-	50 (100.00)
Lodha	W.B.	100	9 (9.00)	20 (20.00)	71 (71.00)
	Orissa	50	-	36 (72.00)	14 (28.00)
Mahali	W.B.	100	23 (23.00)	17 (17.00)	60 (60.00)
	Bihar	50	-	-	50 (100.00)
Santal	W.B.	100	12 (12.00)	38 (38.00)	50 (50.00)
	Orissa	50	-	38 (76.00)	12 (24.00)
Munda	W.B.	100	11 (11.00)	29 (29.00)	60 (60.00)
	Bihar	50	-	-	50 (100.00)
Bhumij	W.B.	100	8 (8.00)	35 (35.00)	57 (57.00)
	Bihar	50	-	-	50 (100.00)

N.B. *Figures in the parentheses indicate percentages.*

50.00 per cent Santal families of West Bengal use both inside and outside of their rooms as the cooking place and 12.0 per cent families are cooking their food outside the house. In Orissa 24.00 per cent use both outside and inside as a cooking place. 38.00 per cent Santal family of West Bengal and 76.00 per cent Santal family of Orissa cook inside the house. More or less the same picture is observed in case of the Munda. In West Bengal 60.00 per cent families and in Bihar 100.00 per cent families use both outside and inside of their houses for the purpose of cooking. 57.00 per cent Bhumij families of West Bengal use both inside and outside places for cooking, 35.00 per cent use inside and only 8.00 per cent use outside but all the Bhumij households of Bihar use both inside and outside as places for cooking.

In Midnapur district, generally, most of the poor people use straw and dry leaves as fuel. A very little percentage of people, who are economically strong, buy wood for fuel. But majority of the families who are economically weak cannot use wood as fuel. They solely depend on dry leaves and branches of trees. But in rainy season they face an acute problem of fuel. All dry leaves and straw which are used by them as fuel get wet in rain. Except this, the quantity of fuel which is required for a family does not fulfil the need of the households because jungles are situated at a far distance from the tribal localities and nowadays it is legally prohibited to collect wood from jungles. So the tribal households face a major fuel crisis in West Bengal.

But in case of Purulia district in West Bengal, Mayurbhanj district in Orissa and Hazaribagh and Singbhum districts in Bihar we get some different pictures about fuel. Jungles are situated near the residence of tribal communities. Majority of the tribal households collect fuel from jungles.

Table 7.4 shows the sources of drinking water of six tribal communities of West Bengal. In Birhor of Purulia, majority of the families (91.89 per cent) use well as the source of drinking water.

In case of the Lodha and Bhumij of Midnapur district 55.00 per cent families and 58.00 per cent families use tube-well respectively and 45.00 per cent families of the Lodha and 42.00 per cent families of the Bhumij use well.

It is noticed from the table that the Mahalis mostly depend on tubewell for water. 93.00 per cent families use tubewell and 7.00 per cent use well as sources of water for drinking.

In case of the Santal, 77.00 per cent families use tubewell, and 8.00 per cent families use well for drinking water, 7.00 per cent families use both tubewell and well and only 8 per cent families use tap water of the railways as a source of water.

It is noticed from the above table that in the Munda community, a higher percentage of families (56.00 per cent) depend on well for water, and 44.00 per cent families use tubewell.

TABLE 7.4
SOURCES OF DRINKING WATER

Tribe	State	No. of family	Sources of Drinking Water: Tubewell	Well	Tubewell and well	Tap
Birhor	W.B.	37	3 (8.11)	34 (91.89)	-	-
	Bihar	100	-	100 (100.00)	-	-
Lodha	W.B.	100	55 (55.00)	45 (45.00)	-	-
	Orissa	50	21 (42.00)	16 (32.00)	13 (26.00)	-
Mahali	W.B.	100	93 (93.00)	7 (7.00)	-	-
	Bihar	50	-	50 (100.00)	-	-
Santal	W.B.	100	77 (77.00)	8 (8.00)	7 (7.00)	8 (8.00)
	Orissa	50	-	50 (100.00)	-	-
Munda	W.B.	100	44 (44.00)	56 (56.00)	-	-
	Bihar	50	-	50 (100.00)	-	-
Bhumij	W.B.	100	58 (58.00)	42 (42.00)	-	-
	Bihar	50	-	50 (100.00)	-	-

N.B. *Figures in the parentheses indicate percentages.*

In case of the Santal in Orissa all the families (100.00 per cent) depend on well for water, but in the Lodha community 42.00 per cent families use tubewell, 32.00 per cent families use well and both tubewell and well are used by 26.00 per cent families as sources of drinking water. There is no tap facility in their locality.

Considering the sources of drinking water of the Birhor, Mahali, Munda and Bhumij communities of Bihar it is observed that the members of all these communities use well as a source of drinking water.

Age at marriage (in years) and age at first child (in years) of the tribal women have been depicted in table 7.5. In tribal society, the age at marriage of women is lower than that of urban women. Generally, in rural societies, marriage takes place in early ages, tribal societies are no exception. From this table it is clear that in maximum cases marriage takes place among the tribal communities irrespective of states, between 14 and 18 years. In case of the birth of the first child it has been observed that among the tribal communities of the Birhor, Lodha and Bhumij of West Bengal, the Lodha of Orissa and Birhor, Mahali, Munda and Bhumij of Bihar, birth takes place between 14 and 18 years. Except this '14 to 18' years age group of women for giving birth to first child, the age of '18 to 22' years is also remarkable where a good number of tribal women give birth to their first child. The probable reason as has been observed is that a good number of tribal women's marriage take place within 18 years and 10 to 12 per cent marriages also take place within 14 years as these women belong to the older generation depicted in this study.

Early age at marriage is not only the problem of tribal women but also the problem of Indian society as a whole where majority of the people live in rural areas. If the marriage takes place at an early age many related problems emerge side by side. First, they are immature considering their age, but at an early age. Secondly, they are not sufficiently mature to take care of their children. Thirdly, there is an ample scope for giving birth more children frequently, which is harmful for the health of both mother and child. Finally, population explosion may be caused for this particular system which is still prevalent in our society.

Even in this study a good number of tribal women also develop the notion that early marriage is a harmful practice not only for themselves but for the society as a whole. As they have no alternative against this practice, which is going on traditionally, they have to accept it.

Table 7.6 describes the nature of bride price and dowry system which are prevalent among tribal communities of West Bengal, Orissa and Bihar. In previous years only the bride price system was practised among tribal communities but nowadays dowry system has already been introduced among them.

From this table it has been observed that the tribal women in maximum cases are not in favour of dowry or bride price. On the other hand, nearly 25.00 per cent tribal women or their families have given or taken dowry or bride price. In West Bengal, in case of the Santal and Mahali, bride price giving system is still continuing with a greater acceptability than the dowry system. Whereas in case of the Lodha, Munda and Bhumij dowry system is prevalent much more than bride price. So this new trend of dowry system has already been introduced by the other caste people within their communities and particularly among the newly emerged earning male persons. It may be mentioned here that the large group of respondents belong to 'no category' where they are not taking dowry or bride price but in real practice they take bride price in a ritual form, not in cash or in kind remarkably but in a token form. So the tribal people belonging to poor socio-economc status are still attached to their traditional practice.

But the Birhor of West Bengal and Bihar only practise their traditional marriage rites where the bride price is nominal and in case of Orissa the same practice (bride price) continues among the Lodha and Santal. It has been found in most of the cases that the socio-economic status of the Lodha and Santal is extremely poor. But in case of Bihar, except the Birhor, in the communities of the Mahali, Munda and Bhumij both bride price and dowry system are continuing as some boys of young generation have changed their socio-economic positions. As a result, the dowry system has been recently introduced among them. So dowry is a newly emerged problem in tribal societies. After getting education, increasing social awareness and changing their socio-economic position, they are coping with the new problem of dowry which has already proved disastrous among the caste people.

TABLE 7.5
AGE AT MARRIAGE AND FIRST CHILD

Tribe	No. of respon- dent	No. of unmar- ried female	Age at marriage (in years)				No. of Childless female	Age at first child (in years)				Married women with children
			14	14-18	18-22	22+		14	14-18	18-22	22+	
WEST BENGAL												
Birhor	37	-	6	29	1	1	2	-	18	15	2	35
	(100.00)		(16.22)	(78.38)	(2.70)	(2.70)			(51.43)	(42.86)	(5.71)	(100.00)
Lodha	100	-	15	60	21	4	9	1	43	36	11	91
	(100.00)		(15.00)	(60.00)	(21.00)	(4.00)		(1.09)	(47.25)	(39.56)	(12.09)	(100.00)
Mahali	100	2	9	57	30	2	7	-	33	49	9	91
	(100.00)	(2.00)	(9.00)	(57.00)	(30.00)	(2.00)			(36.26)	(53.85)	(9.89)	(100.00)
Santal	100	6	13	53	27	1	11	1	29	42	11	83
	(100.00)	(6.00)	(13.00)	(53.00)	(27.00)	(1.00)		(1.20)	(34.94)	(50.60)	(13.25)	(100.00)
Munda	100	6	11	53	25	5	5	-	33	36	20	89
	(100.00)	(6.00)	(11.00)	(53.00)	(25.00)	(5.00)			(30.08)	(40.45)	(22.47)	(100.00)

(Contd.)

	(100.00)	(1.00)	(15.00)	(61.00)	(21.00)	(2.00)			(52.22)	(35.55)	(12.22)	(100.00)
ORISSA												
Lodha	50	-	9	35	6	-	8	1	18	17	6	42
	(100.00)		(18.00)	(70.00)	(12.00)			(2.38)	(42.86)	(40.48)	(14.29)	(100.00)
Santal	50	-	4	41	5	-	1	-	18	22	6	49
	(100.00)		(8.00)	(82.00)	(10.00)				(36.73)	(44.90)	(18.37)	(100.00)
BIHAR												
Birhor	100	2	16	80	2	-	8	1	57	30	2	90
	(100.00)	(2.00)	(16.00)	(80.00)	(2.00)			(1.11)	(63.33)	(33.33)	(2.22)	(100.00)
Mahali	50	-	6	32	12	-	5	5	32	8	-	45
	(100.00)		(12.00)	(64.00)	(24.00)			(11.11)	(71.11)	(17.78)		(100.00)
Munda	50	-	8	33	8	1	-	8	33	6	3	50
	(100.00)		(16.00)	(66.00)	(16.00)	(2.00)		(16.00)	(66.00)	(12.00)	(6.00)	(100.00)
Bhumij	50	1	4	35	9	1	-	4	33	11	1	49
	(100.00)	(2.00)	(8.00)	(70.00)	(18.00)	(2.00)		(8.16)	(63.35)	(22.45)	(2.04)	(100.00)

N.B. *Figures in the parentheses indicate percentages.*

TABLE 7.6
BRIDE PRICE AND DOWRY DURING MARRIAGE

Tribe	No. of respondent	No. of unmarried women	Dowry/Bride Price		Dowry			Bride Price			Dowry/Bride Price	
			Not Taken	taken	Cash	Kind	Both	Cash	Kind	Both	Supported	Not Supported
WEST BENGAL												
Birhor	37	-	37	-	-	-	-	-	-	-	-	37
												(100.00)
Lodha	100	-	72	28	11	6	5	2	-	4	18	82
					(39.29)	(21.43)	(17.86)	(7.14)		(14.29)	(18.00)	(82.00)
Mahali	100	2	72	26	1	8	-	4	1	12	28	72
					(3.85)	(30.77)		(15.38)	(3.85)	(46.15)	(28.00)	(72.00)
Santal	100	6	67	27	1	5	1	-	14	6	21	79
					(3.70)	(18.52)	(3.70)		(51.85)	(22.22)	(21.00)	(79.00)
Munda	100	6	66	28	2	13	5	3	-	5	27	73
					(7.14)	(46.43)	(17.86)	(10.71)		(17.86)	(27.00)	(73.00)

(Contd.)

Bhumij	100	1	75	24	10	9	2	-	3	-	25	75
					(41.67)	(37.50)	(8.33)		(12.50)		(25.00)	(75.00)
ORISSA												
Lodha	50	-	50	-	-	-	-	-	-	-	-	50
												(100.00)
Santal	50	-	50	-	-	-	-	-	-	-	-	50
												(100.00)
BIHAR												
Birhor	100	2	98	-	-	-	-	-	-	-	-	100
												(100.00)
Mahali	50	-	22	28	10	3	3	2	10	-	17	33
					(35.71)	(10.71)	(10.71)	(7.14)	(35.71)		(34.00)	(66.00)
Munda	50	-	21	29	9	1	3	4	10	2	16	34
					(31.03)	(3.45)	(10.34)	(13.79)	(34.48)	(6.90)	(32.00)	(68.00)
Bhumij	50	1	23	26	11	2	4	3	5	1	14	36
					(42.31)	(7.69)	(15.38)	(11.54)	(19.23)	(3.85)	(28.00)	(72.00)

N.B. *Figures in the parentheses indicate percentages.*

Table 7.7 describes the awareness of tribal women regarding medical advice during pregnancy. It has been observed that the overall awareness regarding the doctor's advice is not very remarkable. Comparing the tribal women of all three states, belonging to different communities, it is found that in West Bengal, except the Lodha, more than 50.00 per cent tribal women take the doctor's advice during their pregnancy. But in case of the Birhor (both the state) not a single woman takes medical advice and they are not at all aware of it. On the other hand, in Orissa about 60.00 per cent tribal women belonging to the Lodha and Santal community do not take doctor's advice. The tribal women in Bihar (all four communities) show little awareness regarding doctor's advice during the pregnancy period.

Three important causes have been found, for which the tribal women do not take the doctor's advice. These are ignorance, less awareness and poor health service from the health centre. Considering these factors, it is found that ignorance proves the most important hindrance to the normal growth of the baby when it is in the womb. The second important factor is that the women attach less importance to the modern modes of medical treatment. They believe that pregnancy is the natural outcome and it will be solved automatically. In Bihar, the third factor, i.e., poor health service from the health centre is also mentioned by the respondents because they do not get any facility from it.

Table 7.8 describes the mother's awareness regarding the vaccination programme for their children. A few families are childless families. Except these, the rest of the families are studied to ascertain whether they have gone through the programme or not. Except the Birhors in Purulia, among the other five sample communities, majority of the mothers are well aware about the vaccination programme of their children. But about 60.00 per cent of them have completed the course in West Bengal, except the Munda (47.76 per cent). In Orissa among the Lodha and Santal a comparatively good picture is observed. But in Bihar the result is completely dissatisfactory for the sample tribal people; though initially a good number of the tribal families started this programme, finally only a few of them like the Mahali, Munda and Bhumij in Bihar completed the course. Generally these vaccination programmes are provided by the rural sub-centre or Primary Health Centre.

TABLE 7.7

WOMEN'S AWARENESS ABOUT PREGNANCY

Tribe	*No. of family*	*No. of unmarried women*	*No. of childless women*	*No. of women taken doctor's advice*	*No. of women not taken doctor's advice*	*Causes*		
						Ignorancy	*Less awareness*	*Poor heaith service*
WEST BENGAL								
Birhor	37	-	2	-	35 (100.00)	35 (100.00)	35 (100.00)	-
Lodha	100	-	9	39 (42.86)	52 (57.14)	42 (46.15)	37 (40.66)	5 (5.49)
Mahali	100	2	7	53 (58.24)	38 (41.76)	30 (32.97)	26 (28.57)	8 (8.79)
Santal	100	6	11	59 (71.08)	24 (28.92)	16 (19.28)	11 (13.25)	8 (9.64)
Munda	100	6	5	55 (61.80)	34 (38.20)	26 (29.21)	18 (20.22)	4 (4.49)

(*Contd.*)

Bhumij	100	1	9	57 (63.33)	33 (36.67)	24 (26.67)	20 (22.22)	5 (5.56)
ORISSA								
Lodha	50	-	8	14 (33.33)	28 (66.67)	22 (58.38)	9 (21.43)	-
Santal	50	-	1	20 (40.82)	29 (59.18)	29 (59.18)	14 (28.57)	-
BIHAR								
Birhor	100	2	8	-	90 (100.00)	90 (100.00)	90 (100.00)	-
Mahali	50	-	5	4 (8.89)	41 (91.11)	41 (91.11)	31 (68.39)	22 (48.89)
Munda	50	-	-	4 (8.00)	46 (92.00)	46 (92.00)	39 (78.00)	34 (68.00)
Bhumij	50	1	-	4 (8.16)	45 (91.84)	45 (91.84)	38 (77.55)	33 (67.35)

N.B. *Figures in the parentheses indicate percentages.*

Table 7.9 depicts the choice of family size by the tribal mothers. Regarding the choice of the family size it has been observed that majority of the mothers of all six sample tribal communities in West Bengal and Orissa prefer small-size family. But in Bihar among the Mahali, Munda and Bhumij, majority of the sample tribal women show their preference for middle-sized family. But the Birhor shows a different picture where 58.00 per cent tribal women prefer small-sized family and 42.00 per cent large and middle-sized families.

So it is clear that the tribal women of West Bengal and Orissa are more aware about the utility of small-sized family than that of Bihar.

Regarding the acceptance of the family planning programme it is observed from Table 7.10 that more than 40.00 per cent tribal women in West Bengal accept the family planning methods but the rest do not accept it. Among them a good number of tribal women show their preference for small-sized family (Table 7.9). So majority of them are convinced about the positive effect of a small-sized family. In Orissa more than 50.00 per cent tribal women accept the family planning programme. But in Bihar the tribal women show a negative and/or ambivalent attitude towards accepting the family planning programme.

Table 7.11 represents various diseases of six selected tribal communities—the Birhor, Lodha, Mahali, Santal, Munda and Bhumij of West Bengal. Generally twelve types of diseases are found among these communities. These are —Problem of eye-sight, headache, weakness, diarrhea, skin disease, cough and cold, asthma, malaria, tuberculosis, worm, dysentery and fever. But men, women and children are not equally affected by these diseases.

In the Birhor community of Purulia district, it is observed, that all male, female and children are free from the problem of eye-sight, asthma, tuberculosis. In case of other diseases like malaria, dysentery, fever and diarrhoea more or less the number of affected men, women and children are the same. But in case of headache and weakness the children are the less affected group. Cough and cold and skin diseases are mostly prevalent among the children.

TABLE 7.8
AWARENESS ABOUT VACCINATION

Tribe	No. of family	No. of Childless family	No. of unmarried	Vaccination taken or not			No. of family in which children taken full course	No. of family in which children taken Incomplete course	Total
				Yes	No	Total			
WEST BENGAL									
Birhor	37	2	-	13	22	35	8	5	15
				(37.14)	(62.86)	(100.00)	(61.54)	(38.46)	(100.00)
Lodha	100	9	-	60	31	91	38	22	60
				(65.93)	(34.07)	(100.00)	(63.33)	(36.67)	(100.00)
Mahali	100	7	2	63	28	91	39	24	63
				(69.23)	(30.77)	(100.00)	(61.90)	(38.10)	(100.00)
Santal	100	11	6	69	14	83	41	28	69
				(83.13)	(16.87)	(100.00)	(59.42)	(40.58)	(100.00)
Munda	100	5	6	67	22	89	32	35	67
				(75.28)	(24.72)	(100.00)	(47.76)	(52.24)	(100.00)

(Contd.)

Bhumij	100	9	1	59 (65.56)	31 (34.44)	90 (100.00)	40 (67.80)	19 (32.20)	59 (100.00)
ORISSA									
Lodha	50	8	-	27 (64.29)	15 (35.71)	42 (100.00)	20 (74.08)	7 (25.93)	27 (100.00)
Santal	50	1	-	31 (63.27)	18 (36.73)	49 (100.00)	29 (93.55)	2 (6.45)	31 (100.00)
BIHAR									
Birhor	100	8	2	52 (57.78)	38 (42.22)	90 (100.00)	11 (21.15)	41 (78.85)	52 (100.00)
Mahali	50	5	-	8 (17.78)	37 (82.22)	45 (100.00)	3 (37.50)	5 (62.50)	8 (100.00)
Munda	50	-	-	11 (22.00)	39 (78.00)	50 (100.00)	4 (36.36)	7 (63.64)	11 (100.00)
Bhumij	50	-	1	12 (24.49)	37 (75.51)	49 (100.00)	5 (41.67)	7 (58.33)	12 (100.00)

N.B. *Figures in the parentheses indicate percentages.*

TABLE 7.9
PREFERENCE OF FAMILY SIZE

Tribe	No. of family	No. of family without children	Choice of family size			Acceptance of Family Planning			No. of unmarried
			Large	Middle	Samll	Yes	No	Total	
WEST BENGAL									
Birhor	37	2	3	8	26	20	15	35	-
	(100.00)		(8.11)	(21.62)	(70.27)	(57.14)	(42.86)		
Lodha	100	9	9	12	79	44	47	91	-
	(100.00)		(9.00)	(12.00)	(79.00)	(48.35)	(51.65)		
Mahali	100	7	8	14	78	50	41	91	2
	(100.00)		(8.00)	(14.00)	(78.00)	(54.95)	(45.05)		
Santal	100	11	22	9	69	38	45	83	6
	(100.00)		(22.00)	(9.00)	(69.00)	(45.78)	(54.22)		
Munda	100	5	16	9	74	36	53	89	6
	(100.00)		(16.00)	(9.00)	(74.00)	(40.45)	(59.55)		

(*Contd.*)

Bhumij	100 (100.00)	9	13 (13.00)	6 (6.00)	81 (81.00)	42 (46.67)	48 (53.33)	90	1
ORISSA									
Lodha	50 (100.00)	8	6 (12.00)	1 (2.00)	43 (86.00)	28 (66.67)	14 (33.33)	42	-
Santal	50 (100.00)	1	17 (34.00)	4 (8.00)	29 (58.00)	26 (53.06)	23 (46.94)	49	-
BIHAR									
Birhor	100 (100.00)	8	39 (39.00)	3 (3.00)	58 (58.00)	-	90 (100.00)	90	2
Mahali	50 (100.00)	5	-	33 (66.00)	17 (34.00)	-	45 (100.00)	45	-
Munda	50 (100.00)	-	-	41 (82.00)	9 (18.00)	-	50 (100.00)	50	-
Bhumij	50 (100.00)	-	-	42 (84.00)	8 (16.00)	-	49 (100.00)	49	1

N.B. *Figures in the parentheses indicate percentages.*

TABLE 7.10
PARTICIPATION IN THE FAMILY PLANNING

Tribe	*No. of family*	*No. of unmarried women*	*No. of family without children*	*Acceptance of family planning programme*		
				Yes	*No*	*Total*
			WEST BENGAL			
Birhor	37	-	2	20 (57.14)	15 (42.86)	35 (100.00)
Lodha	100	-	9	44 (48.35)	47 (51.65)	91 (100.00)
Mahali	100	2	7	50 (54.95)	41 (45.05)	91 (100.00)
Santal	100	6	11	38 (45.78)	45 (54.22)	83 (100.00)
Munda	100	6	5	36 (40.45)	53 (59.55)	89 (100.00)
Bhumij	100	1	9	42 (46.67)	48 (53.33)	90 (100.00)
			ORISSA			
Lodha	50	-	8	28 (66.67)	14 (33.33)	42 (100.00)
Santal	50	-	1	26 (53.06)	23 (46.94)	49 (100.00)
			BIHAR			
Birhor	100	2	8	-	90 (100.00)	90 (100.00)
Mahali	50	-	5	-	45 (100.00)	45 (100.00)
Munda	50	-	-	-	50 (100.00)	50 (100.00)
Bhumij	50	1	-	-	49 (100.00)	49 (100.00)

N.B. *Figures in the parentheses indicate percentages.*

TABLE 7.11
FREQUENCY OF DISEASES

Tribe	No. of family	Problem of Eyesight			Headache			Weakness			Diarrhoea		
		F	M	C	F	M	C	F	M	C	F	M	C
WEST BENGAL													
Birhor	37	-	-	-	9	9	5	12	13	6	22.	20	20
					(24.32)	(24.32)	(13.51)	(32.43)	(35.14)	(16.22)	(59.46)	(54.05)	(54.05)
Lodha	100	12	21	-	24	9	1	41	14	1	17	21	53
		(12.00)	(21.00)		(24.00)	(9.00)	(1.00)	(41.00)	(14.00)	(1.00)	(17.00)	(21.00)	(53.00)
Mahali	100	24	26	-	38	14	1	69	18	1	11	11	9
		(24.00)	(26.00)		(38.00)	(14.00)	(1.00)	(69.00)	(18.00)	(1.00)	(11.00)	(11.00)	(9.00)
Santal	100	39	30	4	36	13	-	49	10	-	6	6	7
		(39.00)	(30.00)	(4.00)	(36.00)	(13.00)		(49.00)	(1.00)		(6.00)	(6.00)	(7.00)
Munda	100	25	17	1	22	9	1	36	18	-	19	21	22
		(25.00)	(17.00)	(1.00)	(22.00)	(9.00)	(1.00)	(36.00)	(18.00)		(19.00)	(21.00)	(22.00)

(Contd.)

Bhumij	100	18	11	2	23	6	-	38	9	-	13	18	15
		(18.00)	(11.00)	(2.00)	(23.00)	(6.00)		(38.00)	(9.00)		(13.00)	(18.00)	(15.00)
ORISSA													
Lodha	50	-	-	-	25	25	13	15	13	7	24	13	26
					(50.00)	(50.00)	(26.00)	(30.00)	(26.00)	(14.00)	(48.00)	(26.00)	(52.00)
Santal	50	2	-	-	32	26	22	28	19	15	40	16	3
		(4.00)			(64.00)	(52.00)	(44.00)	(56.00)	(38.00)	(15.00)	(80.00)	(32.00)	(6.00)
BIHAR													
Birhor	100	-	-	-	81	62	43	71	47	63	46	23	76
					(81.00)	(62.00)	(43.00)	(71.00)	(47.00)	(63.00)	(46.00)	(23.00)	(76.00)
Mahali	50	10	8	-	42	40	22	38	32	29	47	48	36
		(20.00)	(16.00)		(84.00)	(80.00)	(44.00)	(76.00)	(64.00)	(58.00)	(94.00)	(96.00)	(72.00)
Munda	50	5	7	-	35	32	21	34	32	24	46	44	32
		(10.00)	(14.00)		(70.00)	(64.00)	(42.00)	(68.00)	(64.00)	(48.00)	(92.00)	(88.00)	(64.00)
Bhumij	50	-	4	-	39	36	23	33	31	22	48	48	38
			(8.00)		(78.00)	(72.00)	(46.00)	(66.00)	(62.00)	(44.00)	(96.00)	(98.00)	(76.00)

(Contd.)

Tribe	No. of family	Skin disease			Cough and cold			Asthama			Malaria		
		F	M	C	F	M	C	F	M	C	F	M	C
WEST BENGAL													
Birhor	37	3	3	19	11	7	28	-	-	-	25	26	25
		(8.11)	(8.11)	(51.35)	(29.73)	(18.92)	(75.68)				(67.57)	(70.27)	(67.57)
Lodha	100	16	22	55	42	39	61	3	10	-	8	10	9
		(16.00)	(22.00)	(55.00)	(42.00)	(39.00)	(61.00)	(3.00)	(10.00)		(8.00)	(10.00)	(9.00)
Mahali	100	16	16	45	61	52	76	2	4	-	4	5	5
		(16.00)	(16.00)	(45.00)	(61.00)	(52.00)	(76.00)	(2.00)	(4.00)		(4.00)	(5.00)	(5.00)
Santal	100	10	13	58	23	14	43	2	3	-	4	4	-
		(10.00)	(13.00)	(58.00)	(23.00)	(14.00)	(43.00)	(2.00)	(3.00)		(4.00)	(4.00)	
Munda	100	16	13	39	42	39	51	1	7	-	6	10	7
		(16.00)	(13.00)	(39.00)	(42.00)	(39.00)	(51.00)	(1.00)	(7.00)		(6.00)	(10.00)	(10.00)
Bhumij	100	11	9	40	38	33	50	-	1	-	8	10	10
		(11.00)	(9.00)	(40.00)	(38.00)	(33.00)	(50.00)		(1.00)		(8.00)	(10.00)	(10.00)

(Contd.)

						ORISSA							
Lodha	50	12	4	18	16	24	26	-	-	-	41	29	24
		(24.00)	(8.00)	(36.00)	(32.00)	(48.00)	(52.00)				(82.00)	(58.00)	(48.00)
Santal	50	15	6	44	22	16	43	-	-	-	47	32	8
		(30.00)	(12.00)	(88.00)	(44.00)	(32.00)	(86.00)				(94.00)	(64.00)	(16.00)
						BIHAR							
Birhor	100	-	-	3	61	36	86	-	-	-	19	18	11
				(3.00)	(61.00)	(36.00)	(86.00)				(19.00)	(18.00)	(11.00)
Mahali	50	-	-	2	38	34	42	-	-	-	44	42	39
				(4.00)	(76.00)	(68.00)	(84.00)				(88.00)	(84.00)	(78.00)
Munda	50	-	-	3	37	39	41	-	-	-	45	48	36
				(6.00)	(74.00)	(78.00)	(82.00)				(90.00)	(96.00)	(72.00)
Bhumij	50	-	-	4	36	32	39	-	-	-	46	44	41
				(8.00)	(72.00)	(64.00)	(78.00)				(92.00)	(88.00)	(82.00)

(Contd.)

Tribe	No. of family	Tuberculosis			Worm			Dysentery			Fever		
		F	M	C	F	M	C	F	M	C	F	M	C
WEST BENGAL													
Birhor	37	-	-	-	-	-	-	37 (100.00)	37 (100.0)	37 (100.00)	37 (100.00)	37 (100.00)	37 (100.00)
Lodha	100	2 (2.00)	5 (5.00)	1 (1.00)	-	-	21 (21.00)	52 (52.00)	51 (51.00)	47 (47.00)	6 (6.00)	4 (4.00)	5 (5.00)
Mahali	100	-	1 (1.00)	-	-	1 (1.00)	28 (28.00)	50 (50.00)	46 (46.00)	16 (16.00)	39 (39.00)	32 (32.00)	7 (7.00)
Santal	100	4 (4.00)	3 (3.00)	-	-	-	60 (60.00)	30 (30.00)	27 (27.00)	12 (12.00)	30 (30.00)	31 (31.00)	9 (9.00)
Munda	100	-	4 (4.00)	-	2 (2.00)	-	37 (37.00)	48 (48.00)	57 (57.00)	46 (46.00)	4 (4.00)	3 (3.00)	2 (2.00)
Bhumij	100	-	2 (2.00)	-	1 (1.00)	3 (3.00)	15 (15.00)	31 (31.00)	27 (27.00)	37 (37.00)	11 (11.00)	10 (10.00)	5 (5.00)

(*Contd.*)

ORISSA													
Lodha	50	-	-	-	-	-	-	49	39	37	50	50	50
								(98.00)	(78.00)	(74.00)	(100.0)	(100.00)	(100.00)
Santal	50	-	-	-	-	-	30	49	49	41	50	50	50
							(60.00)	(98.00)	(98.00)	(82.00)	(100.0)	(100.00)	(100.00)
BIHAR													
Birhor	100	-	-	-	-	-	-	29	21	11	75	80	85
								(29.00)	(21.00)	(11.00)	(75.00)	(80.00)	(85.00)
Mahali	50	-	-	-	-	-	12	24	21	9	46	44	42
							(24.00)	(48.00)	(42.00)	(18.00)	(92.00)	(88.00)	(84.00)
Munda	50	-	-	-	-	-	6	24	28	13	47	42	44
							(12.00)	(48.00)	(56.00)	(26.00)	(94.00)	(84.00)	(88.00)
Bhumij	50	-	-	-	-	-	9	22	24	11	46	42	43
							(18.00)	(44.00)	(48.00)	(22.00)	(92.00)	(84.00)	(86.00)

N.B. *Figures in the parentheses indicate percentages.*

In case of the Lodha community men suffer more from the problem of eyesight, skin disease and asthma than women. On the other hand, women suffer more from headache and weakness than men whereas children of the Lodha community are more or less free from the diseases—problem of eyesight, headache, weakness, asthma and tuberculosis. Children suffer most from the diseases like diarrhoea, skin diseases and cough and cold.

In the Mahali community of West Bengal women are more affected by headache and weakness than men. The number of men and women of the tribal families suffering from the diseases of problem of eyesight, diarrhoea, skin disease and malaria are more or less the same. Children are highly affected by cough and cold and worm.

In the Santal community, women are more affected by the problem of eyesight, headache, weakness, cough and cold and dysentery than men. Men and women are more or less equally affected by diarrhoea, skin disease, asthma, tuberculosis and fever. The Santal children do not suffer from headache, weakness, asthma, malaria and tuberculosis, but they are seriously affected by skin disease and worms.

In the Munda community the number of women, suffering from the problem of eyesight, headache and weakness more than men. But the men in the Munda community suffer from diarrhoea, asthma, malaria, tuberculosis and dysentery more frequently than the women folk. Children are mostly affected by cough and cold and skin disease.

The female members of the Bhumij community are more affected by problem of eye sight, headache, weakness, skin disease and cough and cold than men. No female patient of asthma and tuberculosis is found in the Bhumij community.

From table 7.11 it has been observed that except the Birhor community, the remaining five surveyed communities of Midnapur district women are more affected by weakness and headache than men. Children greatly suffer from worms. Children of all six tribal communities are highly affected by cough and cold than adult male and female members. On the other hand, none of the children of six communities suffer from asthma.

In Orissa majority of the men, women and children of the Lodha community are free from the problem of eyesight, asthma and tuberculosis. Women and men of the Lodha community are equally affected by headache and fever. Except this the Lodha women are more affected by weakness, diarrhoea, skin disease, malaria and dysentery. It is also noticed from the table that the children are more affected by diarrhoea, skin disease and cough and cold than female and male members of this community.

It is observed from Table 7.11 that except dysentery and fever, (in which men and women of the Santal community are equally affected) asthma, tuberculosis, worms (in which men and women are totally free), women are more affected by the rest of the diseases than men. Men are free from the problem of eyesight, and the children are free from the problem of eyesight, asthma and tuberculosis.

In Bihar among the various diseases, the problem of eyesight is rarely seen among male and female members of all the three communities except the Birhor. Children of all four communities are free from the problem of eyesight.

It is observed from Table 7.11 that headache, weakness and diarrhoea are more prevalent among the female members of all four communities than male members. Skin disease is found only among the children. More or less male, female and children are equally affected by cough and cold. But on the other hand, asthma and tuberculosis are completely absent among the members of four communities.

The male, female and children of the Mahali, Munda and Bhumij communities are also more affected by malaria than the Birhor. But dysentery and fever are common diseases where the children are less affected by dysentery than fever.

TABLE 7.12
ARRANGEMENT OF ALTERNATIVES TO LOOK THE CHILD DURING ABSENCE

Tribe	No.of family	No. of unmar-ried women	No. of childless women	No. of children who need no care	Care taken by individual/institution					No. of children who need care
					Son/ daughter	Adult members	Neighbour	Children with working mother	children in school	
WEST BENGAL										
Birhor	37	-	2	10	21	4	-	-	-	25
					(84.00)	(16.00)				(100.00)
Lodha	100	-	9	11	37	27	9	3	4	80
					(46.25)	(33.75)	(11.25)	(3.75)	(5.00)	(100.00)
Mahali	100	2	6	23	49	14	2	-	4	69
					(71.01)	(20.29)	(2.90)		(5.80)	(100.00)
Santal	100	6	9	14	39	18	4	9	1	71
					(54.93)	(25.35)	(5.63)	(12.68)	(1.42)	(100.00)
Munda	100	6	5	15	38	21	6	3	6	74
					(51.35)	(28.38)	(8.11)	(4.05)	(8.11)	(100.00)

(Contd.)

Bhumij	100	1	8	15	33	17	16	6	4	76
					(43.42)	(22.37)	(21.05)	(7.89)	(5.26)	(100.00)
						ORISSA				
Lodha	50	-	3	22	20	5	-	-	-	25
					(80.00)	(20.00)				(100.00)
Santal	50	-	1	7	32	10	-	-	-	42
					(76.19)	(23.81)				(100.00)
						BIHAR				
Birhor	100	2	8	30	40	20	-	-	-	60
					(66.67)	(33.33)				(100.00)
Mahali	50	-	5	14	23	4	-	-	4	31
					(74.19)	(12.90)			(12.90)	(100.00)
Munda	50	-	-	11	33	3	-	2	1	39
					(84.62)	(7.69)		(5.13)	(2.56)	(100.00)
Bhumij	50	1	-	18	25	3	-	1	2	31
					(80.65)	(9.68)		(3.23)	(6.45)	(100.00)

N.B. *Figures in the parentheses indicate percentages.*

In the Birhor community it is observed that in maximum households (84.00 per cent) the elder son or daughter takes care of his/her younger brother or sister in the absence of his/her parents (Table 7.12).

It is observed in the Lodha community that out of 80 families where children need care in absence of their parents at home, in 46.25 per cent families, the elder son or daughter takes care of the children and in 33.75 per cent families, adult members—grandfather or grand-mother take care of the children.

In the Mahali community of West Bengal we observe that out of 69 families (where children need care in absence of their parents), the children are taken care of in 71.01 per cent families by their elder brother or sister, in 20.19 per cent families by adult members, in 2.90 per cent families by neighbours. In 5.80 per cent families children go to school when their parents are engaged in cultivation work in fields.

In the Santal community out of 100 surveyed women, 6 are unmarried, 9 are childless; the children of 14 families need no care and the children of 71 families need care when their parents are engaged in field. Out of 71 families, in 54.93 per cent families the children are taken care of by their elder brother or sister, 25.35 per cent families by adult members, in 5.63 per cent families by the neighbour and in 12.68 per cent families where the mothers take their children with her in the field.

In case of the Munda it is observed that in maximum cases (51.35 per cent) children are cared by elder brother or sister in absence of their parents. There are very few families in villages where neighbour take care of the children.

More or less the same picture is found in the Bhumij community. Here, also the children of maximum families (43.42 per cent) are cared by elder son or daughter when their parents are involved in agricultural work.

It is found from the Table 7.12 that both in the Lodha and Santal community of Mayurbhanj district in Orissa children are taken care of by the elder sons or daughters and the adult members of the family. Out of 25 Lodha households, the children of 80.00 per cent families are taken care of by the elder brother or sister. Out of 42 Santal households in 76.19 per cent families elder son or daughter take care of younger children whereas in 23.81 per cent families children are taken care of by adult members of the family.

In Bihar, in maximum number of cases the children are taken care of by their elder brothers or sisters. In the Mahali and Bhumij communities out of 50, there are 31 families where children need care. The children of 74.19 per cent Mahali and 80.65 per cent Bhumij are taken care of by sons or daughters. In case of the Munda the number is more or less the same. In these three communities, it has been observed, that in very few families, children are looked after adult members in absence of their mothers. In the Birhor community out of 100 families the children of 60 families need care where the children of 66.67 per cent families are taken care of by elder brothers or sisters and 33.33 per cent by adult members.

It is clear that in tribal societies a good number of children are looked after by their elder brothers and sisters. It is one of the important reasons for which the parents are not willing to send their children to school.

8

Opinions and Attitudes

This chapter deals with the attitudes and opinions of the respondents regarding their life situation.

Table 8.1 depicts married women's perceived position in husband's families. The married respondents of the Lodha, Mahali, Santal, Munda and Bhumij in West Bengal take upon themselves (in more than 50.00 per cent cases) the roles of decision-makers in their families whereas in the other communities in the states of Orissa, Bihar and West Bengal—the Birhor of Purulia, the women do not assume this role in their husbands' family. On the other hand, the women in all communities and states express that their position in husbands' families is good. So it is evident that their position in the family is not affected by whether they take part in decision making or not. In most of the cases they have less awareness regarding the various roles that are performed by women in their families.

Table 8.2 shows that in most of the cases the majority of the tribal women are less aware of different activities in the political field. All tribal women of Bihar and especially the Lodha in Orissa are totally unaware of political events. On the other hand, the Santal women in Orissa (26.00 per cent) and the other tribals of Midnapur district like the Lodha, Santal, Munda, and Bhumij (more than 75 per cent) strongly favour participation of women in political fields and the Birhors of Purulia are not an exceptional one (nearly 50.00 per cent of women of this community also favour it).

So the tribal women of the district of Midnapur in West Bengal seem to be more progressive than their counterparts in other places.

TABLE 8.1
PERCEIVED ROLE OF WOMAN IN HUSBAND'S FAMILY

Tribe	*No. of Respondent*	*Right to take Decision*		*Nature of Position*		*No. of Unmarried Women*
		Yes	*No*	*Favourable*	*Unfavourable*	
WEST BENGAL						
Birhor	37	-	37 (100.00)	37 (100.00)	-	-
Lodha	100	50 (50.00)	50 (50.00)	91 (91.00)	9 (09.00)	-
Mahali	100	81 (81.00)	17 (17.00)	95 (95.00)	3 (03.00)	2 (2.00)
Santal	100	74 (74.00)	20 (20.00)	82 (82.00)	12 (12.00)	6 (6.00)
Munda	100	62 (62.00)	32 (32.00)	87 (87.00)	7 (07.00)	6 (6.00)
Bhumij	100	58 (58.00)	41 (41.00)	83 (83.00)	16 (16.00)	1 (1.00)
ORISSA						
Lodha	50	6 (12.00)	44 (88.00)	50 (100.00)	-	-
Santal	50	3 (06.00)	47 (94.00)	50 (100.00)	-	-
BIHAR						
Birhor	100	-	98 (98.00)	98 (98.00)	-	2 (2.00)
Mahali	50	-	50 (100.00)	42 (84.00)	8 (16.00)	-
Munda	50	-	50 (100.00)	45 (90.00)	5 (10.00)	-
Bhumij	50	-	49 (98.00)	47 (94.00)	2 (4.00)	1 (2.00)

N. B. *Figures in the parentheses indicate percentages.*

TABLE 8.2
WOMEN'S OPINIONS ABOUT POLITICAL PARTICIPATION

Tribe	*No. of Respondent*	*Political Participation*	
		Unjustified	*Justified*
		WEST BENGAL	
Birhor	37	19 (51.35)	18 (48.65)
Lodha	100	20 (20.00)	80 (80.00)
Mahali	100	18 (18.00)	82 (82.00)
Santal	100	25 (25.00)	75 (75.00)
Munda	100	15 (15.00)	85 (85.00)
Bhumij	100	26 (26.00)	74 (74.00)
		ORISSA	
Lodha	50	50 (100.00)	-
Santal	50	37 (74.00)	13 (26.00)
		BIHAR	
Birhor	100	100 (100.00)	-
Mahali	50	50 (100.00)	-
Munda	50	50 (100.00)	-
Bhumij	50	50 (100.00)	

N. B. *Figures in the parentheses indicate percentages.*

Differences of opinion regarding the birth of the child (preference of sex) have been recorded in Table 8.3. It has been observed from the table that the women of Birhor community in West Bengal and Bihar and the women of Lodha and Santal in Orissa do not express strong preference for a particular sex, especially for the male, though in few cases females are mentioned by them. Regarding the acceptance of male and female children they have no such preference. But on the other hand, the tribal women of the Mahali, Munda and Bhumij in Bihar hold a completely different opinion, where majority of the women show their preference for male child and in few cases the alternate preferences are mentioned too. But in the case of West Bengal, the tribal women in Midnapur district show their slow increasing trend of preference for male child than female, though, in majorityy of the cases there is no distinction regarding the preference of sex.

Regarding the causes of preference for male children particularly in Bihar is because of the view that male children will stay and look after their families when the parents will be old. But in West Bengal, in Midnapur particularly, the tribal women gradually changed their views and prefer male children due to the emerging dowry system by which they are acculturized with other caste people.

Table 8.4 depicts different opinions of women regarding

(a) age for marriage of women,

(b) early marriage of female, and

(c) preferred type of marriage.

Four important age groups starting from below 15 to 21 years, have been considered for the age of marriage of the women. Variations are observed from the opinions of the tribal women belonging to various states. Maximum number of tribal women (the Mahali, Munda and Bhumij) in Bihar opine that the marriage of the female should be fixed at 15 to 18 years whereas the Birhor community in the same state slightly deviates from this opinion, 60.00 per cent of Birhor women prefer 18 to 21 years, as the age for marriage. On the other hand, for the Birhors in West Bengal maximum umber of women prefer 15 to 18 years of age group for marriage. The rest of the tribal women in the State of West Bengal and Orissa share a similar opinion. Majority of them in all these communities — Lodha, Mahali, Santal, Munda and Bhumij in West Bengal; Lodha and Santal in Orissa prefer 18-21 years as the age for marriage. They are not in favour of early marriage. Exceptions of course are provided by the Birhors in Purulia.

TABLE 8.3
PREFERENCE OF SEX OF CHILD

Tribe	No. of Respondent	Preference of sex		
		Male	Female	No Preference
		WEST BENGAL		
Birhor	37	-	2 (05.41)	35 (94.59)
Lodha	100	28 (28.00)	3 (03.00)	69 (69.00)
Mahali	100	12 (12.00)	-	88 (88.00)
Santal	100	13 (13.00)	-	87 (87.00)
Munda	100	32 (32.00)	-	68 (68.00)
Bhumij	100	24 (24.00)	1 (01.00)	75 (75.00)
		ORISSA		
Lodha	50	-	4 (08.00)	46 (92.00)
Santal	50	-	7 (14.00)	43 (86.00)
		BIHAR		
Birhor	100	-	6 (06.00)	94 (94.00)
Mahali	50	30 (60.00)	12 (24.00)	8 (16.00)
Munda	50	38 (76.00)	7 (14.00)	5 (10.00)
Bhumij	50	42 (84.00)	1 (02.00)	7 (14.00)

N. B. *Figures in the parentheses indicate percentages.*

TABLE 8.4
OPINION IN RESPECT OF MARRIAGE

Tribe	No. of Respondent	Proper age at marriage				Early marriage of female		Type of marriage preferable		
		Below 15	15-18	18-21	21+	Justified	Unjustified	Negotiation	Love	Both
					WEST BENGAL					
Birhor	37	-	29	8	-	15	22	37	-	-
			(78.38)	(21.62)		(40.54)	(59.46)	(100.00)		
Lodha	100	15	35	46	4	26	74	96	1	3
		(15.00)	(35.00)	(46.00)	(04.00)	(26.00)	(74.00)	(96.00)	(01.00)	(03.00)
Mahali	100	4	24	71	1	14	86	100	-	-
		(04.00)	(24.00)	(71.00)	(01.00)	(14.00)	(86.00)	(100.00)		
Santal	100	5	30	61	4	29	71	86	-	14
		(05.00)	(30.00)	(61.00)	(04.00)	(29.00)	(71.00)	(86.00)		(14.00)
Munda	100	4	27	57	12	16	84	97	-	3
		(04.00)	(27.00)	(57.00)	(12.00)	(16.00)	(84.00)	(97.00)		(03.00)
Bhumij	100	3	23	64	10	12	88	89	5	6
		(03.00)	(23.00)	(64.00)	(10.00)	(12.00)	(88.00)	(89.00)	(05.00)	(06.00)

(Contd)

Tribe	No. of Respondent	Proper age at marriage				Early marriage of female		Type of marriage preferable		
		Below 15	15-18	18-21	21+	Justified	Unjustified	Negotiation	Love	Both
ORISSA										
Lodha	50	-	23	27	-	-	50	50	-	-
			(46.00)	(54.00)			(100.00)	(100.00)		
Santal	50	-	16	34	-	3	47	50	-	-
			(32.00)	(68.00)		(06.00)	(94.00)	(100.00)		
BIHAR										
Birhor	100	-	40	60	-	5	95	100	-	-
			(40.00)	(60.00)		(05.00)	(95.00)	(100.00)		
Mahali	50	7	40	3	-	36	14	50	-	-
		(14.00)	(80.00)	(06.00)		(72.00)	(28.00)	(100.00)		
Munda	50	9	39	2	-	41	9	50	-	-
		(18.00)	(78.00)	(04.00)		(82.00)	(18.00)	(100.00)		
Bhumij	50	4	42	4	-	39	11	50	-	-
		(08.00)	(84.00)	(08.00)		(78.00)	(22.00)	(100.00)		

N.B. *Figures in the parentheses indicate percentages.*

Maximum number of tribal women in West Bengal and Orissa assume that the early marriage of female is not good for the society. The Birhors in Bihar also agree with this opinion but the differences of opinion have been observed in the case of the Mahali, Munda and Bhumij in Bihar. They strike a favourable attitude towards early marriage.

Regarding preferential marriage most of the tribal women belonging to all states show their preference for 'negotiation' marriage. Marriage by love or selection of the spouses by each other is totally rejected by them.

From Table 8.5 the differences of opinion are observed regarding inheritance of parents' property by female and rights to inherit property equally by male and female both. Majority of the tribal women in Bihar, Orissa and Birhor women in West Bengal express a negative attitude towards inheritance of property by female. On the other hand, majority of the tribal women in the district of Midnapur in West Bengal have a favourable attitude regarding the inheritance of property by female and also they claim for equal rights to get the parent's property through male and female children.

Table 8.6 deals with the data, regarding the responses of all female informants about whether divorce is approved or not in society, position of female divorcee and position of male divorcee in the eyes of the respondents.

In case of Birhor in Purulia (W.B.) all (37.00 per cent) the respondents have said that divorce is not approved in society but it is found that all of them have said that the position of female and male divorcees in their eyes are good.

Considering the Lodha community of W.B. it has been observed that 65.00 per cent respondents have said that divorce is approved in society. Again 80.00 per cent of them have said that the position of female divorcee in their eyes is bad and 89.00 per cent respondents have said that the position of male divorcee in their eyes is bad.

TABLE 8.5
INHERITANCE OF PROPERITY

Tribe	No. of Respon-dent	Right to inherit parent's property by female		Right to inherit equally with male	
		Justified	Unjustified	Justified	Unjustified
		WEST BENGAL			
Birhor	37	-	37 (100.00)	-	37 (100.00)
Lodha	100	60 (60.00)	40 (40.00)	39 (39.00)	61 (61.00)
Mahali	100	76 (76.00)	24 (24.00)	33 (33.00)	67 (67.00)
Santal	100	79 (79.00)	21 (21.00)	40 (40.00)	60 (60.00)
Munda	100	66 (66.00)	34 (34.00)	47 (47.00)	53 (53.00)
Bhumij	100	80 (80.00)	20 (20.00)	54 (54.00)	46 (46.00)
		ORISSA			
Lodha	50	-	50 (100.00)	-	50 (100.00)
Santal	50	-	50 (100.00)	-	50 (100.00)
		BIHAR			
Birhor	100	-	100 (100.00)	-	100 (100.00)
Mahali	50	7 (14.00)	43 (86.00)	11 (22.00)	39 (78.00)
Munda	50	4 (8.00)	46 (92.00)	3 (06.00)	47 (94.00)
Bhumij	50	9 (18.00)	41 (82.00)	8 (16.00)	42 (84.00)

N. B. *Figures in the parentheses indicate percentages.*

Out of 100 Mahali respondents 84.00 per cent have said that divorce is approved in society. In the second case 75.00 per cent respondents have said that the position of female divorcee in their eyes is bad whereas in case of position of male divorcee in the eyes of respondents, 80.00 per cent of them have said that it is bad.

In West Bengal out of 100 Santal respondents 96.00 per cent respondents have said that divorce is approved in society whereas only 4.00 per cent of them have said that it is not approved. 75.00 of the respondents have said that the position of female divorcee in their eyes is bad and in case of position of male divorcee in the eyes of the respondent 85.00 per cent have said that it is bad.

Among the respondents of Munda community 24.00 per cent have said that divorce is not approved in society whereas 24.00 per cent have said that in their eyes the position of female divorcee is good and in the eyes of 19.00 per cent respondents the position of male divorcee is good.

In the case of Bhumij only 20.00 per cent respondents have said that divorce is not approved in society whereas 31.00 per cent of respondents have said that the position of female divorcee in their eyes is good and only 13.00 per cent have said that the position of male divorcee is good.

All the Lodha respondents of Orissa have said that divorce is not approved in their society but it has been observed that 84.00 per cent of them have said that the position of female and male divorcees in their eyes is good.

In the case of the Santal of Orissa out of 50 respondents only 4.00 per cent have said that divorce is approved in their society whereas 88.00 per cent respondents have said that the position of both female and male divorcees in their eyes is good.

But in Bihar, majority (more than 90.00 per cent) of the four tribal communities — Birhor, Mahali, Munda and Bhumij have opined that divorce is not approved in their society. Regarding the position of female and male divorcee no extreme opinion can be observed though in all cases 'good position' is occupied by the male divorcees.

It has also been observed that except the Birhors in Purulia, the majority of tribal respondents (women) in the Midnapur district, West Bengal have replied that the position of divorcee is not good. But in the other states like Orissa and Bihar majority of the tribal women have replied that the position of divorcee is not bad.

TABLE 8.6
ATTITUDE TO DIVORCE

Tribe	No. of respondent	Divorce in society		Position of female divorcee		Position of male divorcee	
		Approved	Not approved	Good	Bad	Good	Bad
WEST BENGAL							
Birhor	37	-	37 (100.00)	37 (100.00)	-	37 (100.00)	-
Lodha	100	65 (65.00)	35 (35.00)	20 (20.00)	80 (80.00)	11 (11.00)	89 (89.00)
Mahali	100	84 (84.00)	16 (16.00)	25 (25.00)	75 (75.00)	20 (20.00)	80 (80.00)
Santal	100	96 (96.00)	4 (04.00)	25 (25.00)	75 (75.00)	15 (15.00)	85 (85.00)
Munda	100	76 (76.00)	24 (24.00)	43 (43.00)	57 (57.00)	19 (19.00)	81 (81.00)
Bhumij	100	80 (80.00)	20 (20.00)	31 (31.00)	69 (69.00)	13 (13.00)	87 (87.00)

(Contd.)

Tribe	No. of respondent	Divorce in society		Position of female divorcee		Position of male divorcee	
		Approved	Not approved	Good	Bad	Good	Bad
				ORISSA			
Lodha	50	-	50 (100.00)	42 (84.00)	8 (16.00)	42 (84.00)	8 (16.00)
Santal	50	2 (04.00)	48 (96.00)	44 (88.00)	6 (12.00)	44 (88.00)	6 (12.00)
				BIHAR			
Birhor	100	-	100 (100.00)	59 (59.00)	41 (41.00)	59 (59.00)	41 (41.00)
Mahali	50	3 (06.00)	47 (94.00)	35 (70.00)	15 (30.00)	29 (58.00)	21 (42.00)
Munda	50	4 (08.00)	46 (92.00)	38 (76.00)	12 (24.00)	30 (60.00)	20 (40.00)
Bhumij	50	5 (10.00)	45 (90.00)	33 (66.00)	17 (34.00)	26 (52.00)	24 (48.00

N.B. *Figures In the parentheses indicate percentages.*

Considering the right of the women to divorce it has been observed that the Birhors in Purulia, W.B., as well as in Hazaribagh, Bihar, and the Lodha in Orissa reflect the same trend where the women of those communities have expressed their views that the right of the women to divorce is unjustified, whereas the other tribal communities like the Lodha, Mahali, Santal, Munda and Bhumij of W.B. have expressed that it is justified. The majority of the women of the rest tribal communities of Orissa and Bihar have replied that the right of the women in divorce is justified (8.7).

Table 8.8 depicts the opinion of the tribal women regarding remarriage of the widow. Majority of the tribal women (60.00 per cent - 69.00 per cent) except the Lodha of Midnapur district justified their opinion for widow remarriage. But in Bihar majority of the tribal women consider just as the Lodha of Orissa that widow remarriage is unjustified. But most of the tribal women belonging to all states and districts strongly express their opinions that the position of widow is good in their societies.

It has been observed from the Table 8.9 that all tribal communities and their families mainly depend on allopathic treatment. In all cases cent per cent families depend only on allopathic treatment. But initially in some cases, they depend on local herbal medicines but finally they have to rely on allopathic medicines.

Regarding medical facilities of their villages maximum number of tribal women in West Bengal and Orissa have expressed their satisfaction with the same. But in Bihar, except the Birhor, the tribal communities (Mahali, Munda and Bhumij) are not satisfied with medical arrangements.

Maximum number of respondents in all states and districts express their positive opinion regarding the improved medical facilities in comparison to what existed during the last ten years. Except Birhor in Bihar, the rest of the sample tribal population like the Mahali, Munda, and Bhumij opine that their societies are more affected by diseases, but the other tribal communities in West Bengal and Orissa express more favourable opinions because they observe that their societies are less affected by various diseases in the context of last ten years.

So from the overall observation it is evident that they are satisfied with improved medical facilities.

TABLE 8.7
DIVORCE AND SOCIETY'S REACTION

Tribe	*No. of Respondent*	*Position of divorce in society*		*Right of the women to divorce*	
		Good	*Bad*	*Justified*	*Unjustified*
		WEST BENGAL			
Birhor	37	37 (100.00)	-	4 (10.81)	33 (89.19)
Lodha	100	19 (19.00)	81 (81.00)	56 (56.00)	44 (44.00)
Mahali	100	25 (25.00)	75 (75.00)	76 (76.00)	24 (24.00)
Santal	100	25 (25.00)	75 (75.00)	88 (88.00)	12 (12.00)
Munda	100	37 (37.00)	63 (63.00)	52 (52.00)	48 (48.00)
Bhumij	100	23 (23.00)	77 (77.00)	77 (77.00)	23 (23.00)
		ORISSA			
Lodha	50	42 (84.00)	8 (16.00)	41 (82.00)	9 (18.00)
Santal	50	44 (88.00)	6 (12.00)	5 (10.00)	45 (90.00)
		BIHAR			
Birhor	100	59 (59.00)	41 (41.00)	3 (06.00)	97 (97.00)
Mahali	50	35 (70.00)	15 (30.00)	38 (76.00)	12 (24.00)
Munda	50	32 (64.00)	18 (36.00)	40 (80.00)	10 (20.00)
Bhumij	50	36 (72.00)	14 (28.00)	35 (70.00)	15 (30.00)

N.B. *Figures in the parentheses indicate percentages.*

Table 8.10 represents the attitude of the respondents towards happy life. Respondents express different opinions regarding happy life which includes (*a*) sufficient money, (*b*) better accommodation, (*c*) adequate food, (*d*) favourable environment, (*e*) employment opportunity for children, and (*f*) communal facilities such as supply of water, medical, facility, good communication etc.

TABLE 8.8
WIDOW REMARRIAGE

Tribe	*No. of respon-dent*	*Widow marriage*		*Widow's position in the society*	
		Justified	*Unjustified*	*Good*	*Bad*
		WEST BENGAL			
Birhor	37	25 (67.57)	12 (32.43)	36 (97.30)	1 (02.70)
Lodha	100	45 (45.00)	55 (55.00)	83 (83.00)	17 (17.00)
Mahali	100	68 (68.00)	32 (32.00)	84 (84.00)	16 (16.00)
Santal	100	69 (69.00)	31 (31.00)	81 (81.00)	19 (19.00)
Munda	100	59 (59.00)	41 (41.00)	88 (88.00)	12 (12.00)
Bhumij	100	65 (65.00)	35 (35.00)	83 (83.00)	17 (17.00)
		ORISSA			
Lodha	50	23 (46.00)	27 (54.00)	43 (86.00)	7 (14.00)
Santal	50	43 (86.00)	7 (14.00)	44 (88.00)	6 (12.00)
		BIHAR			
Birhor	100	6 (06.00)	94 (94.00)	61 (61.00)	39 (39.00)
Mahali	50	23 (46.00)	27 (54.00)	36 (72.00)	14 (28.00)
Munda	50	22 (44.00)	28 (56.00)	34 (68.00)	16 (32.00)
Bhumij	50	18 (36.00)	32 (64.00)	31 (62.00)	19 (38.00)

N.B. *Figures in the parenthesesindicate percentages.*

In Birhor community all are in support of 'sufficient money' to ensure a happy life. 'Sufficient food' is also as important as 'sufficient money' (as mentioned by 89.19 per cent) of the respondents. None of the respondents stress the factor of 'employment opportunity for children' for a happy life.

In Lodha community it is observed that maximum people feel that 'sufficient money' is the main factor for a happy life.

TABLE 8.9
PREFERENCE OF TREATMENT

Tribe	*No. of family*	*Physician*				
		Allopathy	*Home-opathy*	*Allo.+ Hom.*	*Quack*	*Allo.+ Quack*
		WEST BENGAL				
Birhor	37	35 (94.59)	-	-	-	2 (05.41)
Lodha	100	85 (85.00)	-	3 (03.00)	4 (04.00)	8 (08.00)
Mahali	100	91 (91.00)	-	2 (02.00)	3 (03.00)	4 (04.00)
Santal	100	81 (81.00)	1 (01.00)	4 (04.00)	-	14 (14.00)
Munda	100	84 (84.00)	3 (03.00)	7 (07.00)	-	6 (06.00)
Bhumij	100	73 (73.00)	3 (03.00)	12 (12.00)	-	12 (12.00)
		ORISSA				
Lodha	50	50 (100.00)	-	-	-	-
Santal	50	50 (100.00)	-	-	-	-
		BIHAR				
Birhor	100	100 (100.00)	-	-	-	-
Mahali	50	6 (12.00)	-	-	11 (22.00)	33 (66.00)
Munda	50	6 (12.00)	-	-	11 (22.00)	33 (66.00)
Bhumij	50	10 (20.00)	-	-	5 (10.00)	35 (70.00)

(Contd.)

Medical facilities			*Improvement in last 10 years*		*Frequency of disease*	
Very good	*Good*	*Bad*	*Yes*	*No*	*Decreased*	*Increased*
			WEST BENGAL			
37	-	-	32	5		
(100.00)			(86.49)	(13.51)		
70	22	8	83	17	67	33
(70.00)	(22.00)	(08.00)	(83.00)	(17.00)	(67.00)	(33.00)
87	7	6	97	3	88	12
(87.00)	(07.00)	(06.00)	(97.00)	(03.00)	(88.00)	(12.00)
80	12	8	92	8	66	34
(80.00)	(12.00)	(08.00)	(92.00)	(08.00)	(66.00)	(34.00)
54	41	5	76	24	75	25
(54.00)	(41.00)	(05.00)	(76.00)	(24.00)	(75.00)	(25.00)
72	21	7	71	29	65	35
(72.00)	(21.00)	(07.00)	(71.00)	(29.00)	(65.00)	(35.00)
			ORISSA			
50	-	-	50	-	50	-
(100.00)			(100.00)		(100.00)	
50	-	-	50	-	50	-
(100.00)			(100.00)		(100.00)	
			BIHAR			
100	-	-	100	-	100	-
(100.00)			(100.00)		(100.00)	
-	17	33	36	14	11	39
	(34.00)	(66.00)	(72.00)	(28.00)	(22.00)	(78.00)
-	16	34	39	11	9	41
	(32.00)	(68.00)	(78.00)	(22.00)	(18.00)	(82.00)
-	17	33	33	17	8	42
	(34.00)	(66.00)	(66.00)	(34.00)	(16.00)	(84.00)

N.B. *Figures in the parentheses ndicate percentages.*

In Mahali community maximum number of respondents (91.00 per cent) speak of 'sufficient money', next (70.00 per cent) respondents mention 'sufficient food' as a requirement for happy life.

TABLE 8.10
IDEAS OF BETTER LIFE

Tribe	*No. of family*	*Sufficient money*	*Better accommodation*	*Sufficient food*	*Favourable Environment*	*Employment opportunity for children*	*Communal facility*
				WEST BENGAL			
Birhor	37	37 (100.00)	7 (18.92)	33 (89.19)	6 (16.22)	-	16 (43.24)
Lodha	100	85 (85.00)	59 (59.00)	62 (62.00)	32 (32.00)	09 (09.00)	50 (50.00)
Mahali	100	91 (91.00)	77 (77.00)	70 (70.00)	28 (28.00)	18 (18.00)	77 (77.00)
Santal	100	79 (79.00)	60 (60.00)	56 (56.00)	30 (30.00)	12 (12.00)	78 (78.00)
Munda	100	82 (82.00)	55 (55.00)	77 (77.00)	25 (25.00)	20 (20.00)	53 (53.00)
Bhumij	100	74 (74.00)	63 (53.00)	60 (60.00)	39 (39.00)	17 (17.00)	59 (59.00)

(Contd.)

Tribe	*No. of family*	*Sufficient money*	*Better accommod-ation*	*Sufficient food*	*Favourable Environment*	*Employment opportunity for children*	*Communal facility*
				ORISSA			
Lodha	50	50 (100.00)	21 (42.00)	46 (92.00)	9 (18.00)	2 (04.00)	28 (56.00)
Santal	50	49 (98.00)	34 (68.00)	47 (94.00)	17 (34.00)	9 (18.00)	29 (58.00)
				BIHAR			
Birhor	100	100 (100.00)	98 (98.00)	88 (88.00)	12 (12.00)	2 (02.00)	43 (43.00)
Mahali	50	48 (96.00)	45 (90.00)	40 (80.00)	15 (30.00)	16 (32.00)	25 (50.00)
Munda	50	46 (92.00)	41 (82.00)	39 (78.00)	17 (34.00)	36 (72.00)	31 (62.00)
Bhumij	50	45 (90.00)	44 (88.00)	43 (86.00)	20 (40.00)	43 (86.00)	39 (78.00)

N.B. *Figures in the parentheses indicate percentages.*

Among the Santal community to 79.00 per cent women, happy life means 'sufficient money', to 60.00 per cent women 'better accommodation', and to 78.00 per cent 'communal facility'.

In Munda community 82.00 per cent respondents are in favour of 'sufficient money' as a way to have a happy life. From the answers of 77.00 per cent respondents it is found that 'sufficient food' is also an important factor.

In Bhumij community 74.00 per cent women speak of happy life which comes through 'sufficient money'. 'Better accommodation' and 'sufficient food' are also mentioned by them —63.00 per cent and 60.00 per cent respectively.

In Orissa both in the Lodha (100.00 per cent) and Santal (98.00 per cent) communities' women respondents consider 'sufficient money, as one of the important factors of happy life. Except this, they also include 'sufficient food' for making a man happy. Out of 50 informants of each community 58.00 per cent of the Santal women and 56.00 per cent of the Lodha women mention different communal facilities for making a happy life.

In Bihar all tribal groups have mentioned 'sufficient money' as a prime factor for happy life. In Mahali community 80.00 per cent responses are in favour of 'sufficient food', which is 86.00 per cent in Bhumij, 78.00 per cent in Munda and 88.00 per cent in Birhor communities to ensure a happy life. But in Bihar except a few of the Birhor community, 'employment opportunity for children' is also considered as one of the factors of happy life. In comparison to the other communities Bhumij people attach more importance (86.00 per cent) to it as well as to communal facility (78.00 per cent).

9
Policy Recommendations

The tribal women are backward in all respects in comparison to the general non-tribal people of the country. They suffer from extreme poverty, massive illiteracy and many other allied problems. The prestige they receive from their society is by no means unequal to that enjoyed by their male counterparts. This is mainly because the women in tribal societies take more or less equal responsibility in the economic sphere, help their families financially, and receive the honour of having equal status from the members of the society. In their families and also in the society in which they live they have opinions and different roles to play in the decision-making process. In short, tribal society allows more liberty to the subjugated sex. They are free to choose their partners and equally free to divorce them and select new partners. Widow remarriage is also permissible and selection of a new husband can be made either from their own families or from their own community. Female children are not unwanted in their society.

II

Apart from this the tribal women have several problems, but a few are highlighted by the researcher through this project where their problems are categorised into four different parts—occupational, educational, problems in their living pattern and problems of awareness and attitude towards better living. The last part of this chapter deals with some suggestions, and some recommendations have been for their development.

In this book the six tribal communities, identified by

hunting-gathering economy (Lodha and Birhor), basket-making profession (Mahali), settled agriculturist trends (Santal and Munda) and Hinduised tribal characteristics (Bhumij), who live in a similar ecological setting, have been studied in detail. The study shows that the tribal people are more conservative in nature and are always trying to engage themselves with their traditional occupations through which they try to maintain their core on traditional culture, where most of the time, the welfare programmes fail to do any good for them.

It is found that all sample women irrespective of tribes and states participate in economic activities and all females are earners. This may be due to their poor socio-economic condition, or perhaps in a tribal society the idea of gender role has not yet so much developed. In case of the Birhor (Purulia, W.B. and Hazaribagh, Bihar) all tribal women are associated with their traditional economy, rope-making along with cultivation and daily labour, which substantially further their family income. Among the Mahalis (Midnapur, W.B. and Singhbum, Bihar) the same trend has been observed, where almost all women are engaged in basket making along with cultivation and daily labour. Among the Santals, (Midnapur, W.B. and Mayurbhanj, Orissa) most of the women are engaged in different types of agricultural activities, only a few are occupied with other non-agricultural pursuits. 2.67 per cent women are permanent service holders. In case of the Lodha (Midnapur, W.B. and Mayurbhanj, Orissa) a different category of occupational activities has been observed. Most of the Lodha women in Midnapur district are engaged in agricultural activities as they are now settled in different villages too far from the forest. Hunting gathering economy no more sustains their traditional economy. But the Lodhas in Mayurbhanj mainly depend on forest and forest products. There, majority of them are engaged in different types of work associated with the raw materials provided by the forest, though a few of them are engaged in agricultural labour. Most of the Munda and Bhumij women of Midnapur, West Bengal and Singhbhum (Bihar) are associated with agricultural activities, except a few who are housewives.

Majority of the tribal women (housewives) earn Rs. 15 to Rs. 30 daily irrespective of states and groups. Most of the five tribal communities in Midnapur district have expressed their satisfaction regarding their occupation. But the Birhor in Purulia, W.B. are not satisfied. In Orissa among the Lodha and Santal, majority of them of which the Lodha are more (72 per cent) in number express their dissatisfaction with jobs. But in Bihar majority of the tribal women (not more than 60 per cent) are not satisfied with their present occupational status. Regarding income, majority of the tribal women in West Bengal are not satisfied but in case of the Santal and Bhumij women show little satisfaction, which is better than the other tribal groups. In Orissa and Bihar, the majority of the sample tribal population express their dissatisfaction with their income.

Considering the nature of their annual family income it has been observed that majority of the tribal family about (80 per cent), Birhor, Lodha, Mahali, Munda, Bhumij earn Rs. 5001 to Rs. 15000. But in case of the Santal only 56 per cent belong to the above mentioned category while the rest (38 per cent) earn more than Rs. 15001 annually. In Orissa each of the majority of the Lodha and Santal families earn annually Rs. 5001 to Rs. 15000. In Bihar majority of the sample tribes earn Rs. 5000 to 15000 annually, and the annual family income of 10 per cent Bhumij families' is above Rs. 25001.

Majority of the tribal people except the Mahali and Bhumij in West Bengal have taken various steps including government help to increase their income level. Regarding occupational training majority of the tribal communities in West Bengal are not at all interested. Only a few of them have shown their eagerness for taking training in tailoring, rope making and basket making. In Orissa and Bihar (except the Munda in Bihar) majority of them are interested in taking some training either in basket making (the Mahali and Bhumij) or rope making (Birhor, Santal, Lodha) or leaf work (Santal and Lodha). Majority of the tribal women of the sample finally show their preferences for clinging to their traditional occupation.

III

In general the literacy level of the tribal people is very poor. The study reveals, irrespective of all tribes belonging to different states, that the number of female literates is lower than that of male literates. On the other hand, the number of female illiterates is more in all tribal communities irrespective of states. Female literates are more in West Bengal than in Bihar and in Orissa. In West Bengal the female literacy rate among the Munda community is relatively high (52 per cent), and lowest among the Birhors.

The educational status of the sample tribal women also shows the sample picture where the Munda women in both the states, West Bengal (53 per cent) and Bihar (24 per cent) are literates where in West Bengal (34 per cent) can only sign. The sample tribal women of the Birhor, in both the states, West Bengal and Bihar, are all illiterates. The tribal women of West Bengal are yet to show better educational performance than the other tribal women of Orissa and Bihar.

The reasons behind their iilliteracy are same in all states. In maximum cases the respondents opine that poor economic condition is the main cause of their illiteracy. According to them another important cause is that women's education is not at all demanded by the members of their society. In a few cases inadequacy of schools have also been mentioned by them.

Among the literate women the reasons for dropouts as mentioned by them are poor economic condition, early marriage, lack of adjustment with other caste students, looking after younger siblings in their houses.

Apart from giving formal education the Government has been trying to increase the level of women literacy through the Adult Education Programmes as most of the women are illiterate. Except West Bengal, other states, Orissa and Bihar do not have succeeded in implementing any Adult Education Programme. Only in West Bengal, a few participants have been enlightened by this programme, where the Munda and the Bhumij have shown their development through it.

IV

The problems of the tribal people are immense. Though they are suffering from economic, housing, land, fuel, cloth, water, hygiene, social, educational and food problems, in most cases they cannot locate them and sometimes they are not even aware of the particular problem which are most important to them, due to their lack of consciousness. In majority of the cases they have mentioned that extreme poverty is their main problem.

Most of the tribal people under study live in mud built houses with only one room. The problem of accommodation has been mentioned by a good number of respondents. Except during rainy seasons most of the tribal families use the courtyard as their cooking place, as majority of them have no separate kitchen. But the tribal people, because of their lack of awareness, do not think this to be a problem at all and accept this system as quite natural. But it is a good sign that these people have developed consciousness regarding the necessity of clean drinking water and most of them use tubewells for this purpose. In few cases they use wells for drinking water.

It has been found that in most of the cases, irrespective of communities and states the age at the marriage of girls has been decided to be between 14 and 18 years. Naturally it has been observed that the age at first child of most of the tribal mother is 14 to 18 years. It is important to note that a good number of tribal people think that this practice of early marriage is harmful both for the women concerned and also for the wider society.

The study has shown that the dowry system has already been introduced in the tribal society along with the system of bride price. A good number of tribal families under study have taken bride price and/or dowry.

The study reveals lack of awareness of the tribal women regarding the necessity of doctor's advice during the pregnancy period. However, the situation is to some extent favourable among the tribal women of West Bengal. It is found that the most important cause for which most of the tribal women do not take doctor's advice during pregnancy is their ignorance. The second major cause is that they attach little importance to the modern medical facilities. But majority of the tribal mothers are well aware about the necessity of the vaccination programme for their children. In 40 per cent cases (W.B.) children take vaccination from the village sub-centre or primary health centre. Initially they start vaccination but discontinue the course due to various problems. But in Orissa and Bihar the result is more unsatisfactory.

The need for small-sized family has been felt by a good number of tribal women of West Bengal and Orissa, and hence they have accepted the family planning programme. But the picture regarding the acceptance of the family planning programme is somewhat different in Bihar. The tribal women of Bihar have shown a somewhat negative attitude towards the family planning programme.

Twelve important common diseases like problem of eye sight, headache, weakness, diarrhoea, skin disease, cough and cold, asthma, malaria, tuberculosis, worms, dysentery and fever are visible among the tribal men, women and children. The Birhor community in Purulia district is a little exception to the other communities of Bengal as the whole Birhor community in that district is free from the problem of eyesight, asthma, tuberculosis and worms as mentioned by them. But apart from this community, members of other communities are mostly affected in varied nature and degree by the above mentioned diseases. Though it is very difficult to categorise them according to particular diseases, it has been observed that apart from suffering from many diseases most women are facing the problem of general weakness and headache than their male counterparts. Children mostly suffer from worms, cough and cold and the problem of asthma and tuberculosis are found more in male than in female and there is not a single child who is affected by asthma and tuberculosis.

In Orissa the tribal communities of Lodha and Santal suffer from the above mentioned diseases except the problem of eyesight, tuberculosis, asthma and worms. Children are more affected by diarrhoea, skin disease and cough and cold.

In Bihar the male, female and children of the Mahali, Bhumij and Munda are more affected by malaria and the problem of eyesight than those of the Birhor community. But dysentery and fever are common diseases in four communities whereas skin diseases and diarrhoea are mostly found among the children.

Irrespective of districts and tribal groups, all tribal mothers engage their adult children in taking care of the younger ones. And generally the elder sisters of tribal communities have to do different household works, including looking after the younger brothers and sisters when their parents are not at home.

The attitudes and opinions of the women regarding their life situations are studied through various questions relating to the role of decision makers in husband's family, women's awareness in political life, preference for male child or female child, preferred age for children's marriage, various opinions regarding widow remarriage, position of the widow, position of the divorced woman in a society, preference for medical treatment, understanding of happy life etc.

In most of the cases the women in different communities respond to different questions by which their attitude, whether progressive or conservative, is expressed. In some areas particularly the tribal women in Bengal, specially of Midnapur district, are more democratic and more conscious than their counterparts in other states. Many new information are collected from the tables and discussions of the chapters. Tribal women are very simple and innocent. After marriage they come and settle in the husband's family gladly. In most of the cases they are quite indifferent to or show a little interest in taking decisions in the husband's family. Except Birhor, the other five communities like the Lodha, Mahali, Santal, Munda and Bhumij (more than 50 per cent) play the role of decision makers, when it is required.

The tribal women in West Bengal are more aware of the different political issues of the community and they show their political conscience by expressing the opinion that women should participate in different political activities, whereas the tribal women in Bihar, and Orissa show their negative ambivalent attitude regarding assumption of different political roles. The tribal women in West Bengal are more progressive and democratic minded than the other women of different states.

Generally the tribal women are a little bit indifferent about the preference of male or female child excepting in Bihar (excluding Birhor) where they prefer male child. But gradually the tribal women throughout West Bengal, Bihar and Orissa are developing a particular preference for male child as they are influenced by the idea of dowry system which is now an ongoing practice of the caste people.

Other important opinions as to the marriage of the tribal women have been studied, where the maximum number of tribal women except the Mahali, Munda and Bhumij of Bihar prefer 18 to 21 years as age for marriage but above mentioned tribal women of Bihar prefer early marriage (15 to 18 years). But regarding the selection of bridegroom they all express their preferences for negotiation marriage.

Majority of the tribal women in West Bengal, except Birhor, and the tribal women of Bihar and Orissa, show their favourable attitude towards the inheritance of property by female and also they claim equal rights to get their parent's property.

All tribal women argue that divorce is approved by their society but the position of divorcee either for male or female, is not good in West of Bengal except in Purulia where they show a reverse attitude. But in Bihar and Orissa the position of divorcee is better as stated by the tribal women. Except the Birhor of Purulia (W.B.) and Hazaribagh (Bihar) and Lodha in Orissa all tribal women opine that if the relationship between husband and wife is disturbed they may claim divorce.

Tribal women in all districts argue that the position of widow is good and widow remarriage is justified by their society except among the tribal women in Bihar and the Lodha of West Bengal and Orissa.

Tribal women in all districts, except the Mahali, Munda and Bhumij, express their satisfaction regarding medical facilities. Their societies are being more free from diseases and most of them have good faith in allopathic treatment. The maximum number of tribal women in various districts believe that happy life denotes better comfort in their day-to-day life, and all of them argue that only sufficient money leads to happiness.

Policy Recommendations

The problems of the fair sex of the weaker section are many and varied. Sometimes it is difficult to define and locate them properly, naturally their development becomes much more complex and problematic to achieve. After Independence various measures have been taken through constitutional safeguards, planning commissions, tribal welfare departments of different states and NGOs for overcoming their problems as well as bringing about their upliftment in society. But till today many such attempts have not shown great promise. Except in a few cases the conditions of the tribal women throughout the country is far from satisfactory. Illiteracy is one of the important causes for their backwardness. Only education and economic security through employment can improve their socio-economic condition along with the real enlightenment of the whole population.

Six tribal communities of West Bengal, Orissa and Bihar, under study show a similar picture. Realizing the need of education the Government has launched and implemented the Adult Education Programme in different states of the country. But unfortunately the villages of Bihar and Orissa under study are yet to be the beneficiaries of this programme. To increase the level of literacy among the tribal people of these villages the Adult Education Programme should be implemented as soon as possible. In West Bengal, though this programme has been started, it is found that the rate of participation in it is very low. To achieve the desired goal people's participation is a must and large-scale campaigning through processions, posterings, video shows, street corner meetings etc, is essential. Before launching the programme, attempts should be made to generate awareness among the tribal people, most of whom do not know the importance of education even to this day. It is found in majority of the cases, that the short time allotted to the courses engenders disinterest among the adult students, who prefer earning to learning. Continuity of the courses for a long span of time along with the follow-up sessions is necessary. Besides the governmental efforts, political leaders, educated persons and other social workers should join hands with the government to make the policy successful. The teachers of the Adult Education Programme should be properly remunerated. Voluntary services of the teachers for a long time may give rise to negligence which may harm the students.

The numbers of dropouts among the tribal people is very high and attempts should be made to stop it by preventing the school students from doing household work, from going to the fields with their parents and at the same time by creating consciousness among the guardians about the necessity of education. Methods of teaching in the school should be attractive and interesting. The environment of many schools is not appropriate for study. The government should establish more schools in the tribal concentrated areas.

Teachers of the schools in tribal areas should be given special training in tribal languages, practices and culture.

Knowledge about the tribal ways of life may help them to deal with the tribal students properly which may in turn create a lot of interest among the tribal students. Above all, the most important requirements are the advice, suggestions and recommendations of the enlightened people of the society. To increase the literacy level of the tribal people their involvement is necessary as they are quite aware of the tribal problems and of the values and ethics embedded in their lifestyle.

Regarding the improvement of economic conditions, not a uniform measure should be taken into consideration as all these six groups have been selected from various economic strata and pursuits. All of them cling to their traditional economy which prescribes a particular way of life.

As for example, the Birhor and Lodha are the hunting-gathering group. Among them the Birhors are more primitive and considered as the Primitive Tribal Group (PTG). They live in jungles. Naturally the forest exerts tremendous effect on their minds. But since mid-nineties restrictions have been imposed on entering or utilizing the jungles for the tribal groups. Before alienating them from the forest, provisions for their alternative economic pursuits should be made. In many cases the tribal women prefer to have traditional economy. So traditional economy should not be replaced. Let them understand the nature of changing the necessity of proper utilization of available resources and of comfortable life slowly and gradually.

On the other hand, the Lodha were once identified as criminal tribes due to their adoption of many illegal means for maintaining their life and now in many places resort to agriculture. Women are lazy, less worthy and impatient. Very few women show their eagerness for training in different small-scale industries for self-sufficiency. The new generation may be the trial group. Compulsory training-cum-production centre should be opened with constant efforts to make them aware about better life.

The basket-maker Mahali community prefer to continue its traditional occupation. Most of the women are associated with basket making, which offers them scope for earning to substantiate their family income. Naturally, for this group basket-making practice should be formalized and a training-cum-production centre should be established under the supervision of the Tribal Welfare Department in which they should be apprised of the modern methods of basket-making according to the demands of the local market.

The Santal, Munda and Bhumij women are basically unskilled agricultural labourers. They should be encouraged in some small-scale cottage industries which can provide them extra financial assistance that can increase their family income and strengthen the economy.

Majority of the tribal women of West Bengal are less interested in modern occupational training. It is found that in West Bengal except the Birhor all other groups want training in tailoring and basket-making. But most of the communities of Bihar, except the Munda, feel the necessity of modern occupational training and demand training in rope and basket-making. This is due to the fact that the Birhors live in forests, and naturally this action pattern pivots around them. But in Orissa, the Lodha and Santal show a completely different outlook on the issue of occupational training. Most of them live in and around the forests in Mayurbhanj district and majority of them prefer training in preparing leaf made cups and plates as well as rope objects. On the other hand, the Lodha and Santal of West Bengal have developed a different outlook for better life where the forest plays no significant role. So the tribal women of West Bengal should be given training in tailoring and basket making and their counterparts in Bihar and Orissa should be given training in rope-making and leaf-making. This special training, in consonance with their demands can be helpful to make them competent among the competitors in the market.

The housing problem is a very common problem which is faced by the tribal people too. The housing schemes for the tribals should properly be implemented as in most cases the dissatisfaction of the people has been expressed. Though in some cases the government allotted ready-made houses for their living purposes, due to poverty or unawareness proper maintenance of the houses could not be done. The government should be more alert and also sanction many follow up schemes for the same.

The early age of marriage is another problem. To combat it mass awareness is needed through large-scale campaigning.

After Independence many welfare schemes have been introduced for protecting the health of the mother and the child but in reality their is a gap between the interaction of the health clinics and the poor tribal mothers. So proper arrangement should be made, so that the rural health centres can function properly with the help of the medical officers, local leaders and the participation of the tribal mothers. In a word, the awareness of the tribal mothers should be increased so that they can protect themselves as well as their children with the help of the personnel of the rural health centres. At the same time they should be made aware of the usefulness of the Family Planning Programme though in many cases they express their positive feelings towards the small-sized family, but in reality they are till now denying the positive mode of functioning of the Family Planning Programme.

Apart from considering the various problems and their suggested remedial measures, the tribal women still enjoy much more freedom in taking decisions in different socio-political issues in their societies. Reflecting on the pattern of living of tribal women in three afore-mentioned states, it is observed that the West Bengal's tribal women are much more rational, progressive and democratic minded. The literacy rate of the women, though very poor, is promising in comparison with that of the other two states.

Bibliography

Adhikari, A. K. (1984). Society and World View of the Birhor. Calcutta.

Basu,, S. K. and Saha, R. N. (1987). The Mundas— A Profile. Calcutta.

Basu Roy, I. (1992). Literacy Among the Tribal Women in West Bengal. In Bulletin of the CRI Vol. XVIII No. 1-2.

Bhowmick, P. K. (1963). The Lodhas of West Bengal. Calcutta.

———————— (1985). Education for Tribal Women: A Suggestion, in *Tribal Women and Development* (ed.) by Singh and others. Udaipur.

———————— (1991). Dynamics of Tribal Development. New Delhi.

———————— (1992). Chenchus of the Forests and Plateaux. Calcutta.

Bodding, P. O. (1940). How The Santals Live. Calcutta.

Bose, N.K. (1972). Some Indian Tribes. New Delhi.

Chowdhury, A. B. (1985). Santal Samaj, *Daini -o- bartaman Sankat.* Calcutta.

Dalton, E. T. (1872). Descriptive Theology of Bengal. Calcutta.

Das, A. K.; Raha, M. K. and De, S. K. (1990). Tribal Situation in West Bengal. Calcutta.

Elwin, V. (1975). Tribal Women, in *Indian Women* (ed.) by D. Jain. New Delhi.

Lowie, R. H. (1920). Primitive Society. New York.

Majumdar, D. N. and Madan, T. N. (1957). An Introduction of Social Anthropology. Bombay.

Malinowski, B. (1949). Sex and Repression in *Savage Society.* London.

Moser, C. N. (1991). General Planning in the Third World: Meeting Practical and Strategic Gender needs, in *Changing Perceptions* (ed.) Tina Wallace with Candida March.

Nandi Basu, A. (1993). Mundas in Transition — A Study in Cultural Geography. Calcutta.

Palchowdhury, D. (1991). Women Welfare and Development: A source Book. New Delhi.

Piza Lopez, E. (1991). Overcoming of the Barriers: Woman and Participation in Public lifes in *Changing Perceptions* (ed.) Tina Wallace with Candida March.

Risley, H. (1891). The Tribes and Castes of Bengal. Calcutta.

Risley, H. (1981). The Tribes and Castes of Bengal (Vol. I). Calcutta.

Rowbotham, S. (1992). Woman in Movement. New York.

Roy, S. C. (1912). The Mundas and Their Country. Calcutta.

———— (1925). The Birhors: A Little-Known Jungle Tribe of Chotanagpur. Ranchi.

———— (1978). The Birhors. Ranchi.

Roy, U. K.; Das, A. K. and Basu, S. K. (1982). To be with Santals. Calcutta.

Sachchidananda (1979). The Changing Munda. New Delhi.

———— (1985). Tribal Women in the Throes of Development, in *Tribal Women and Development* (ed.) by Singh and others. Udaipur.

Sengupta, S. K. (1969). The Portrait of Mahali Economy in Midnapur. Calcutta.

Singh, J. P., Vyas, N. N., Mann, R. S. (1985). Tribal Women and Development (ed.). Udaipur.

Singh, S. (1967). Village Survey Monograph on Bhumij Dhansol. Delhi.

Singh, Y. (1995). Contemporary Social Crisis in India and its Dimensions, in *Sociology of Rural Development* (ed.) by Nahar and Chandani. Jaipur.

Index